The Operas of
Johann Adolf Hasse

Studies in Musicology, No. 2

George Buelow, Series Editor

Professor of Music
Indiana University

Other Titles in This Series

The Operas of
Johann Adolf Hasse

by
Fredrick L. Millner

UMI RESEARCH PRESS
Ann Arbor, Michigan

Library of Congress Cataloging in Publication Data

Millner, Fredrick L   1946-
The operas of Johann Adolf Hasse.

   (Studies in musicology ; no. 2)
   Bibliography: p.
   Includes index.
   1. Hasse, Johann Adolph, 1699-1783. Operas.
I. Title. II. Series.

ML410.H35M5 1979   782.1'092'4   79-11832
ISBN 0-8357-1006-8
ISBN 0-8357-1007-6 pbk.

CONTENTS

PLATES

TABLES

DIAGRAMS

EXTENDED MUSICAL EXAMPLES

Examples are by Hasse unless otherwise indicated.

STYLISTIC PRACTICES

Italian words for which there are no English equivalents are not italicized: opera seria, maestro di cappella, primo uomo, festa teatrale, serenata, allegro, and the like. Italian plurals are used in such cases: libretti, intermezzi, and so forth.

Most library abbreviations are those used by *RISM* (*Répertoire International des Sources Musicales*):

A-Wgm,   Austria, Gesellschaft der Musikfreunde, Vienna

A-Wn,   Austria, Österreichische Nationalbibliothek, Vienna

B-Bc,   Belgium, Bibliothèque du Conservatoire, Brussels

B-Br,   Belgium, Bibliothèque royale, Brussels

D-Bds,   Germany, Deutsche Staatsbibliothek, Berlin (East)

D-Dl,   Germany, Sächsische Landesbibiothek, Dresden

D-Mbs,   Germany, Bayerische Staatsbibliothek, Munich

D-SWl,   Germany, Mecklinburgische Landesbibliothek, Schwerin

D-W   Germany, Herzog August Bibliothek, Wolfenbüttel

DK-Kk,   Denmark, Det kongelige Bibliotek, Copenhagen

F-Pn,   France, Bibliothèque nationale, Paris

GB-Lam,   Great Britain, Royal Academy of Music, London

GB-Lbm,   Great Britain, British Museum, London

GB-Lcm,   Great Britain, Royal College of Music, London

GB-Lk,   Great Britain, King's Music Library, London

GB-Och,   Great Britain, Christ Church College, Oxford

I-Bc,   Italy, Biblioteca del Conservatorio, Bologna

I-Fm,   Italy, Biblioteca Marucelliana, Florence

I-Mb,   Italy, Biblioteca nazionale di Brera, Milan

I-Mc,   Italy, Biblioteca del Conservatorio, Milan

I-MC   Italy, Biblioteca dell' Abbazia, Montecassino

I-MOe,   Italy, Biblioteca Estense, Modena

I-Nc,   Italy, Biblioteca del Conservatorio, Naples

I-PAc,   Italy, Biblioteca del Conservatorio, Parma

I-Rc,   Italy, Biblioteca Casanatensis, Rome

I-Rn,   Italy, Biblioteca nazionale, Rome

I-Rsc,   Italy, Biblioteca del Conservatorio Santa Cecilia, Rome

I-Vc,   Italy, Biblioteca del Conservatorio, Venice

I-Vnm,   Italy, Biblioteca nazionale Marciana, Venice

PL-Wn,   Poland, Biblioteka Narodowa, Warsaw

US-AA,   United States, University of Michigan, Ann Arbor

US-BE,   United States, University of California, Berkeley

US-CA,   United States, Harvard University, Cambridge

US-LA,   United States, University of California, Los Angeles

US-NH,   United States, Yale University, New Haven

US-NYp,   United States, New York Public Library, New York City

US-Wc,   United States, Library of Congress, Washington, D.C.

STYLISTIC PRACTICES

The following abbreviations are also used:

Grove's Dictionary: *Grove's Dictionary of Music and Musicians*, ed, by Eric
Blom, 5th Ed., London: St. Martin's Press, 1954.

MGG: *Musik in Geschichte und Gegenwart*, ed. by Friedrich Blume,
Kassel & Basel: Bärenreiter, 1949-1973.

JAMS: *Journal of the American Musicological Society*

D-Bpk: Germany, Berlin, Library of the Preussische Kulturbesitz,
Dahlem (formerly at the University of Tübigen)

PREFACE

Johann Adolf Hasse was one of the most important operatic composers of the eighteenth century. Only recently has he begun to be recognized as a founder of the "Classical" style, of the new idiom that was reacting against the complexities of the seventeenth century and that was to become, itself, the style of Mozart and Haydn some forty years later. Yet the last extensive work on Hasse, and the only one on his operas, was written in 1925; this deals only briefly with Hasse's artistic development, and not at all with his career. Hasse's operas themselves remain, with two exceptions, out of print, and the complex circumstances of their composition and revision have never been adequately treated. *The Operas of Johann Adolf Hasse* attempts, in the most basic way, to begin to rectify these conditions.

The origins of this present work were in a seminar on eighteenth-century Italian opera seria taught by Daniel Heartz and Harold Powers at the University of California at Berkeley in the winter and spring of 1970. Due to the generosity of Sven Hansell, who was then teaching at the University of California at Davis, many microfilm copies of Hasse scores were made available to the students of the seminar.

These microfilm copies were of twenty-nine autograph scores found in the library of the Milan Conservatory. They had been listed in the library's nineteenth-century manuscript catalogue, but had been misplaced during the Second World War. It was only through the persistent questioning of Professor Hansell that these had been rediscovered; and it was he who identified them as autographs.

This collection amounted to an enormous, untouched source of information on Hasse, his operas, and eighteenth-century operatic practice. I was fortunate to be given full access to all of the information and microfilms that Professor Hansell had collected. With his encouragement, I began studying what these scores told us of Hasse's compositional practices.

It soon became apparent that the subject could not be limited to the autographs themselves. Hasse had set several of the operas found among the autographs several times, and the problem of identifying the proper performance and date for each autograph score was difficult. This search led to an attempt to clarify the situation of Hasse's revisions and later productions.

Identifying the later productions, in turn, necessitated a study of available libretti, and a tracing of Hasse's life, to determine the likelihood of his presence at, or supervision of productions in various cities. Since the last complete biography of Hasse was written in 1906, it became necessary to bring up to date the chronology of his life, using the research that had been done since the beginning of this century. Theories concerning his career were also made and utilized, when they could clarify aspects of Hasse's life.

Large amounts of material collected in the preparation of this thesis are not present in the finished draft. A catalogue of arias found in scores, libretti, and aria collections, especially, was highly important in the tracing of lost or doubtful performances and operas. The painstaking comparison of many libretti also led to conclusions concerning the otherwise problematical productions. The form of this thesis has been determined by the various necessities described above, and the chapters group themselves around the central idea: the composition and revision of Hasse's operas.

Thus this work begins with a biography, incorporating the new documents brought to light since 1906, and rational assumptions derived from a careful study of Hasse's known career. This biography is not intended to be a complete one, of all the known facts about Hasse, but merely an outline of the main events in his life, centered around his operas and their revisions.

The biography is followed by a description of Hasse's musical style, and the conventions employed in his operas; Chapter III discusses the autographs, their appearance, and what they demonstrate of the original composition of the operas. These two chapters are necessary introductions to the revisions.

The fourth chapter is the heart of this book. It is concerned with which operas were revised, how many times, to what extent, in what ways, and why. Such a broad chapter cannot hope to be more than an introduction. I sincerely hope that I have reduced the amount of confusion concerning Hasse's revisions, yet much work certainly remains to be done. The fact remains that this sort of broad survey has never before been made.

The conclusion, too, is in several parts. It is divided into a chapter on Hasse's position in music history, and one on Hasse's position in criticism. The second of these closes with an attempt to analyze a Hasse aria, the central art-form of his career, on its own terms.

Compiling the material gathered here would not have been possible without the aid and assistance of many people. My research in Europe was supported by an Alfred Hertz Memorial Travelling Fellowship, granted by the University of California. The staffs of the libraries of the Naples, Bologna, Parma, and Venice Conservatories of Music, the Bavarian State Library, the Austrian National Library and the Library of the Friends of Music in Vienna, the Este Library in Modena, the National Libraries of Venice (Marciana) and Milan (Brera), the British Museum, Royal Academy of Music, National Library in Paris, and Royal Library of Copenhagen all deserve my thanks.

Plates VIII-XXVIII are reproduced with the generous permission of the libraries of the Conservatorio di Musica "Guiseppe Verdi" of Milan and the Conservatorio di Musica "Benedetto Marcello" of Venice.

Special appreciation is due Gilda Grigolato of the Milan Conservatory, and Ortrun Landmann of the Saxon State Library for their help.

Alan Curtis has been reading and offering helpful suggestions since 1970. Sven Hansell has offered a continuous stream of support and encouragement, along with, as mentioned above, free use of his notes and some sixty microfilms of Hasse operas. Daniel Heartz, as my advisor, has seen this project from beginning to completion. By his constant striving after historical accuracy and literate clarity, he has made this book much more than it otherwise could have been.

CHAPTER I

HASSE'S LIFE AND OPERATIC CAREER

Johann Adolf Hasse was born on 23 or 24 March 1699, in Bergedorf, a small village near Hamburg.[1] His baptismal certificate was signed on the 25th, in the presence of three witnesses including his godfather, Johann Adolf Klessing. Hasse came from a moderately distinguished family of organists. His great-grandfather was Peter Hasse, organist of the Marienkirche in Lübeck, who had gained some fame as a composer. His grandfather, father, and brother successively held the position of organist in Bergedorf. Johann's father, Peter, was the son-in-law of Bartram Klessing, the mayor of Bergedorf, and it was through Klessing that Peter Hasse was made administrator of a certain charity originally intended for the poor of Bergedorf.

Hasse's family was not well-off; the position of organist paid less than four Taler a year. It was fortunate, even if apparently nepotic, that the young Johann, already showing much talent at age 15, could be made beneficiary of this charity. He was given a stipend of 20 2/3 Taler (later 26 Taler) a year, and was sent to Hamburg to study voice, for the four years between 1714 and 1718.

In 1718 Hasse was hired as a tenor by the Hamburg opera company. He had been recommended for the position by Johann Ulrich König, private secretary and poet of the Saxon court at Dresden, responsible for German texts of the court festivities. Reinhard Keiser, the director of the Hamburg opera, was on leave from 1717 to 1722, so Hasse never met him; but he gained a thorough knowledge of his music by his participation in performances.[2]

König also recommended Hasse for his next position, that of tenor of the opera at Wolfenbüttel, the residence of the Duke of Brunswick. Hasse's name first appears on a libretto at this time: as the singer of the *Dankwart*, or licenza, in Schürmann's *Heinrich der Vogler*, first performed in the Carnival of 1721.[3] He also sang in operas by F. Conti and Caldara, but the most important result of his Wolfenbüttel stay was the composition and performance of his first opera, *Antioco*, in the summer fair of 1721.[4] Hasse sang the title role in this production, and Schürmann sang the role of Seleuco. According to the custom at Wolfenbüttel, the opera was probably given with German recitatives and Italian arias and choruses. Only six arias survive.[5]

It was evidently on the basis of this work that Hasse decided to devote his life to composition. In 1722 he left Wolfenbüttel for Italy, presumably at the expense of the Brunswick court. He traveled throughout the country for three years, spending a few months each in Venice, Bologna, Florence, and Rome, before settling in Naples.[6] In

1725 he began studying with Niccolò Porpora, one of the most famous teachers of the century, but he apparently did not get along with him, for he soon began taking lessons instead with Alessandro Scarlatti. This could not have been for long, since the master died on 29 October 1725.[7] J. J. Quantz's autobiographical sketch in Marpurg confirms the state of Hasse's position at this time.[8] Hasse had helped Quantz to obtain a position as a student of Scarlatti's. Quantz then says that up until 1725, Hasse had not written anything major for the stage, but in that year he received a commission from a banker for a serenata for two voices. The work was presumably *Antonio e Cleopatra*; the singers, according to Quantz, were Carlo Broschi *detto* Farinelli and Vittoria Tesi, two of the most famous singers of the time. As a result, Quantz adds, Hasse was commissioned to compose operas for the court theatre in May of that year.[9]

    Antonio e Cleopatra has been called a cantata on the basis of its limited cast and plot development, and because it was obviously planned for chamber performance.[10] It is quite lengthy, with a three-part sinfonia followed by eight arias and two duets, and could easily be considered a serenata, especially if it had been staged.[11]

    The title page of *Antonio e Cleopatra* lists the composer as "Giovanni Hasse, detto il Sassone," the first time that this appellation appears. The name was a result of Hasse's birth in Lower Saxony, a geographical, not a political, area, and not a part of the Electorate of Saxony. Although Handel (from Halle, also not a part of Saxony proper) was also known sometimes as "il Sassone," the two were not countrymen.[12]

    With *Antonio e Cleopatra*, Hasse's apprenticeship was at an end. The young composer found himself accepted by the Neapolitan court, and he began an uninterrupted period of seven years of composition for the court of Naples. By the time this period ended, Hasse had become a composer of international fame.

The Neapolitan Period

    The Kingdom of Naples was, between 1713 and 1735, ruled by Charles VI, the last emperor of the direct Hapsburg line, and father of Maria Theresa, Empress of the Holy Roman Empire. Court opera was presented in the Teatro San Bartolomeo throughout Hasse's stay in Naples, with lighter comedies presented at a variety of smaller theatres. Hasse's first work for the Royal Opera was *Sesostrate*, on a libretto by Angelo Caresale, performed on the ninth birthday of Maria Theresa, 13 May 1726. The libretto names Hasse as maestro di cappella to the Duke of Brunswick. One copy of the score remains.[13] Hasse also composed his first intermezzo for this production, though there is some doubt that the intermezzo was actually separate from the opera. The score differs in many respects from the libretto. The characters of the intermezzo (*Miride e Damari*) appear in the opera seria proper, and in the score they sing arias in the seria part of the production.[14] The score has, thus, no separate intermezzo, but rather uses Miride and Damari as comic characters in the manner of 17th- and early 18th-century operas. In contrast, the libretto seems to be revised to suit later tastes: all of Miride and Damari's arias are consolidated in the intermezzo.[15]

In the autumn of 1726, another serenata was produced: *Semele, o sia la richiesta fatale*. The libretto, like that of *Antonio e Cleopatra*, was by Ricciardi.[16] This work is not mentioned in any source on Hasse, and there is no libretto or record of its production. The manuscript is in the same format and by the same copyist as *Sesostrate* and *Antonio e Cleopatra*. The work is for three voices and is in two sections, or *parte*, and would logically have been another privately-produced serenata, though the title page gives no indication of the patron.[17]

Hasse's second work for the Neapolitan stage was *Astarto*.[18] It was produced in December of 1726, and included *Larinda e Vanesio*, an intermezzo in three scenes. The libretto of the opera was one of Apostolo Zeno's, revised by Pariati. Antonio Salvi was the author of the intermezzo.

Most biographies state that Hasse made a trip to Venice in 1727 to begin serving as maestro di cappella for the *Ospedale degli Incurabili*. Documents recently brought to light by Hansell make this extremely doubtful.[19] Though a visit to Venice by the ambitious young composer would have been logical and in fact likely, there is no evidence that Hasse became a permanent resident of that city until three years later.

A third serenata was performed in 1727, though the libretto does not give the exact date. *Enea in Caonia*, on a libretto by Luigi Maria Stampiglia, may have been commissioned for the same patron as that of *Antonio* and *Semele*. This is listed as a cantata by Abert,[20] but in length and forces (a three-section sinfonia, followed by fifteen arias and a final coro, with a cast of five singers), it must be considered a festa teatrale.[21]

Hasse's third full-scale opera for Naples was *Gerone, tiranno di Siracusa*, on an anonymously-revised version of a seventeenth-century libretto by Aurelio Aureli. This was produced on 19 November 1727, in honor of the birthday of the Empress, Elisabeth Christine. The intermezzo, *Porsugnacco e Grilletta*, is in the three-scene format. Its plot is an anonymous adaptation of Molière's *Monsieur de Pourceaugnac*.

In the spring of 1728, *Attalo, rè di Bitinia* was produced. Giovanni Carestini, one of the most famous castrati of the epoch, sang the title role. The librettist was Aurelio Aureli. With *Attalo*, the intermezzo *Pantaleone e Carlotta*, a three scene work on an anonymous libretto, was presented.

According to the schedule of operas, Hasse could have written a work for the fall of 1728. If he did, it has been lost. He did write a two-scene intermezzo, *La Contadina*, on a libretto by Belmuro, which was produced with Pietro Scarlatti's *Clitarco*.[22]

Three new operas were performed during 1729. The first, *Ulderica*, had its premiere on 19 January. The score has been lost, but the libretto (whose author is unknown) does exist. Several arias survive in isolated copies, including one taken from *Enea in Caonia*. The three-scene intermezzo *La Fantesca*, on a libretto by B. Saddumene, was performed with it.

La Sorella amante followed in the spring. It is described in the libretto as a *commedia*, though there is a strict division made between dialect- and Italian-speaking roles.[23]

Tigrane was also produced in the winter, on 4 November, celebrating the name-day of the Emperor, Charles VI. The prima donna was Vittoria Tesi, and a three-scene intermezzo was included: *La Serva scaltra, ovvero la moglie a forza.* The libretto identifies Hasse as an official member of the royal chapel, calling him "maestro sopranumerario della Real Cappella di Napoli." The libretto of *Tigrane* was by Silvani.[23a]

Venice and Dresden

By 1730, Hasse's fame had spread beyond Naples. In the Carnival season of that year he produced his first opera in Venice. While Neapolitan opera was at this time the most stylish in Italy, such an invitation indicated that Hasse had joined Scarlatti, Porpora, Leo, and Vinci in conquering the city that still dominated the field in quantity of operas produced. In contrast to that of Naples, the Venetian opera was a public-supported enterprise. More important, it offered more opportunities for a man who, however successful, otherwise would have remained a "supernumerary" composer at Naples. But two immediate results were to have enormous significance to his life and career: he met and subsequently married Faustina Bordoni; he received the offer of the position of maestro di cappella at Dresden.

The opera he set in Venice was Metastasio's *Artaserse*, the first Metastasian text he had used, and a very new one.[24] It had only been set once before, in the same Carnival season, by Leonardo Vinci, at that time the most successful composer of Italian opera seria.[25] Hasse's opera was well-liked by the Venetian public, and the result was a stream of operas composed for Venice that lasted until 1758. The success was aided by the participation of Farinelli as Arbace and Francesca Cuzzoni as Mandane.[26]

In June, Johann Hasse and Faustina Bordoni were married in a private ceremony.[27] Faustina, born in 1693 or 1700,[28] had been a famous soprano since 1716, and the marriage may well have been one of convenience for both participants. Hasse's career was rapidly advancing, but he was still relatively unknown. Faustina was already famous, with a superb voice still in its prime, but no longer considered a prodigy, and her career may have been temporarily at an ebb. Whatever the reasons, their marriage was a long, and, by all accounts, a happy one.

During the preceding years, the Saxon ambassador to Venice, Count Villio, had been seeking out and training young Italian singers to be hired for the new opera company being organized in Dresden. The previous court opera company had been dissolved in 1720, and in 1724 and 1725 the start of a new one was made through the hiring of some singers and a theatre decorator. The Elector of Saxony at this time was Frederick Augustus I, known as "the Strong," and though he was pleasure-loving and an enthusiastic patron of the arts, the impetus for the new company may well have come from his son, the Electoral Prince, who was to succeed his father in 1733 as Frederick Augustus II, and secure the title of King of Poland in 1735 as Augustus III.

The future Frederick Augustus II had known Faustina for some time. She had first sung in Pollaroli's *Ariodante*, performed in Venice in May 1716, and the libretto, and thus the production, was dedicated to the 20-year-old Electoral Prince, then on an extended trip through France and Italy. It is inconceivable that he did not take the oportunity to meet Faustina.

In 1730 the Dresden court was clearly dissatisfied with its musical directors. Ristori, the opera composer in residence, produced only a few comic operas in the 1720's. When the maestro di cappella Johann David Heinichen died in July 1729, he was not replaced by his expected successor, concert-master Jean-Baptiste Volumier, who died himself three months later. The third in line, the composer Jan Dismas Zelenka, was not promoted. He was an extremely individualistic composer, highly chromatic and polyphonic in his style, and was not what either the Elector or his son wanted for an opera composer. In 1735, however, he was appointed church composer.

Villio may have been under orders to hire Faustina at any cost. More likely, he was looking for both a prima donna and a maestro di cappella, around whom a spectacular Italian opera company could be built.[29] Sometime during 1730 Hasse and Faustina were invited to join the Dresden company. The date for their arrival was set for the middle of 1731, and Hasse was either given, or began to use on his own, the title of maestro di cappella to the Electoral court. This appears on the libretto of each of the three operas of 1730 that follow *Artaserse*:[30] *Dalisa*, produced in Parma in April and in Venice during Ascension;[31] *Arminio*, performed on 28 August in Milan, in honor of the birthday of the Empress Elisabeth Christine, with Carestini as Arminio and Faustina as Tusnelda; and *Ezio*, produced in Naples sometime during the year, either at Carnival or, as Schatz suggests, the fall.[32] *Dalisa*, on a text by Minato, probably extensively revised by Domenico Lalli (the pseudonym of Sebastiano Biancardi), is lost, except for isolated arias. The two-scene intermezzo to *Ezio*, *Il Tutore*, was one of Hasse's most popular works, being produced at least eight more times in later years. *Arminio* was on a text by Antonio Salvi, completely different from the one by Claudio Pasquini that Hasse was to set in 1745.

In addition to these four operas, Hasse also began contributing musically to the *Ospedale degli Incurabili* during 1730. About this time he composed a *Miserere* for the orphan girls of this charitable institution.[33]

In early 1731 Hasse made his first documented trip to Vienna, where his oratorio *Daniello* was performed on 15 February.[33a] He was delayed from leaving for Saxony in June, as he had originally planned, by an attack of gout, an ailment that would afflict him throughout his life. He and Faustina arrived in Dresden on 7 July and the next day performed for the king, who was understandably anxious to hear his new employees.

The first performance of *Cleofide* took place on 17 August. This was a private performance, presumably for the Elector, his family, and a few chosen members of the court. The official premiere was on 13 September. The specific holiday, if there was one, is not known.

The opera was presented in the Electoral Theatre of the Zwinger, the palace of the Elector, where during the next thirty-two years Hasse would present thirty-four other operas. The theatre had been constructed in 1719, along with the Zwinger itself, at the incredible cost of 150,000 Taler.[34] It did not front on the Zwinger courtyard, but was placed behind one of the galleries designed by M. D. Pöppelmann. (Plates I and II) The interior was the design of Alessandro Mauro. (Plates III and IV) It was rather old-fashioned, having three rows of loges instead of boxes, and a U-shaped amphitheater on the parterre, but it was the largest theatre in Germany at the time, seating 2000 spectators.[35] It was redecorated and rearranged with boxes in 1738 by the stage-designer A. Zucchi (Plate V) and in 1749-1750 Giuseppe Galli-Bibiena enlarged it and revamped the interior completely (Plates VI and VII).[36] Throughout Hasse's stay in Dresden the theatre remained non-commercial. It was open without admission charge, with the populace assigned seats on the basis of rank.[37]

The cast of *Cleofide* included Maria Catanea (soprano), Domenico Annibali (alto), Venturo Rochetti, *detto* Venturino (soprano), Antonio Campioli (alto), Nicolo Pozzi (alto), and Faustina Bordoni. Catanea, Annibali, and Rochetti had never sung in another opera company before; they had been hired between 1725 and 1728, along with

Campioli, who had been engaged as their trainer. Faustina, Annibali, and Rochetti were to remain active into the 1750's, Pozzi until 1742.

The libretto of *Cleofide* was a revision of Metastasio's *Alessandro nell' Indie*, liberally rewritten by Boccardi: of the twenty-nine arias, thirteen are not the original Metastasian ones. Dislike for the text was probably not the only reason for changing it; five of the substitutes are from earlier operas: *Gerone, Tigrane, Ezio*, and *La Sorella amante*; at least two more are contrafacta, from *Gerone* and *Attalo*.

Johann Sebastian Bach probably attended the premiere of *Cleofide*. He had journeyed to Dresden that week with his son Friedemann, and gave a concert in the St. Sophia Church on the day following the performance; Hasse presumably heard him in turn. The two composers seem to have respected each other, perhaps even enjoyed a friendship. C. P. E. Bach wrote in 1775 to Forkel that "In his last years, Bach esteemed highly the former imperial Oberkapellmeister Fux, Handel, Caldara, Reinhard Keiser, Hasse, both Grauns, Telemann, Zelenka, Benda, and in general everything that was worthy of esteem in Berlin and Dresden. The first four he did not know personally, but the others, he did."[38] Forkel himself relates:

> In Dresden, at the time that Hasse was maestro di cappella, the orchestra and the opera were quite brilliant and excellent. Bach had had, even in his earlier years, many acquaintances there, all of whom honored him. Also Hasse, with his wife, the celebrated Faustina, had come often to Leipzig and admired his great talents. He was therefore always received in an especially respectful manner at Dresden, and often went there to hear the opera. His eldest son usually accompanied him. A few days before he left, he would say in joke, 'Friedemann, shall we not go again to hear the lovely little Dresden songs?' As innocent as this joke is in itself, I am convinced that Bach would not have said it to anybody except this son, who, at that time, already knew what is great in art and what is only pretty and pleasant.[39]

Cleofide was performed three more times, the last presentation being on 26 September.[40] On 7 October, Faustina sang in Hasse's cantata, *La Gloria sassonia*, composed for the Electoral Prince's birthday. No copy remains of this work.

The next day, on 8 October, the couple departed for Italy. Fürstenau reports that Hasse was paid 500 gold ducats for his services and Faustina 1000.[41] Mennicke mentions only a figure of 6000 Taler in reference to Faustina's payment. This was the equivalent of eight years' pay for a singer such as Annibali or Rochetti.[42]

PLATE I

"The Dresden opera house according to its reconstruction by Giuseppe Galli-Bibiena in 1749, and its connection to the Zwinger."

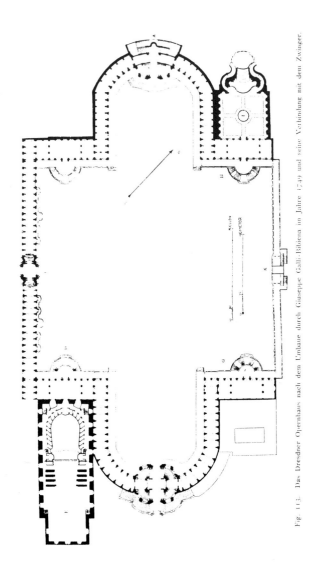

Martin Hammitzsch, *Der moderne theaterbau, der höfische theaterbau, der anfang der modernen theaterbaukunst, ihre entwicklung und betätigung zur zeit der renaissance, des barock, und des rokoko.* (Berlin: E. Wasmuth, 1906) p. 185.

PLATE II

Bernardo Bellotto, *detto* Canaletto, "Zwinger Courtyard," c. 1750.
View of southeast end of Zwinger courtyard. Facade in right-hand
corner (facing viewer) is of galleries in front of opera house. Roof
directly behind, with single row of six dormer windows, is that of opera
house.

Rodolfo Pallucchini, *La Pittura Veneziana del settecento*, (Venice and Rome: Instituto
per la collaborazione culturale, 1960) plate 586.

PLATE III

Interior of opera house. Caption of plate:
"Lateral view of the great royal theatre, with the loges and the parterre."
(Vue laterale du grand theatre roial, avec les Loges et le Parterre.)

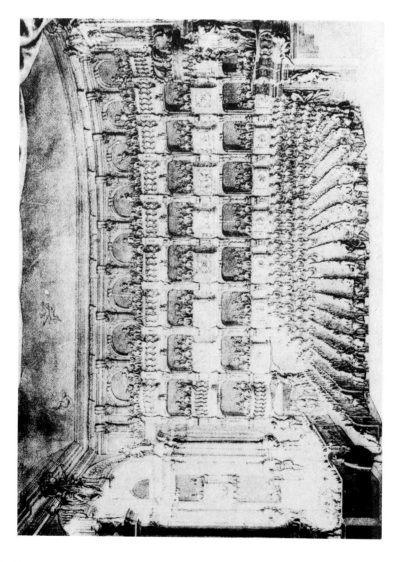

Löffler, Fritz, *Das Alte Dresden. Geschichte seinger Bauten*, (Dresden: Sachsenverlag
Dresden, 1955) p. 354, plate # 125.

PLATE IV

"The great opera house in Dresden, by Alessandro Mauro (constructed 1718-1719)."

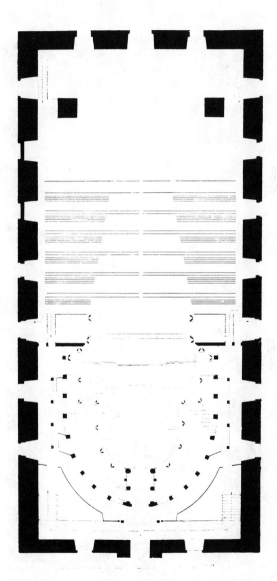

Hammitzsch, *op. cit.*, p. 136.

PLATE V

"The great opera house of Dresden, after the rebuilding by Andrea Zucchi of 1738."

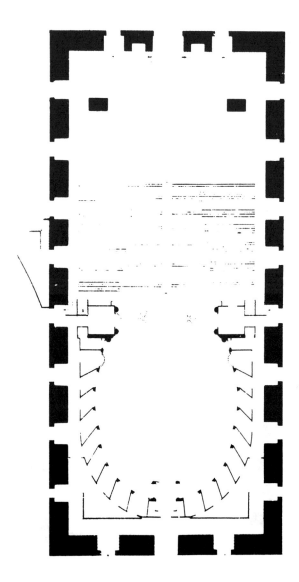

Hammitzsch, *op. cit.*, p. 138.

PLATE VI

"The Dresden opera house in 1749: View of the electoral box."

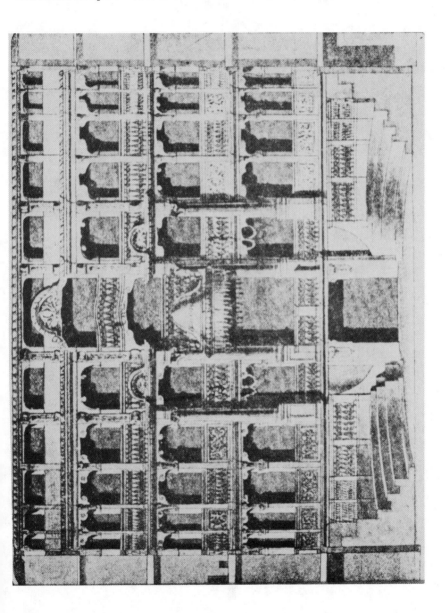

Hammitzsch, *op. cit.*, p. 167.

PLATE VII

"The Dresden opera house in 1749: Lateral elevation of the auditorium."

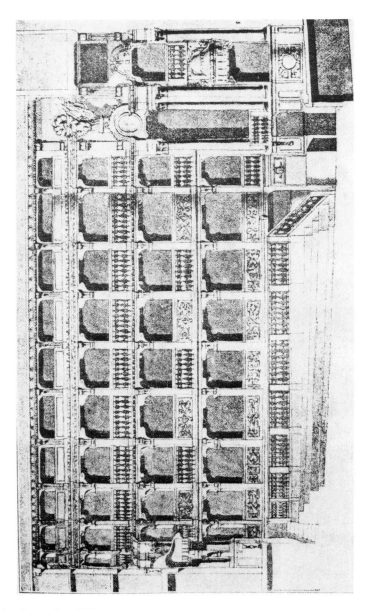

Hammitzsch, *op. cit.*, p. 166.

Hasse made a quick journey back to Italy, for his *Catone in Utica* was to be performed in Turin on 26 December 1731. This work, on another of Metastasio's librettos, has disappeared.[43] The cast included Farinelli, Tesi, and Filippo and Caterina Giorgi. Faustina was pregnant and did not participate. Hasse probably was not involved with a revival of *La Contadina*, performed in the autumn in the Teatro San Angelo in Venice and at the same time in Trieste.[44]

Hasse then had to make another fast journey, for on 12 January at the Teatro Capranica in Rome, *Cajo Fabrizio* was produced. Zeno's libretto was much altered: only four arias and the final chorus are original. One of the new arias is found also in *Catone in Utica*; it is not Metastasian, so it may have been composed originally for either opera. The cast included Annibali and two other singers who would become quite famous: Angelo Maria Monticelli, a soprano, then sixteen years old, who would join the Dresden company in 1752, and Felice Salimbeni, then a nineteen-year-old soprano who was to have a flourishing career in Vienna, Berlin, and Dresden.[45]

Hasse also produced two operas for Venice in 1732: *Demetrio* and *Euristeo*. The first was performed in the Carnival season, with Faustina as the prima donna.[46]   The prima donna of *Euristeo* (at Ascension) was Francesca Cuzzoni, which may explain why Faustina did not sing in this production. Lalli, the regular poet at the Teatro San Giovanni Grisostomo, rewrote the libretto of the latter, which is based in general on a libretto of Zeno's.[47] *Demetrio* was Hasse's fifth Metastasian libretto.

Issipile, another Metastasian *dramma per musica*, was the last of the long series of operas composed for Naples that had begun with *Sesostrate* in 1726. Hasse could only have participated in the performance if it took place in the fall. But since no librettos survive, it is not known when it was performed.[48]

After the activity of 1730-1732, Hasse enjoyed a year of relative quiet. Throughout 1733 he stayed in Venice, perhaps composing pieces for the *Incurabili*. He produced only one new opera, and that was in Bologna, a one- or two-day trip from Venice. *Siroe*, again on a Metastasian libretto, was performed on 2 May, with Farinelli and Tesi singing the first roles. Gaetano Majorana, *detto* Caffarello, who had sung in *Cajo Fabrizio* and *Euristeo*, Filippo Giorgi, and Elisabetta Uttini, who had sung in *Ezio*, were also in the cast. The opera was performed some twenty-six times, quite an impressive record, and Hasse received 1260 lire for his participation in nineteen performances and for the further use of his score.

Hasse may have received an invitation to become composer for the London opera company (the "Opera of the Nobility") competing against Handel in this year, but there is no solid evidence for such an invitation, and it is almost certain that Hasse never went to London.[49] Handel's pasticcio *Cajus Fabricius*, produced on 4 December 1733 in London, shows that Hasse's music had quickly reached England. Of the twenty-six arias in the work, nineteen are from Hasse's *Cajo*, and two others are from his *Ulderica* and *Tigrane*.[49a]

In 1733 Frederick Augustus I died. During the period of mourning, Hasse probably began his official connection with the *Ospedale degli Incurabili* in Venice.[49b] With the accession of Frederick Augustus II, the musical activity of the Saxon court immediately increased. Count Villio received instructions to notify Hasse and Faustina that they were expected to be in Dresden by the end of 1733. Faustina was pregnant at that time, and it was not until 7 January, after the birth of their second child, that the couple left Venice.[50] They arrived in Dresden either on 3 February or in the beginning of March.[51] Hasse immediately began preparations for an opera. He and Faustina had been on the royal payroll as of 1 December 1733, with a combined salary of 6000 Taler a year, and a travel allowance (that year only) of 500 Taler.

On 8 July 1734 Hasse produced a revised version of *Cajo Fabrizio*. The date was an uncommon one for opera in Dresden, and may have been set because Hasse had arrived too late to produce one for the Carnival season. The opera was almost identical to the 1732 version, the main differences being that all of Angelo Monticelli's arias were rewritten for Faustina, who sang the role of Sestia in Dresden. The intermezzo was *L'Artigiano gentiluomo*, a version of *Larinda e Vanesio* of 1726, shortened and revised to two parts.

There were four performances of *Cajo Fabrizio* and on 15 July the Elector journeyed to Danzig for the summer. Upon his return on 2 August a cantata or serenata was performed, "*Sei tu, Lidippe.*"[52] Hasse's normal duties at this time may also have included private performances for the court, but there is no information on what was performed, or how often such concerts took place.

On 3 November, the court journeyed to Warsaw. Under the conditions of his employment, Hasse was not required to remain in Dresden when the court was absent. Thus he was free to do as he wished until the return of the court on 7 August 1736, a year and a half later. On 5 November 1734, Hasse and Faustina left for Venice. Their activities during the next two years have not been adequately documented. Evidently they stayed in Venice much of the time, for they rented a house at the "*calle grande o di Ca' Zen*" in 1735 and 1736.[53] Hasse did some writing for the *Incurabili*, including a *Salve regina* performed some time in 1736[54] but the Venetian performance of *Cajo Fabrizio* of the 1735 Carnival, ascribed to Hasse in the libretto, was probably a pasticcio: seventeen of the arias were new, and none of the singers was associated with Hasse.[55]

Hasse did write one opera in 1735, *Tito Vespasiano*. This work, on a Metastasian libretto, was commissioned for the opening of the Teatro Pubblico del Sole in Pesaro which took place on 24 September 1735. The cast was quite impressive: Faustina and Carestini were the prima donna and primo uomo, and Amorevoli sang the title role.[56]

For the Carnival of 1736 Hasse presented, in the Teatro San Giovanni Grisostomo, *Alessandro nell' Indie*. Though the libretto was the same as that from which *Cleofide* was derived, the work was new in almost every respect. All of the arias were either newly composed or heavily revised. Only one aria of the new opera was not taken from the original Metastasian libretto. Faustina did not take part in this; Tesi and Amorevoli sang the parts of Cleofide and Alessandro.[57]

Though the Elector had returned to Dresden in August of 1736, Hasse obtained permission to stay abroad for several more months. He returned to Saxony only on 28 January 1737,[58] though what had detained him is not known.[59]

Hasse spent 1737 and 1738 in Dresden. He was kept quite busy with court requirements during this period. The 1737 Carnival was the first that Frederick Augustus II had spent in Dresden, and Hasse produced *Senocrita* on 27 February for the occasion. This was the first opera that he had set on a libretto of Stefano Benedetto Pallavicino, the court poet and son of the composer Carlo Pallavicino. The libretto does not list the singers, but a score in Munich gives them: Faustina in the title role, supported by other members of the company hired in 1730-31: Negri, Bindi, Rochetti, Campioli, and Pozzi.[60]

26 July was the name day of Czarina Anna of Russia, and a second new opera of the season, *Atalanta*, also on a text by Pallavicino, was performed in her honor.[61] Again, Faustina sang the title role. This work was apparently written in the space of thirty-seven days, for a letter from Prime Minister Brühl to Hasse written on 17 June asks him to write "quelque petite operette" for the occasion.[62] By 24 July the work was ready to be performed at a dress rehearsal for the court and the première was on 26 July. It was short (sixteen arias and a chorus), but the autograph does not show any specific signs of haste, unless a large amount of simple da capo arias (lacking a new ritornello following the second verse, *i.e.* not dal segno) can be considered as such. Also performed was *Don Tabarano*, a slightly revised version of *La Contadina*.

Eight days later, 3 August, was the first performance of yet another opera, *Asteria*, in honor of the name-day of the King. Although Pallavicino called it a *pastorale* in his libretto, it is indistinguishable in form from an opera seria. The reason for the term was evidently the mythological subject matter of the work. The cast included Faustina, Bindi, Pozzi, Negri, Rochetti, Campioli, and Catanea.[63]

Hasse was not required to produce a new opera for the King's birthday on 7 October. Instead, *Asteria* was repeated. In later years, this date, rather than that of 3 August, would become the customary date for an opera presentation.

For the 1738 Carnival season, Hasse revised *Tito Vespasiano*. He now had an alto and two sopranos singing the parts originally given to a tenor and two altos. Faustina, again singing the part of Vitellia, was only given one new aria, and many of the other arias were only transposed, but twelve pieces from the second half of Act II and from Act III were completely rewritten. The premiere of this work took place on 17 January, the third anniversary of Augustus' coronation as King of Poland. It was quickly followed by a completely new opera, *Irene*, on another Pallavicino libretto. This was first performed on 8 February, the birthday of Czarina Anna.[64] Annibali had returned to Dresden after a two-year trip to London; he sang in both productions.

On 9 May Princess Maria Amalia, daughter of Frederick Augustus II, married Charles, King of the Two Sicilies, later Charles III of Spain. Two days later, the event was celebrated with an opera, *Alfonso*, on an appropriately Spanish story, versified by Pallavicino. The Dresden opera house was rebuilt and redecorated for the occasion, and the production was lavish, utilizing the King's Life-Guard in the battle scenes. The cast was the usual: Faustina, Rochetti, Annibali, Negri, Bindi, and Pozzi, but Ricci, a visitor, sang the tenor part of Pelagio. With *Alfonso* was sung the intermezzo *Il Tutore*, revised to a two-scene version. *Alfonso* was Pallavicino's fifth libretto in two years, and he was rewarded with the position of legation counsellor in the private court of Electoral Prince Frederick Christian, and given a vacation of two and a half years with the Prince on a tour through Italy.

On 22 September 1738 the court left for Poland, and Hasse and Faustina again journeyed to Italy. They rented a house in the "*contrada di S. Maria Zobenigo*" in Venice during the fall of 1738 and all of 1739.[65] Faustina sang in four operas during this period, while Hasse produced one, *Viriate*. This was a revision by Lalli of an anonymous *Siface* (possibly by Metastasio), and was presented during the Carnival of 1739, probably with the intermezzo *Pandolfo*, another name for *Il Tutore*. Faustina and Angelo Monticelli sang in *Viriate*, and Margherita and Cosimo Ermini performed in the intermezzo.[66] Another Hasse intermezzo, *Il Bottegaro gentiluomo*, actually identical to *L'Artigiano gentiluomo*, was also performed by the Erminis, between acts of Chiarini's *Achille in Sciro*, at the Teatro San Angelo.

The Hasses may have left Venice shortly after the Carnival season, for the court returned to Dresden on 11 April. There is no evidence for any activity on the part of Hasse, however, until 11 January 1740, when he presented *Tito Vespasiano* again. If this was a second revision, the extent of the changes is not known. On 8 February 1740, on the other hand, the production of *Demetrio* was of an opera that was radically different from the 1732 Venetian version. Only four arias in the first act and one in the second remained the same.[67] Faustina, Annibali, Bindi, Rochetti, and two guests, Filippo and Caterina Giorgi, made up the cast. The Erminis sang in the intermezzo, Pergolesi's *La Serva padrona*.[68]

On 7 September 1740, Prince Frederick Christian returned from his journey through Italy. His return was feted on 9 September with a new production of *Artaserse*. The opera had been revised to a moderate extent, with Faustina receiving five of the nine new arias. The cast included a new member of the cappella, Sofia Denner (also known as Dennerin; after her marriage in 1747 she was referred to by her married name, Pestel, or Pestelin), who was to remain active until 1751.

There were no further operas for a year. It is not known how Hasse spent this time. In 1741, the King's birthday, 7 October, was celebrated in the royal hunting lodge at Hubertusburg with a performance of a new opera and intermezzo, *Numa* and *Pimpinella e Marcantonio*, both set to librettos by Pallavicino. The intermezzo was Hasse's first completely new one since 1730. The two works were repeated on 3 November, the feast-day of St. Hubert.

In the following years, the schedule of 1740 became standard: one or two operas during the Carnival, and, in October, a new opera for the King's birthday.

The 1742 Carnival production, presented on 18 January, was *Lucio Papirio*, again on a libretto by Pallavicino. A new bass singer, Joseph Schuster (or, in Italian, Giuseppe Calzolaro) performed for the first time in this work. He was to remain with the cappella for the next ten years.[69]

Politics again entered Hasse's life at this point. The War of the Austrian Succession, in its localized form known as the First Silesian War, had been continuing since 1740. Frederick the Great, allying himself with Saxony, had invaded and conquered Silesia, a neighboring state belonging to the Austrian Empire. On 19 January 1742, he entered Dresden to sign the treaty that would give him control of Silesia. According to an anecdote related by Fürstenau, the talks ended abruptly on the 19th so that Frederick could attend a performance of *Lucio Papirio*.[70] Though he must have heard of Hasse, this was his first acquaintance with a complete opera, and the result was a long series of productions of Hasse's operas in Potsdam and Berlin, beginning the next year with *Tito Vespasiano* (performed as *La Clemenza di Tito*) and extending to 1786, the year of Frederick's death.

Hasse's next opera was again for the King's birthday on 7 October: *Didone abbandonata*. Metastasio's first opera seria was one of the few that Hasse had not yet set. The cast included Faustina, Negri, Rochetti, Bindi, Annibali, and Schuster.[71] Its libretto was altered by Algarotti, since the small stage in the Hubertusburg hunting lodge would not accommodate the final scene, the burning of Carthage.[72] According to the 1742 libretto, Didone had a long solo scene in accompanied recitative, culminating in an aria, "Ombra cara, ombra tradita," none of which is Metastasian. The opera then closed with dialogue between the other characters, and was followed by a licenza and chorus in honor of Frederick Augustus. Existing scores make a compromise between the two versions, and include both the "Ombra cara" scene and Didone's death scene, ending in the destruction of Carthage. It may be assumed that this second version was performed at the court theater in the Carnival of 1743.

A repeat of *Numa* opened the Carnival season on 14 January, 1743. It was followed by *Didone abbandonata* on 31 January. Again, Hasse remained in Dresden through the summer, though his next production was not until 7 October. The cast of this work, *L'Asilo d'amore*, is not known, but the scoring (four sopranos, alto, and tenor) suggests Faustina, Negri, Rochetti, Bindi, Annibali, and the tenor Angelo Amorevoli who had been hired in 1742 but was not listed in any libretti until 1744.[73]

Hasse's next two productions were quite important. His *Antigono* was the first setting of the Metastasian libretto, which had been commissioned specifically for Hasse by the Electoral Court. Rehearsals in the Queen's aparments took place on 9, 13, and 16 January 1744, a dress rehearsal was given on 18 January in the theatre, and the first open performance was presented on 20 January. Angelo Amorevoli, who had long been associated with Hasse's operas in Italy, sang the title role. He was to remain with the cappella until its disbanding in 1763. By 18 February, *Antigono* had been given fourteen times, quite a large number for the Dresden court.[74]

8 January also saw the first performance of *Ipermestra*, in Vienna, presented at the marriage of Maria Anna of Austria to Charles Alexander of Lorraine. This libretto, written "in great haste"[75] for the Austrian Imperial Court, had also never been set before. Hasse, who had never before had the honor of giving a Metastasian libretto its first setting to music, found himself setting two of them, and producing them withing twelve days of each other. Though he probably was present in Vienna to supervise rehearsals, he may not have presided at the actual performance. The music of the licenza was written by the

Vizekapellmeister Predieri, and the ballets were composed by Holzbauer; the performance was probably directed by Predieri since the post of maestro di cappella was vacant at the time.

On 5 May 1744 Hasse left Dresden for Italy, stopping at Vienna on the way south. He did not return until the late summer of 1745. During this year he was quite active in Italy, probably taking over Carcani's duties as maestro di cappella of the *Incurabili*.[76]   In the Carnival season of 1745 he presented a new opera, *Semiramide*, at San Giovanni Grisostomo in Venice. This was actually first performed on 26 December 1744, St. Stephen's Day.[77]   The cast included Tesi and Carestini: the libretto was by Metastasio.

By the middle of 1745, Hasse was probably occupied with the composition of *Arminio*. Pallavicino had died in 1742 at the age of 68, and in 1744 Claudio Pasquini, a protégé of Metastasio, was appointed court poet. Letters were sent to him in Vienna from the Dresden court in October 1744 asking him to finish the text of *Arminio* and send it to Hasse act by act so that it could be set to music. The opera was completed, rehearsed, and performed by 7 October 1745. In a change from custom, the holiday was not celebrated in Hubertusburg, but in Dresden. The cast included Faustina, Rochetti, Annibali, Amorevoli, Bindi, Negri, and Schuster.

Again in 1745, politics affected Dresden's musical life. In the Second Silesian War of 1744-45, Saxony changed its allegiance, and supported Austria when Frederick the Great invaded Bohemia. The Prussians were successfully expelled, but they defeated the Saxon-Austrian Army at Kesselsdorf and forced the compromise Treaty of Dresden, where Prussia recognized Maria Theresa's husband as Emperor Francis I (and ended this phase of the War of the Austrian Succession) in return for the legal cession of Silesia to Prussia. Frederick entered Dresden on 18 December with all the prestige of a conqueror, to negotiate the treaty. By his command, *Arminio* was performed the next day and Hasse and Faustina were asked to give chamber concerts for Frederick every night for his nine-day stay. Upon his leaving Dresden, Frederick gave Hasse a "costly" ring, and the cappella 1000 Taler for its trouble. Frederick also had *Arminio* performed in Berlin one year later, in January of 1747, for the performance rights of which Pasquini received 100 ducats.

Frederick Augustus II had fled to Prague, but although he returned on 4 January 1746 there was no Carnival opera given that year. The artistic requirements of the nobles were met by the travelling opera company of Pietro Mingotti, which spent July and August in Dresden. Mingotti received permission to build a wooden theatre in the Zwinger courtyard. This was the first commercial theatre in Dresden, and its prices are worth noting: a first or second row loge was 24 ducats a season or two ducats a night. Individual seats were 16 groschen each. A third-row loge was 12 ducats a season, one ducat a night, or twelve groschen for individual seats in loges five through ten, sixteen groschen for seats in loges one to four and eleven to fourteen and parterre. The most expensive seats were those closest to the stage.

One of Mingotti's productions, on 26 July, was of Hasse's *La Clemenza di Tito* (*Tito Vespasiano*), but Hasse may not have stayed to observe the performance. By late July he had left for Venice. On the way south he visited the Electoral Bavarian Court in Munich, where he met the artistically-inclined Princess Maria Antonia Walpurgis, elder sister of the Elector of Bavaria. The marriage of Maria Antonia with Frederick Christian had certainly been arranged by this time, and Hasse was becoming acquainted with his future employer.

Once in Venice, Hasse began revising *Semiramide* for its Dresden debut.[78] The autograph, in the Venice Conservatory, shows the haste involved in the revision.[79] A court letter of 28 December says that Hasse journeyed back by way of Munich, where he was stricken with gout and delayed. Thus he had to send the completed manuscript of *Semiramide* ahead of him, using he mounted courier of the Saxon ambassador, Count von Gersdorf. The King and Queen had been in Warsaw from 12 September to 17 December and Hasse apparently returned to Dresden after they did. The reason for haste was the imminent formal request by the French ambassador, the Duc de Richelieu, for the hand of Princess Josepha in the name of the Dauphin of France. This announcement was made at a celebration on 7 January 1747, and *Semiramide* was performed in honor of the betrothal on 11 January.[80] The cast included Faustina, Rochetti, Annibali, Amorevoli, Bindi, and Denner. Six of the arias were completely new, others were transposed, and three were extensively revised; Hasse was thus not successful in creating a totally new work for the occasion.

A very important event for Hasse and the artistic life of Dresden took place on 13 June 1747 with a double marriage, between Frederick Christian and Maria Antonia, and the Saxon Princess Maria Anna and Bavarian Elector Maximilian Joseph. The celebration lasted from 10 June to 3 July, and included a reference to Maria Antonia in the title of Hasse's opera, written for the occasion by Pasquini, *La Spartana generosa*, performed on 14 June. The cast included Carestini, in Dresden for a four-year stay.

The same summer, Hasse probably met Gluck, for the latter was in Dresden with the Mingotti opera company, presiding at the performance of *Le Nozze d'Ercole e d'Ebe* on 15 September 1747. A more fateful meeting was with his former teacher Porpora, hired by Maria Antonia as her singing teacher. On 18 July, Hasse presided at a performance of Porpora's *Filandro*, given in the court theatre. Caterina

Regina Mingotti, the young wife of impresario Pietro Mingotti, and a student of Porpora's, was the prima donna. This was the first time since Hasse had become maestro di cappella that he had produced an opera seria by another composer, and the first time that a prima donna other than Faustina had sung.

The impetus for this change came from the new Princess Maria Antonia Walpurgis.[81] She had great artistic pretensions, and was an avid amateur of painting, composing, and versifying. Her poetry was edited by Metastasio, and her music by Hasse, though she did not really appreciate any aid beyond the most general suggestions, hidden behind compliments.[82]

The true condition of the relationship between Hasse and Maria Antonia will never be known. While she was obviously proud to have such a renowned composer in her court, he may not have been diplomatic enough in correcting and finishing her compositions. She also had insulted him deeply by hiring a well-known composer, though this may well have been unintentional, a result of a desire for a more glittering musical establishment. Likewise, the hiring of the 19-year-old Regina Mingotti may have been necessitated by a failing of Faustina's vocal powers--she was 47 or 54 years old at the time--but it was extremely unpolitic not to let Faustina and Hasse determine the successor. The situation also shows quite clearly the lack of power that Hasse had, even after fourteen years as maestro di cappella.

On 7 October, a new Pasquini opera, *Leucippo*, was produced, with a cast including Carestini, Faustina, Amorevoli, Denner, Rochetti, and Schuster. This, as usual, was in Hubertusburg. *La Spartana generosa* was repeated at the opening of the 1748 Carnival season. (The exact date does not seem to be known.) This was followed on 9 February by *Demofoonte*, on a Metastasian libretto. For this season, the opera house had been enlarged and completely redecorated by Giuseppe Galli-Bibiena, who remained as stage designer until 1753.

Both Faustina and Mingotti sang in this production, which produced a battle reminiscent of the Faustina-Cuzzoni rivalry of 1726 in London. While Faustina was the prima donna, her role was that of a princess in disguise as a handmaiden, and as such she was forced to give precedence on stage to Mingotti, playing a princess of lower rank, but undisguised. Metastasio was appealed to as a judge of the dispute, and all of his abilities as diplomat were necessary as he wrote in succession to Pasquini (10 and 16 February), Baron Diesskau, the court impresario or "Directeur des plaisirs" (21 February), and Hasse himself (21 February), attempting to convince them that Faustina must indeed give precedence to Mingotti.[83]

As a further blow, Porpora was created maestro di cappella on 13 April 1748. This meant that Dresden had two holders of that position, though Hasse continued to serve all of his usual functions.

On 27 May the court left for Warsaw. Though it returned on 8 February 1749, this was too late for the usual Carnival celebrations, and Hasse's leave was probably easily extended. There is no actual evidence that Hasse went to Venice,[84] but in the Carnival season of 1749 a version of his *Demofoonte* was performed at San Giovanni Grisostomo, with Carestini again in the title role. Eight or nine arias were rewritten, and much of the new music survives under Hasse's name.[85] In May, for Ascension, Hasse revised *Leucippo* for Venice; once more Carestini sang the title role. This version was almost identical to the Dresden production, with only two substitute arias, one of which was taken from *Didone abbandonata*. This was to be Hasse's last production for Venice for ten years.

After returning to Dresden, Hasse prepared *Il Natal di Giove*, presented in Hubertusburg on 3 August, the name-day of the king.[86] This "azione teatrale" of Metastasio's was one act in length. Hasse was then busy setting to music another important libretto, *Attilio Regolo*. This libretto had been written by Metastasio in 1740 for the name day of Charles VI. The Emperor had died, however, and the work was put away for a decent length of time before it was allowed to be set.[87] Metastasio was quite proud of it, and since Hasse was giving it its first setting, he wrote him a long letter giving advice on how to treat the characters and text.[88] Hasse followed the advice, almost to the last detail, as to which words should be set to accompanied and which to simple recitative. On 12 January 1750 the opera had its premiere, with Faustina, Annibali, Amorevoli, Mingotti, Negri, Schuster, and Rochetti in the cast.

From April through October of 1750 the court was in Warsaw, and Hasse and Faustina took advantage of this to make a trip to Paris. The Dauphine, Maria Josepha of Saxony, was well-acquainted with the Hasses and provided a warm welcome for them. Hasse had been made Oberkapellmeister on 7 January of that year, but Porpora and Mingotti remained at court, and a certain desire for appreciation might have lain behind this journey. Hasse could not have expected to find a new position in Paris, where Italian-French musical tastes were so polarized, but he may have gained some leverage in Dresden merely by making such a journey.[89]

One of Dresden's few triumphs over Berlin came in 1751, when, through the diplomacy of Brühl, Frederick the Great's favorite castrato was lured away by the Saxon court.[90] Felice Salimbeni was an internationally-known figure, and admired by all who heard him. He was hired as of 1 January 1750, with a salary of 4000 Taler, compared to the 3000 he had been receiving in Berlin, and with the understanding that he could make a trip to England and Italy before arriving at Dresden. Thus, it was not until 7 January 1751 that he made his court debut in the title role of *Leucippo*. For this production, Hasse rewrote all of the arias for the primo uomo. But Salimbeni was ill with consumption, and he left Dresden after Easter, with a 4000 Taler pension, in hopes of his eventual return after another stay in Italy. He never arrived in Italy, but died in Ljubljana in the last days of August 1751, at the age of 39. Carestini had been allowed to leave, and actually replaced Salimbeni in Berlin for several successful years, so in a sense Frederick the Great had again out-maneuvered Saxony.

On 20 January, 1751, the second opera of the season was presented, *Ciro riconosciuto*, on one of Metastasio's librettos. Faustina and Salimbeni both appeared on the stage for the last time in this opera. Faustina retired after a Good Friday (10 April) performance of Hasse's oratorio, *I Pellegrini al sepolcro di N.S.* She kept the largely honorary title of *virtuosa di camera*, and retained her salary of 3000 Taler a year, quite a sizeable amount for what was in effect a pension.

Hasse does not seem to have left Dresden that summer; a Mass in D minor and a *Te Deum* were performed on 29 June to celebrate the dedication of the new Court church, designed by Gaetano Chiaveri and begun in 1738, though not finished until 1755. Its organ, inaugurated in 1754, was the last instrument designed by Silbermann, who died in 1753.[91]

A greatly-revised version of *Ipermestra*, with twelve new arias, was produced on 7 October in Hubertusburg. The cast included Mingotti, Rochetti, Albuzzi, Annibali, Amorevoli, and a visiting tenor, Lodovico Cornelius.[92] Most of Ipermestra's arias remained untouched: four (including a duet) are copied from 1744. Only two arias are new, perhaps a sign of Hasse's unwillingness to write for this unwelcome prima donna.[93]

On 7 January 1752 the Carnival season opened with a repeat of *Ipermestra*, and on 17 January a new opera, *Adriano in Siria*, was presented.[94] The cast of this opera (on a Metastasian libretto) included Mingotti, Annibali, Amorevoli, Rochetti, Albuzzi, and Anton Führich, a bass who was originally hired in 1746 to sing in the comic opera company of Campagnari, producing in the summer seasons.

From August 1752 to the end of the year, the King and court were in Warsaw, but Hasse stayed in Dresden, according to letters from Count Wackerbarth, and presided at evening concerts for Maria Antonia and Frederick Christian, who also remained in Saxony.

There was no King's birthday celebration in 1752 since the court was absent. This was fortunate for the singers, since a major reorganization of the opera company was taking place this year. Porpora had been pensioned by a decree of 1 January 1752, receiving 400 Taler a year. Regina Mingotti was released without a pension on 31 July 1752, and was replaced by Albuzzi. This was no doubt due in part to Albuzzi's connection with Brühl, though the animosity between the Hasses and Mingotti was certainly another large factor. Führich had been hired earlier, as mentioned above, as an alternate to Schuster. Four new singers had all been hired in 1752: Angelo Maria Monticelli (mezzo-soprano) in January, to replace Annibali (alto); Caterina Pilaja in April, to take the place Albuzzi had vacated when she became prima donna; Giovanni Belli in July, (to replace Bindi), and Bartolomeo Putini also in July (to replace Rochetti until 1755).

Thus in two years the entire cappella of 1731 had been retired: Negri, Faustina, Annibali, Bindi, and for the time being, Rochetti. Replacement was not limited to the singers. Pasquini had been pensioned in 1749, and in his place Giovanni Ambrogio Migliavacca was hired as court poet in 1752. Migliavacca, a pupil of Metastasio's, was a mediocre poet and, worse for Hasse, not a prolific author. In four years he produced only two original opere serie, far too few for Dresden requirements.

The next opera to be produced was *Arminio*, on 8 January 1753, opening the Carnival season. This was a greatly-revised version of the original 1745 opera.[95] Nine arias had new texts, and four had new or greatly revised music. Of the original cast, only Amorevoli and Schuster remained.

Migliavacca's dissatisfaction with his own poetry is very much apparent in Hasse's next work, *Solimano*, first performed on 5 February, after the tenth performance of the revised *Arminio*.[96] The autograph is filled with sections of recitative that were rejected, perhaps by the librettist, after they had been set to music by Hasse. Later copies of *Solimano* do not include these sections, nor does the libretto. The opera was produced with much pomp; Selim's grand entrance in Act I, scene 7 included elephants, horses, camels and other beasts, and literally hundreds of soldiers. The chronicler of the *Curiosa Saxonica* was also very impressed with the scenery, designed by Giuseppe Galli-Bibiena: the final set depicted the Turkish encampment on the banks of the Tigris as seen by night, with Babylon in the background and many ships on the river.

Hasse made another visit to a royal court in March 1753, this time to Frederick the Great in Berlin. He attended a performance of Graun's *Silla*, and received a snuff-box and a ring as a gift from the King. Whether he was offered a position has not been recorded.

In April, on Good Friday, Hasse directed an oratorio, and then was free to prepare for the new opera to be presented on 7 October.[97]

This work, Metastasio's *L'Eroe cinese*, included Amorevoli, Monticelli, Albuzzi, Pilaja, and Belli in the cast.

As was customary, the Carnival of 1754 opened with an old work, *Solimano* in this case, presented on 7 January. This was followed on 6 February by *Artemisia*, the second and last libretto written by Migliavacca for Hasse. From now until the end of his career, Hasse was to be concerned solely with the librettos of Metastasio.[98] The cast included one new member, Pasquale Bruscolini, an alto, who had been a colleague of Salimbeni's in Berlin.

On 17 June 1754 the court departed for Warsaw, where it remained until December. Hasse took the opportunity to go to Italy, though he did not produce any operas there. On his return, he stopped in Leipzig; he and Faustina are known to have attended a concert there on 21 November, and Count Wackerbarth wrote in a letter of 27 November that he was still in that city. On 7 October there had been a repeat of *L'Eroe cinese* in Warsaw, but Hasse was probably not present.[99]

The court had returned in time for the Carnival season, for *Artemisia* was repeated on 7 January 1755. The new opera of the season was *Ezio*, which opened on 20 January. Hasse had set this libretto once before, in 1730, but his second version was apparently entirely new.[100] It is likely that Hasse set the new version using the 1730 opera as a reference point, and then destroyed the 1730 version as being superfluous. He seems to have followed this pattern with the versions of *Tito*, *Artaserse*, and *Siroe*. *Ezio* was even more spectacular than *Solimano*: it included 8000 lamps and candles, carried by 250 supernumerary actors, and the triumphal entry of Ezio in Act III included 400 men, 102 horses, five wagons, eight mules, and eight Bactrian camels, and lasted a total of twenty-five minutes. It had to take place in the Zwinger garden next to the Court theater, for the stage was not big enough. The closing ballet, composed by the Dresden church composer Johann Georg Schürer, and choreographed by Pitrot, included 300 dancers and lasted forty-five minutes.[101]

Again, Hasse's activity after Good Friday has not been documented. His next production was *Il Rè pastore*, on Metastasio's libretto, presented on 7 October in Hubertusburg. This was repeated on 3 November, the Feast of St. Hubert. The cast included Monticelli, Albuzzi, Pilaja, Belli, and Bruscolini. The following Carnival season opened on 7 January 1756 with *Il Rè pastore*, continued with *Ezio*, and ended with a new opera, *L'Olimpiade*, again on a Metastasian libretto, given six times between 16 February and 2 March. Another new singer, Giuseppe Perini, an alto, sang in this.

On Good Friday, Hasse presided at a performance of *I Pellegrini*, and on Easter Sunday, *La Conversione di S. Agostino*. The latter, on a libretto by Princess Maria Antonia, had first been performed in 1750.

Hasse had already begun rehearsals for the 7 October opera, when the musical life of Dresden was completely upset by the outbreak of the Third Silesian War, more widely known as the Seven Years War.[102]   On 9 September, the Prussians marched into Dresden; in October the Saxon army was surrounded at Lilienstein, and Brühl and Frederick Augustus fled to Warsaw.   On 14 November, the Battle of Pirna resulted in the defeat and capture of the Saxon army, and for the rest of the seven years, until 1763, Saxony served as a battleground for other armies.[103]

Hasse and Faustina were on good terms with Frederick the Great, and performed for him while he was in Dresden, notably on 22 November, St. Cecilia's Day.   In December, Frederick's maestro di cappella Georg Benda arrived from Berlin, and Hasse was given permission to leave.   On 20 December, he and Faustina departed for Italy.

The Last Years

Though Hasse was to produce operas for the Electoral Court in exile in Warsaw, and even present one more in Dresden, an epoch was clearly at an end in 1756. Hasse was never again to be the sole arbiter of musical taste for an entire country and court. The decline had been in the making for quite some time, and it did not necessarily take a world-wide war to destroy Hasse's livelihood. He had not produced an opera in a commercial theatre since *Leucippo* in 1749, and, aside from *Nitteti*, in 1758, was not to do it again in his life. The enormous resources required to support opera seria were slowly becoming unavailable to the classes which enjoyed the art form. The destruction and impoverishment of Saxony was only the first in a chain of upheavals which would eventually severely reduce court opera at Naples, Vienna, and Berlin. Hasse himself made only the most minor gestures towards more modern ideas of drama, preferring to continue in the path he had always followed. He made no attempt, at age 57, to move into the more dramatic and fast-moving forms of either opera seria or buffa.

Hasse and Faustina reached Venice by the spring of 1757, for Metastasio wrote to him there on 26 March. During Holy Week, Hasse may have conducted his oratorio *Giuseppe riconosciuto*, given at the Oratorio di San Filippo Neri, though it was not a first performance.[104] On 3 September Hasse wrote to Algarotti in Vienna, saying that Padre

Martini had flattered him with compliments and he wished to visit him in Bologna. He had taken none of his music with him, and he wished Algarotti to make a copy of Didone's accompanied recitative from the last act of *Didone abbandonata* and send it to him so that he could show it to Martini.[105] The copy was made, and Hasse visited Martini, for the monologue survives in the hand of one of Hasse's copyists, with the preceding recitativo semplice added in Hasse's own hand on the back, as if Martini had asked him to include what led up to it.[106] Also in the letter, Hasse made a passing reference to a planned return to Dresden in the near future, a trip of which nothing is known.[107]

Nitteti was given in the Carnival season of 1758 in Venice, in the Teatro San Benedetto. Hasse took advantage of his removal from Dresden, and included in it arias from *Il Rè pastore, Arminio*, and *Ezio*. Giuseppe Belli, of the Dresden company, had the part of Sammete, the primo uomo. Hasse also presided at a performance at the Monastero di San Lorenzo on 10 August, according to an eyewitness, Pierre Jean Grosley de Troyes.[108]

Venice was not a royal court, however, and Hasse had evidently lost much of his popularity with the paying public. He was not to produce any more operas for this city.

Yet he did not lack commissions during these years. In January of 1758 Hasse had written to the court in Warsaw, asking for permission to write operas for the Neapolitan court; he was to remain active in Naples for the next two years.

On 4 November 1758, a new version of *Demofoonte* was peformed at the Teatro San Carlo; this was completely different from the 1748 opera. And on 20 January, a new version of *Tito Vespasiano*, entitled *La Clemenza di Tito*, was presented.[108a] A letter from Warsaw of 20 June 1759 then gave Hasse further permission to write two more operas for the next winter season in Naples: *Achille in Sciro*, presented on 4 November 1759, and *Artaserse*, on 20 January 1760. Metastasio's libretto of *Achille in Sciro* was completely fresh to Hasse, but *Artaserse*, like *Demofoonte* and *La Clemenza di Tito*, was a complete re-setting of an old libretto (except for three arias taken from the earlier versions of 1730 and 1740).

During these years, Hasse was in close touch with the Saxon court, and may have visited Warsaw in the summers. Perhaps also his extended vacation was permitted on the condition that he supply music for the court without the obligation of directing the cappella-in-exile, and he may have merely forwarded operas to be produced by others. Thus on 3 August 1759 *Nitteti* was performed, on 7 October the new version of *Demofoonte*, and on 3 August 1760 the new *Artaserse*.

On 19 July 1760 the forces of Frederick the Great, marching in retreat across Saxony, bombarded Dresden in a vain effort to gain entrance to the city, then occupied by the Austrians. In the bombardment, the residence of Hasse was destroyed, along with a collection of manuscripts that had been prepared for publication by Breitkopf. These may have included the early autographs, which have not survived. More likely, only copies were destroyed, for Hasse apparently took most of his own scores to Venice some time after 1756.[109]

In 1760, Hasse received an invitation to come to Vienna, and the next three years were spent in activity there. On 8 October 1760 the marriage of Archduke Joseph, later Emperor Joseph II, to Maria Isabella of Parma was celebrated with the festa teatrale *Alcide al bivio*, the first setting of this Metastasian text, in the *grossen Redoutensaale* of the Imperial Palace, with Manzuoli in the title role.[110] This was performed in conjunction with Gluck's *Tetide*.

From December 1760 through January 1761 Hasse held the post of music master for the archduchesses Maria Carolina and Maria Antonia. He composed for them a *Complimento* for the birthday of the Emperor, Francis I. The two archduchesses were eight and five years old; the first was later to become the wife of Ferdinand I of the Two Sicilies, the second (as Marie Antoinette) the wife of Louis XVI of France. The cantata, "*Apprendesti, o germana*," was meant to be followed by the opera *Il Rè pastore*, according to instructions in the autograph, but there exists no evidence of Viennese performance of this work.

In January 1761 the entire Hasse family settled in Vienna. In the Carnival, Hasse directed a new opera, *Zenobia*, on Metastasio's libretto of 1740. In February, *Alcide al bivio* was repeated, and in March he presented a Litany of the Blessed Virgin.

Though he could not have directed a repeat of *L'Olimpiade* in Warsaw during the 1761 Carnival, Hasse now had time to journey there, for his next Viennese production was not until April 1762. *Arminio* was repeated in Warsaw in August 1761, and *Zenobia* in October. That *Zenobia* was intended from the first for Warsaw is obvious from the autograph title page: *La Zenobia/ messa in musica/ per il teatro reale di Varsavia/ da Giov: Adolfo Hasse,/ detto il Sassone./ Vienna 1761.* He may or may not have remained for the repeat in the Carnival season of 1762 of *Ciro riconosciuto*.

Upon returning to Vienna, he presided at *Il Trionfo di Clelia*, presented on 27 April, an opera written by Metastasio expressly for the birth of a child to the Archduchess Isabella of Bourbon. Then, he apparently returned to Warsaw for the August, October, and Carnival operas of 1762-1763: *Il Trionfo di Clelia, Il Rè pastore*, and *Siroe*.[111]

Siroe was certainly planned for Warsaw: a libretto was printed and the title page of the autograph score reads "*Varsavia, 1762*" suggesting it was written there. An end to the Seven Years War was imminent at the beginning of 1763 and the Carnival entertainment may have been cancelled as the court prepared to return to Dresden. But, with a lack of evidence to the contrary, it can be assumed that *Siroe* was performed in the first week of January 1763.[112]

The Peace of Hubertusburg was signed on 15 February 1763. The court returned to Dresden on 2 April, and Hasse must have followed soon thereafter.[113] The court theatre had been turned into a magazine by the Prussians, and extensive remodelings were necessary before opera could again be produced. On 3 August, *Siroe* was presented. Three of the pre-war company were in the cast,[114] Amorevoli, Bruscolini, and Pilaja, with three others, Giuseppe Gallieni, Elisabeth Teyber,[115] and Antonio Pio Fabri, replacing Albuzzi (who had died in Prague in 1760), Monticelli (who had died in Dresden in 1758), and Putini (who had gone into service with the Russian court in St. Petersburg).

The next scheduled opera was for the King's birthday on 7 October. *Leucippo* was revived yet a fifth time by Hasse, and was rehearsed on 2 October in the King's apartment. It was to be performed by nobles: Maria Antonia, the Princesses Elisabeth and Cunigunde, Countess Mniszech, Count Brühl, and Chamberlain von Rechenberg.[116] The dress rehearsal was set for 5 October but Frederick Augustus II died suddenly that day of a stroke, and the opera was never performed.

Instead, with the loss of power of Brühl, massive economies were put into effect by the new King, Frederick Christian. On 7 October, instead of being rewarded for his latest opera, Hasse found himself, with Faustina, released without pension. A certain amount of back pay owing to him may also have been cancelled.[117]

The new King did not reign very long. On 17 December of that year, after a four-day bout with smallpox, Frederick Christian died, leaving his minor son to reign as Frederick Augustus III. Frederick Christian's ministers remained in control of the government, and Maria Antonia was unable to bring about any loosening of the purse strings towards the arts. Hasse remained in Dresden through 7 February 1764, conducting the funeral services to their completion, and receiving 1000 Taler for supplemental expenses for November and December. On 19 January 1764 he received the title of Honorary Electoral Oberkapellmeister, a position without pay, and on 20 February he and Faustina left for Vienna. Several singers who had not been active for several years received pensions: Annibali (600 Taler), Margherita Ermini (300 Taler), Denner (400 Taler), and Negri (200 Taler). Amorevoli remained as a church singer, along with two singers from the subsidiary comic opera: Wilhelmine Denner and Salvatore Pacifico.[118]

Hasse found quite a friendly atmosphere in Vienna, though he was not to receive any official post. In April 1764 he produced a new festa teatrale, *Egeria*. This libretto was commissioned from Metastasio and Hasse for the coronation of Joseph II as co-regent. Later that year it was also performed in Naples.

Sometime during that year *Siroe* was also produced in Vienna. Whether this was produced by Hasse is not known. In 1764 Hasse revised *L'Olimpiade* for performance in Turin during the 1765 Carnival, beginning on 26 December 1764. There was no special event associated with the performance, but it was not a pasticcio, for part of this version is bound in with the autograph of the 1756 opera, and a full copy (without recitatives) remains.[119]

Another Imperial Austrian commission followed the next year. In August 1765, the Archduke Leopold (later Leopold II) married Maria Luisa of Bourbon, and on 6 August *Romolo ed Ersilia* celebrated the occasion. Again, this was a joint effort of Metastasio and Hasse, by now considered the two staunchest defenders of the tradition of opera seria.[120] The work was also presented later in the year in Naples' San Carlo theatre.

Early in 1766 Hasse made a trip to Venice, but he was soon back in Vienna. On 9 September 1767 he presided at the premiere of *Partenope*, a two-act festa teatrale of Metastasio's, celebrating the marriage of Ferdinand IV of Bourbon, King of the Two Sicilies, with Maria Josepha, Archduchess of Austria. The obviously topical subject was given again at Naples, (founded by the siren Parthenopea, according to myth) on 20 September, in the Teatro San Carlo. Elisabeth Teyber, one of the last-hired singers of the Dresden company, sang the part of Elpinice, the prima donna, in both locations.

Hasse's penultimate drama was produced for amateurs. *Piramo e Tisbe*, called an *intermezzo tragico* by the librettist, was a two-part drama for two sopranos and a bass. It was commissioned by "a French-woman",[121] who, with a friend, sang the roles of Piramo and Tisbe. The poet, Marco Coltellini, sang the part of Tisbe's father. The performance took place in November of 1768.

Hasse had remained in touch with his Venetian friends, and in June of 1768 he was asked to suggest a director for the *Ospedale degli Incurabili*. He suggested Sarti or Traetta, but approved of the final choice, Galuppi. One of his voice pupils at this time was Marianne di Martinez, the ward of Metastasio and also a pupil of Haydn. Burney tells us that the Davies sisters lived in the same house as Hasse and also received lessons, in return for teaching English to his daughter Peppina.[122] In 1769 Cecily Davies sang in a Hasse cantata, *L'Armonica*, presented in Schönbrunn. Her sister, Mary Ann, performed the "title role," playing the glass harmonica, recently perfected by Benjamin

Franklin.   About this time Hasse met Leopold and Wolfgang Mozart, and wrote a letter of recommendation to his Venetian friend Abate Giovanni Maria Ortes for them.

Piramo e Tisbe was planned to be repeated at Easter 1769, but the performance was held off until September 1770 when a version, "changed and improved,"[123] was performed in the Laxenburg Palace Theatre, the summer residence of the Viennese court. Hasse received a ring from the Empress as a present.

Hasse's last opera was again a royal commission, shared with Metastasio. Ruggiero, ovvero l'eroica gratitudine was to be Metastasio's last opera seria, also.[124] It was presented at the wedding of Archduke Ferdinand with Maria Beatrice d'Este, Princess of Modena. Hasse was again suffering from gout, as the autograph shows, and Mennicke says he dictated parts to his daughter Peppina.[125] He approached the task with much apprehension, unwilling to write a "dramma da balarsi"; he thought that the libretto also had too much recitative and not enough spectacle.[126] In August of 1771 he traveled to Milan to begin rehearsals. One of the first to visit him was the young Mozart, commissioned to write the serenata, Ascanio in Alba, for the same occasion.

From his letters to Ortes we learn the exact schedule of rehearsals: the first instrumental rehearsal was 21 September; the fourth rehearsal, the first with singers and instrumentalists together, was 5 October; on the 13th was the seventh rehearsal. On the 16th, the day after the wedding, was the first performance. The opera was a failure at first; Hasse wrote that everything that could have gone wrong did; that the later performances were better, but in Italy, it was the first one that counted.[127]

On the 17th was the first performance of Ascanio, and Leopold wrote with obvious glee, "I'm sorry; the serenade of Wolfgang's has so completely struck down Hasse's opera that I cannot describe it."[128] But the young Mozart must have been greatly impressed by Hasse's sheer musicality: he wrote a few days later: "Tonight is Hasse's opera; since however Papa is not going out, I cannot see it. Luckily, I know almost all of the arias by heart, and thus I can stay at home and see and hear it in my mind. . ."[129] Hasse wrote that the prima donna, Girelli, had lost her voice on 30 October; Ruggiero was finally given a fourth performance on 4 November, while the last performance of Ascanio, the fifth, had been on 28 October.

By the end of November, Hasse was back in Vienna, after a stop in Venice to visit Ortes. On 7 December he wrote to Ortes that he had had an audience with the Empress on the preceding Sunday, at which Peppina was given a golden box with a pair of earrings set with diamonds, and he received a large box of "most magnificent gold," and a ring with white brilliants. He said he had never been so well-paid for writing an opera.

In December 1772 his *St. Elena al Calvario* oratorio was presented. This work was a second version of the Metastasian libretto, a revision of the oratorio dated 9 April 1746.

Hasse had decided by this time to retire to Venice. He moved there in April 1773. One last letter to Ortes was written on a short visit to Vienna in November of that year, but otherwise he led a quiet life with his wife and daughter, teaching and composing cantatas and religious music: a *Te Deum* in 1776, a Mass for Maria Antonia of Saxony in 1779, and in 1781 a *Credo* and a *Tantum ergo* which the younger Joseph Schuster, by this time the church composer at Dresden, took back with him after visiting with Hasse on an Italian trip. Though he was troubled with loss of much of his income[130] he was never impoverished.

Hasse's last composition was a *Requiem* for Pope Pius VI, requested by the Dominican monks of Venice. It was performed on 16 May 1782, under the direction of Galuppi at San Marco.

Faustina Bordoni-Hasse, his companion of fifty years, died of "a cancerous ulcer" on 4 November 1781, at the age of 81 or 88. Hasse survived her by a little over two years. He died on 16 December 1783, at the age of 84. The death report of the Church of San Marcuola, where he was buried, listed the cause of death as "chest inflammation," (perhaps pneumonia), brought on by a severe attack of gout.

Hasse was not a forgotten man when he died, but the obscurity which had begun to envelop him in his last years is evident in the only obituary which seems to have been published. In 1784, Carl Friedrich Cramer noted:

> 10) From Italy, on the Third of January) In Venice, the famous Electoral Saxon Oberkapellmeister, Mr. Hasse, has departed this life, at an advanced age.

This is followed by the obituary proper, in a footnote:

> It goes without saying that one does not eagerly give the public the naked, tragic, news that "he, also, lives no longer," referring to the death of one of the most honored composers, who has been, in his art, one of the greatest figures of the century. Hasse has recognized as his equals in the realm of theatrical vocal music, within the entire German nation, only Handel, Graun, Gluck, and Benda. At this time, I know nothing about how it comes to pass that, beyond the known facts, not one biographical detail has been published about him. What we know is that: "He was born in Bergedorf. At one time he competed with Handel in London. Afterwards, for many

years, he, with his wife Faustina, was the father and pride of the most glorious stage of Europe that was Dresden.   After his release he continued his private life in Vienna (where *Piramo e Tisbe* became his last, and perhaps also, through the inspiring competition of Gluck, his best work).   Now, in Venice his life has ended." Beyond these details, there are only his works, of which I may eventually give a more complete review in this magazine.   Anyone who is better acquainted with his life history than I am, and can send me an accurate essay, or even any sort of data that he might wish to communicate, can certainly count upon the good will of the friends of art, as well as on the gratitude which I would gladly owe to him.[131]

Hasse was not forgotten by music historians (see Chapter VI), but performances of his operas became exceedingly rare.   In Dresden, there seems to have been no official notice taken of his passing.   In 1784 he was still listed as Oberkapellmeister, in the court calendar.   In 1785, his name disappeared, without a comment.

CHAPTER II

HASSE'S OPERAS: THEIR FORMS AND CONVENTIONS

Hasse began his career as an opera composer at the moment that reform of the libretto was being accomplished by Zeno and Metastasio. With the banishing of comic characters and situations was born the genre which eventually came to be called "opera seria."[1] Hasse devoted most of his efforts throughout his long life to this genre, writing an average of more than one a year during his active career.[2]

The typical opera seria libretto was a three-act *dramma per musica*, with between five and seven characters, usually six: two pairs of lovers, a king, and a general, confidant, or sage. The subject of the drama was usually taken from classical antiquity, and the three acts could often be conveniently separated into exposition, crisis, and resolution. The third act was usually shorter than the two preceding ones, and ended typically with the revealing of the villain and the pairing off of the lovers.[3]

The musical means were also narrowly delineated. The great bulk of the opera consisted of twenty to thirty da capo arias, separated by simple recitative. As a rule, the arias fell at the ends of scenes, and were followed by the exit of the singer. Other standard elements of the music included a three-part sinfonia in the fast-slow-fast Italian manner, a closing *coro*, or ensemble of the remaining principals, and perhaps one duet and one cavatina.[4] Two or three sections of accompanied, or obbligato, recitative enlivened the long stretches of simple recitative. In the former, the support of strings, and later woodwinds, was added to the continuo accompaniment. Trios and quartets were seldom encountered. An isolated march might be included, to accompany an entrance of a king and his court.

Hasse followed these conventions religiously throughout his career. The libretto of *Antioco*, his first opera seria, based on a drama by Minato of 1666, and revised successively by Zeno, Pariati, and Feind, shows most of the above characteristics, though most of the music has been lost. The work is in three acts, and includes six characters: two pairs of lovers, a king, and a general. There are thirty-two arias, a few more than usual, but presumably all are in da capo form, for they consist of the usual two stanzas. The first act has eleven arias that close scenes, a duet that ends the act, and one aria that opens a scene. In later operas, an opening aria would have been set as a cavatina, but it appears from the text that this too was a da capo aria. The second act has twelve arias, only one of which does not end a scene. The third act is shorter, with eight scene-closing arias, a ninth in the middle of a scene, and a tenth that opens a scene. The opera closes with a simple coro, sung specifically by the six characters.[5]

Hasse's second opera seria, *Sesostrate*, (Naples, 1726), is an anachronism, for the libretto shows it to be a typical opera seria, but the one surviving manuscript indicates that it was probably a mixed-genre production, including comic characters and scenes within the body of the opera, in the manner of operas of the previous decades. The manuscript includes thirty arias, while the libretto has only twenty-three (eight, eight, and seven, in the three acts), with a cavatina in the second act. There is no final coro in either source. The difference in numbers is caused by the presence of the comic characters in the opera proper in one case, and in separate intermezzi in the other.

Of the more than fifty opera seria libretti that were set by Hasse after *Sesostrate*, only one other, *La Sorella amante* (Naples, 1730), also included comic characters. This is also one of the few to include eight singers. The only other libretti with this number that were set by Hasse were *Alfonso* (Dresden, 1738), *Lucio Papirio* (Dresden, 1742), and *Demofoonte* (Dresden, 1748 and Naples, 1758). The former were on libretti by the Dresden court poet, Stefano Pallavicino, the latter on one by Metastasio.

Only two operas are not in three acts. The above-mentioned *Alfonso*, and *Senocrita* (Dresden, 1737), also by Pallavicino, have five acts each.[6] The total length of these operas is not any different, since *Alfonso* has twenty-five arias, a cavatina, and two cori, and *Senocrita* has twenty-one arias and a coro; both are well within the normal limits for an opera seria. Only minor adjustments have to be made for the extra acts: ballets are not found between all of the acts, and several acts have only one set-change. The only real dramatic requisite, the set change for the final denouement, in the last act, is found in both operas.

Only nineteen of Hasse's operas have duets. Most of these, like the majority of the arias, are in da capo form. No opera has more than one full-scale duet, but one, *Alessandro nell'Indie*, has also a duet-cavatina: two voices singing a short arioso passage.

Five operas have trios: *Arminio I, Tito Ia* (though this is problematic), *Viriate, Arminio II,* and *Nitteti*. While Claudio Pasquini, the court poet who succeeded Pallavicino, was writing the second *Arminio* libretto in 1744-45, Hasse may have asked him to include a trio, remembering the one in the Antonio Salvi libretto that he had set in 1730.

A lone quartet is found at the end of Act II of *Il Rè pastore*. It is in the Metastasian libretto and Hasse set it as if it were no different from a normal aria, albeit slightly longer. Likewise, *Antigono* ends with a sextet in both libretto and opera, set by Hasse in standard da capo format. The 1753 revision of *Arminio II, Il Rè pastore*, and *Nitteti* are the only operas to have more than one small ensemble.

While all operas but three end with cori,[7] only twenty-two include real opportunities for choral interjections during the course of the opera. Only five operas have more than two such choruses, the most striking being *Achille in Sciro* (Naples, 1759), which has many of the attributes of the festa teatrale. (See below, pp. 49 ff.) This work also includes three non da capo arias, a relatively high number, but the structural points are an opening chorus and two adjacent choruses in the middle of the second act. The first chorus serves as the third movement of the sinfonia, following, as it does, movements in F and B♭. The chorus is through-composed, in F, and marked 3/8, allegro, e con spirito ma non troppo presto. It is accompanied by a stage orchestra ("di sopra") and a normal orchestra ("di basso").

The first of the Act II choruses is in ABA form, with the B reserved for, remarkably, a solo bass voice. The second is in rondo form, with verses sung by Achille and the refrains sung by the chorus. There is a simple concluding coro in Act III, but there is no doubt that the large chorus took part in this along with the principals. Aside from the latter, the choruses are full-scale, elaborate pieces of music that do far more than run through the text once, homophonically. They look forward to the Viennese feste teatrale that Hasse was to set in the late 1760's. The only major difference is the lack of extensive obbligato recitatives: there are only three such pasages in *Achille*.

The specific forms used in the operatic numbers are almost as strict as the materials themselves. The opening sinfonia is usually in three-part Italian style, though five operas open with a French "ouverture," beginning with a slow, dotted, C movement and continuing with three or four succeeding movements: *Euristeo* and *Issipile* (which share the same overture), *Irene, Olimpiade a, Demofoonte II*, and *Ruggiero*. Five others have four-movement sinfonie: *Cleofide* and *La Spartana generosa* include a third movement minuet (the former predating Georg Monn's famous four-movement symphony by nine years); *Arminio II* a polacca, *Ipermestra b* and *L'Eroe cinese* moderate dances in 4/4 time. *Adriano in Siria*, like *Achille in Sciro*, opens with two movements followed by a fast chorus which serves as a conclusion. *Ciro riconosciuto* has three movements marked allegro di molto, allegro, and allegro![8]

The usual form for the aria was the so-called "five-part da capo."[9] The text was composed of two stanzas, A and B, each usually of four lines, though three-, five-, six-, and eight-line stanzas also exist. The typical aria opens with an instrumental ritornello (the A ritornello), which stays in the tonic. The soloist then sings the first stanza of text (A_1), using the theme introduced in the ritornello, but adding sections of coloratura or fioritura, and the aria modulates to the dominant, if in major, or to the relative major, if in minor. At the close of the first stanza, a very short ritornello (the A_1 ritornello), often employing a motive from the theme, is heard. The first stanza is then sung again (A_2), usually modulating quite quickly back to the tonic, and occasionally even opening in the tonic. This makes use of the main theme, newly composed and not simply repeated. Often, there are brief digressions to other keys during this stanza, which is always longer than A_1. It can include a fermata near the final cadence, at which point the singer adds a cadenza. A closing ritornello (the A_2 ritornello) then confirms the tonic.

The second stanza (B) follows. It is often sung to material related to the melody of the first stanza, though it can also be completely new, going so far as to have a different meter and tempo. It begins in a new key, most commonly the submediant, but also the tonic minor or subdominant, and usually modulates to still another key, usually the minor mediant, or minor dominant. At this point, the simplest procedure is the sign "da capo," or "D.C.," which indicates that the singer and orchestra are to return to the very beginning of the aria. More common after 1730 is the "dal segno," or "D.S.," indicated simultaneously with some sort of sign (Hasse liked to use §), in which a ritornello following the second stanza substitutes for the A ritornello, usually not using the same themes, and cadencing much more quickly. At the end of this ritornello (the B ritornello), the sign directs the performer to a similar sign, usually at the beginning of A_1. The B ritornello never cadences in a key other than the tonic of the aria.

Schematically, the major-mode aria can be diagrammed:

A rit.	A_1 stanza	A_1 rit.	A_2 stanza	A_2 rit.	Fine	B stanza	D.C.
I----I	I---------V	V----V	V---------I	I-----I	‖	vi-----iii	

or:

A rit	§A_1	A_1 rit.	A_2	A_2 rit.	Fine	B	B rit.	§D.S.
I----I	I---V	V----V	V--I	I-----I	‖	vi-iii	iii or I--I	

In the minor mode, the dal segno appears as:

A rit.	§A_1	A_1 rit.	A_2	A_2 rit.	Fine	B	B rit.	§D.S.
i----i	i--III	III-III	III--i	i------i	‖	III--v	v or i--i	

Hasse used this format throughout his career, and while minor changes were common, there was no large-scale departure from the outlines described above. Concerning the mode, arias in minor keys are so rare as to be highly noticeable when they occur. Only two or three at most are found in any one opera. These almost always modulate to the relative major; only three or four examples of minor key arias modulating to the minor dominant are to be found in Hasse's operas. Almost as rare as minor-key arias are major-key arias which modulate to the supertonic.

The A_1 ritornello usually both begins and ends in the dominant, but sometimes other situations prevail. It can serve as a modulation from dominant to tonic, in which case A_2 stays in the tonic.[10] At times, A_1 will end on a deceptive cadence (the submediant of the new key), and the authentic cadence will come only at the end of the A_1 ritornello, or even on the first downbeat of A_2. The ritornello can even be omitted, or made to be the accompaniment for an interjection ("Dio," "cara," "ah,") in later operas, though this is extremely rare.

Several times in each opera, Hasse will write an aria without an A ritornello. This is not often on his own initiative, but occurs when the singer of the aria in question has not been the one to conclude the recitative of the scene. The effect is highly dramatic, since it is not anticipated, but, like many of Hasse's uncommon effects, it stems from the imagination of the librettist. Still, it would be possible, though much less dramatic, to have the new speaker wait through fifteen or twenty measures of ritornello before responding to the concluding speech. This type of aria always has a B ritornello, so that the singer can rest between the B stanza and the repeat of A_1. The lack of an A ritornello is one of the few considerations that Hasse ever makes to the dramatic situation, and he wisely uses it rarely.

In operas after 1745, Hasse tends to increase the number of arias in which the B stanza is in a new tempo and meter. These are inherited from the old Venetian opera of the late seventeenth century, and occur from the beginning of his career: *Sesostrate* includes two. *Semiramide a* (1745), *Artaserse II* (1760), and *Siroe b* (1763) all have six, a considerable increase.

Another type of two-tempo aria, much rarer, alternates fast and slow tempos between lines of the A stanza, so the aria may look like:

A   ritornello: adagio
A_1, lines 1-2:   allegro
A_1, lines 3-4:   adagio
A_1 ritornello: allegro

A_2, lines 1-2:   allegro
A_2, lines 3-4:   adagio
A_2 ritornello: allegro

B: allegro
B ritornello: allegro

as in "Se tu non senti, o Dio," (II, 11), from *Cajo Fabrizio a* (Rome, 1732), or:

A   ritornello: adagio
A_1, lines 1-2:   allegro
A_1, lines 3-4:   adagio
A_1 ritornello: allegro
A_2, lines 1-2:   allegro

A_2, lines 3-4:   adagio
A_2 ritornello: allegro

B: allegro
B ritornello: allegro

as in "Se torbido aspetto," (III:11), from *Gerone, tiranno di Siracusa* (Naples, 1728). These arias do not become more frequent in later operas.

Another later development, concurrent with the trend to giving the B stanza its own tempo and meter, is a tendency to have B stanzas begin in the tonic, and then modulate to the new key, or at least have a descending melodic scale at the end of the A_2 ritornello to provide an introduction to the following key. Similarly, the B ritornello, eventually, opens in the key in which the B stanza has cadenced, and then modulates to the tonic, instead of starting out afresh in the tonic after the singer has cadenced on vi or iii.

The most noticeable changes in the da capo form are the various permutations known collectively as the half da capo aria.[11] In these, the A stanza is only sung once on the "da capo." This is accomplished in several ways. The most common arrangement is to provide an A_3 opening stanza after the B ritornello, that is merged, with a D.S., to the A_2 stanza at an appropriate point. Also common is a modulation of the B ritornello to the dominant instead of the tonic, and the D.S. thus refers simply to the unchanged opening of A_2. The consequent disruption of the tonal structure of the aria, providing a long bridge from the beginning of the B stanza to the end of A_2 without a complete tonic cadence, is quite adventuresome.

The most drastic step is the complete writing-out of an A_3 stanza. This usually consists of the first half of A_1 and the last half of A_2. In about half of the arias with shortened da capos, the third repeat of the A stanza begins and ends in the tonic.

These three methods can be diagrammed as follows:

```
1: A rit.    A₁     A₁ rit.   A₂      A₂ rit.   Fine    B        B rit.   A₃      D.S.
   I----I    I--V   V----V    V-§-I   I-----I    ‖      vi-iii   iii-I    I--§

2: A rit.    A₁     A₁ rit.   A₂      A₂ rit.   Fine    B        B rit.            D.S.
   I----I    I--V   V----V    §V-I    I-----I    ‖      vi-iii   iii-V    §

3: A rit.    A₁     A₁ rit.   A₂      A₂ rit.    B       B rit.   A₃      A₃ rit.
   I----I    I--V   V----V    V--I    I-----I    vi-iii  iii-I    I-I     I-----I

                                               Or:      iii-V    V-I     I-----I
```

The first aria with the half da capo format of type 1 above is "Vorrei spiegar l'affanno," (I:4), in *Semiramide a*, performed in Venice in the 1745 Carnival season. This, however, merely uses the opportunity of an A_3 opening to rewrite in minor details the opening of A_1. The da capo then continues through the second half of A_1 and all of A_2 and is not shortened at all. This aria is best considered a more elaborate expression of the usual dal segno, where not only the A ritornello is rewritten, but also the beginning of the A_1 stanza.

The first true half da capo aria is the duet, "Vanne a regnar," (I;7), in *Il Rè pastore* (Dresden, 1755). This is quite early in the historical development of the form, though it may have been preceded by other half da capo arias in the works of Jommelli. There are no other half da capos in *Il Rè pastore*; the fact that this was a duet, and thus already exceptional, may have led Hasse to begin this practice at this point.

Use of half da capo arias does not increase dramatically; the next use is not until 1758, with three examples found in *Demofoonte II* (Naples). None of the following operas has more than three (and some actually do not have any) until *Ruggiero, ovvero l'eroica gratitudine* (Milan, 1771), which has ten of them. Altogether, Hasse did not write more than twenty-five half da capo arias during his operatic career.[12]

The use of free or through-composed forms for arias begins earlier than half da capos, with *Arminio IIa*, first performed in Dresden in 1745. The aria "No, del tuo figlio il sangue," (III:2), is one of the earliest uses of a non-da capo form for a full-scale aria in an opera seria. This one has five verses, which was the obvious impetus for the break from the traditional form, though the opera was experimental in several respects.[13] The aria is in two tempos: the A ritornello (C presto) is followed by a slow (3/4 un poco lento) first couplet, returning to C presto for the second couplet, and cadencing in the dominant. The second stanza returns to 3/4 and stays in the dominant; the third stanza is C presto and modulates to the tonic; the fourth and fifth stanzas are 3/4 lento and C presto respectively, and remain in the tonic.

Through-composed arias are not used much after this early experiment: only three more are found in the following opere serie. More common are ternary arias, in which could be described as A_1-B-A_2 form. This form becomes the standard pattern for the opera seria aria by the end of the century. There are ten examples of ternary arias in Hasse's operas, starting with "Povero cor, tu palpiti," (II:1), in *Nitteti* (Venice, 1758), and continuing with examples in *Achille in Sciro* (1759), *Zenobia* (1761), *Il Trionfo di Clelia* (1762), *Olimpiade b* (1765), and *Ruggiero*. While ternary arias may have the structure I-V, V-I, I-I, it is more common for A_2 to open in a key other than the tonic; often the sequence is I-V, V-IV, IV-I.

A binary structure is also significant in the later development of opera in the eighteenth century. Most of Hasse's binary movements are actually cavatinas, but there are two or three true examples of full-scale arias having the structure of A_1-A_2, with the standard key arrangement of I-V and V-I. The earliest of these is the duet, "Va; già palesi," (I:9), which closes the first act of *Artemisia* (Dresden, 1754). After *Achille in Sciro*, there are no further examples.

Hasse was famous for his recitativo obbligato, but he always used it very sparingly, in keeping with Italian custom.[14] *Siroe b* (1763) has five examples, the most in any opera, but none of the passages is very long. As early as 1733, *Siroe a* had four such passages. The feste teatrali, which include more examples of recitativo obbligato, are described later in this chapter.

Cavatinas can be of two types. In the first, the text is sung once and is interrupted without a full cadence, such as in the famous last scene of *Didone abbandonata* (Dresden, 1742), "Vado . . . Ma dove? Oh Dio!" (III:20). In the second type, the text is sung twice, duplicating a complete A_1 and A_2 section of an aria, though on a smaller scale. An example of this is "Regina!   Tradita!" (II:4), of *Artemisia*.

Choruses show a complete lack of unity of form. The most simple cori can be twenty-measure syllabic renditions of a four-line stanza. The most complex effects can be rendered with the use of the full chorus, up to the rondo in *Achille in Sciro*, "Se un core annodi," (II:7), which alternates soloist with chorus.

Closing cori are never complex, but range from an A form, as with "Sempre in soglio," (III:12), in *Viriate* (Venice, 1739); to A_1-A_2, as with "Giusto rè, la Persia adora," (III:11), in *Artaserse II* (Naples, 1760); to A_1-A_2-A_3, "Più non turba un mesto orrore," (III:14), *Lucio Papirio* (Dresden, 1742); through A-B (two stanzas of text, sung to similar music, and having a key structure of I-V, V-I, thus otherwise being the same as A_1-A_2), "Della via nel dubbio cammino," (III:13), *Ezio II* (Dresden, 1755); and A-B-A, "Del nostro Cesare altro maggiore," (III:13), *La Clemenza di Tito II* (Naples, 1759).

These are mostly variations on the da capo, sometimes matching the cavatina structure, but usually having the key plan of I-V and V-I. The full da capo is occasionally encountered also. *Attilio Regolo*, which ends with Attilio's departure to Carthage and certain execution, needs an unusually weighty close, and thus draws the coro out, with the use of the da capo: "Onor di questa sponda," (III:10).

A surprising departure from this pattern is found in *Atalanta* (Dresden, 1737), where the sections of the da capo coro "Il feschio orribile del mostro ucciso," (III:7, repeated in III:8), are separated by recitative passages. This chorus also has instructions for a complete repeat using new words, an occasional occurrence.

There are only rare instances of a chorus being intended for more than the principals of the opera, aside from those in feste teatrali, and the exceptional *Achille in Sciro*. *Attilio Regolo* includes rare examples of choral interjections ("Regolo resti," (III:9)), which, however, were probably also sung by the principals, perhaps off-stage, though Metastasio has clearly labeled them to be sung by the "popolo."

By far the greatest amount of music in a Hasse opera, at least in amount of text set, is recitativo semplice, or recitative accompanied solely by the continuo: harpsichord and violoncello. Hasse's recitative is indistinguishable from that of his contemporaries, at least to modern ears; it was certainly composed in the minimum amount of time, and with the minimum of effort possible. Despite this facility, Hasse's recitative is always very carefully fitted to the words, with accents placed correctly and the flow of the dialogue running uninterruptedly.

Noteworthy are Hasse's recitative cadences. These are of several types, written down rhythmically as they are to be performed. Early in his career, the following types are to be found:

1:   The standard, tonic-to-dominant cadence in the voice part, with the bass moving from dominant to tonic, a beat later:

In performance, this was altered, with an appoggiatura, to:

In *Cajo Fabrizio a*, a typical case, nineteen of the twenty-four cadences preceding arias are of this type.   In eight of these, the tonic of the cadence becomes the dominant of the following aria.   In the others, the cadence is a major third above the key of the aria six times, a minor third above once (before the only minor-key aria), on the key of the aria twice, on the subdominant once, and on the submediant once.

2: The mediant-to-tonic cadence:

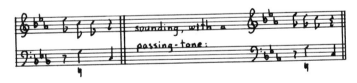

This occurs once in *Cajo*, and from one to three times in most operas.

3:   The phrygian cadence, performed without appoggiaturas or passing tones:

If, as is occasionally done, the penultimate chord is figured "#6," the cadence becomes an emphatic ♭VI-V. In this case, as with the other

cadences, the plurality are on the dominant of the following aria.
Within recitatives, most cadences are of the first type rhythmically, though the progression can be to I^6, IV^6, or another chord.

4: Also found three times in *Cajo* are cadences of the first type, with a delayed resolution:

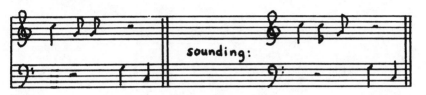

Since Hasse carefully differentiates between types 1 and 4, it must be assumed that the rhythms are intended to be performed as written at all times.
During the years 1752 to 1756, there is a gradual change in the preferred cadence, from type 1 to type 4.   Table I illustrates this:

TABLE I

Year	Opera	Number of type 1 cadences	Number of type 4
1752	*Adriano*	20	3
1753	*Solimano*	14	11
1753	*L'Eroe Cinese*	10	7
1754	*Artemisia*	9	18
1755	*Ezio*	6	16
1755	*Il Rè pastore*	1	16
1756	*L'Olimpiade*	0	20

After this year, type 1 cadences are not used at all.   Types 2 and 3 remain as rare as formerly.   As with the earlier operas, from 1/3 to 2/3 of the cadences are on the dominant of the following aria; the rest cadence on I, iii, IV, or vi.
Within passages of recitative, a compromise of 1 and 4 becomes standard:

This is also occasionally used as the final cadence before an aria. *Ruggiero*, for example, uses it three times before arias, although types 2 and 3 are not used at all.

Occasionally, cadences are found which conform to none of these types. These are interspersed for the sake of variety:

(*Achille in Sciro*, I:14 cadence)

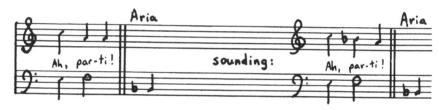

(*Zenobia*, I:6 cadence)

A further advance in contrasting cadences is the cadence into the aria, in which the tonic of the continuo comes on the first beat of the aria proper: either as tonic or dominant. A typical example of this is:

In this cadence, it is expected that the last note will be divided into two eighths:

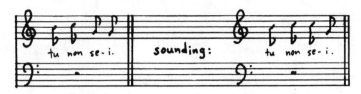

(*Demetrio b*, I:4 cadence)

Despite the time we have just spent on exceptions, the fact remains that most of Hasse's operas remain formally and structurally almost indistinguishable from one another, and are made up of a limited number of interchangeable parts. Only slightly more individualistic are the ten large dramatic works that are often referred to as serenate, feste teatrali, favole pastorali, azioni teatrali, and other similar terms, though in English they all seem to be categorized as operas.

These ten works lie on the boundary of relevancy to this thesis, and shall only be referred to in this chapter. They demonstrate by their contents the boundaries of the genre known as opera seria.

TABLE II

Antonio e Cleopatra: Naples, 1725:	dramma per musica, serenata, or cantata
Semele, o sia la richiesta fatale: Naples, 1726:	dramma per musica, serenata, or festa teatrale
Enea in Caonia: Naples, 1729:	serenata
"*Sei tu, Lidippe*,": Dresden, 1734:	cantata pastorale, or serenata
L'Asilo d'amore: Dresden, 1743:	festa teatrale
Il Natal di Giove: Dresden, 1749:	azione teatrale or serenata
Alcide al bivio: Vienna, 1760:	festa teatrale
Egeria: Vienna, 1764:	festa teatrale

Partenope: Vienna, 1767:   festa teatrale

Piramo e Tisbe: Vienna, 1768, 1770:   intermezzo tragico

Hasse's two small secular dramatic forms are quite well-defined: the cantata and the intermezzo comico. In describing these, it will become apparent that the ten works referred to above all have some of the characteristics of opera seria, but very little resemblance to either the cantata or the intermezzo.

Hasse's cantatas are small pieces, not meant to be staged, for one or two voices, usually without any independent instrumental pieces, and without any real plot development. Two of the above works may be called cantatas for these reasons: *Antonio*, and "*Sei tu, Lidippe*."[15] These are larger than usual cantatas, and include sinfonie.[16] "*Sei tu, Lidippe*" has four voices.[17]

The intermezzo comico is so obviously a separate genre that little discussion of it is necessary here. Suffice it to say that the usual comic intermezzo is in two or three parts, with three or four arias in each part; it is meant to be performed between the acts of an opera seria; it has only two singing parts (though other composers wrote intermezzi for three or more voices, Hasse never did); it has no instrumental introduction; it has a plot and setting based on bourgeois life and mores. There has yet to be any important work done on Hasse's intermezzi, though Irene Mamczarz has correctly pointed out Hasse's importance in the early development of the genre, in her book on the comic intermezzo.[18] Hasse wrote only nine intermezzi in his career, the last coming rather early in 1741.

The serenata or festa teatrale was usually composed for a festive occasion: a wedding or important visit. It was desirable for an opera to be presented at such an occasion, but a shorter work was more easily rehearsed and performed on short notice. Each of the ten works in this general category has its own specific form; thus, each shall be dealt with separately, in chronological order.

First, we should point out that there is a distinction between the serenata and the festa teatrale, albeit a vague and always shifting one. The serenata tends to be like a short opera seria, often in two parts, on a classical or pastoral topic, and without much use of chorus or obbligato recitative. The festa teatrale is more likely to include deities or allegorical characters, is often in only one section, and may rely heavily on the chorus and obbligato recitative. Its topic is often mythological.

The first four works of Table II seem to be more of the serenata type. The next five are all included in the complete works of Metastasio under feste and azioni teatrali, and do indeed conform more closely to that category.[19]

Some opere serie also encroach upon the realm of the serenata and festa teatrale. *Asteria*, written by Pallavicino, and *Leucippo*, written by Pasquini, are called favole pastorali by their authors, since both are based on pastoral subjects, not classical history. *Asteria* includes two gods, and *Alfonso*, also by Pallavicino, ends with the descent of Imeneo (Hymen), an appropriate figure, since the opera celebrated the marriage of Charles, King of the Two Sicilies, and Amalia, Princess of Poland and daughter of Frederick Augustus II. Otherwise, all three of these are normal opere serie (though *Alfonso* has five acts), with a minimum of choruses or obbligato recitative, and normal length and plot development. *Achille in Sciro*, with its abnormal use of chorus, has already been mentioned. Here again, the festive nature of the libretto may have been caused by the exceptional occasion of the performance: the marriage of Maria Theresa, the future empress, to Stephen Francis, Duke of Lorraine and Grand Duke of Tuscany, in 1736.

Hasse's first serenata, *Antonio e Cleopatra*, is quite cantata-like in its cast of only two singers, probable lack of staging, and minimal plot development. Yet it is quite long, with eight arias and two duets, and is preceded by a three-part sinfonia. Quantz called it a serenata (see Chapter I, p. 2) and the title page of the one surviving manuscript states that it is a "*drama per musica.*" It was not written for a festive occasion, but for private chamber performance, as far as can be determined, and served as a test piece, written before Hasse began composing for the Neapolitan court. It was intended to be a sample of the types of arias that Hasse could write, and was performed by two of the greatest singers of the time, Farinelli and Tesi. Being a sample work, the limited cast and lack of staging were sacrifices; the length and sinfonia were not mere augmentations to a cantata. The work is thus an anomaly and does seem very much like a long cantata in effect, but might best be considered a serenata, with a vestigial pause in the middle, after the first duet, and an imitation final "coro," actually another duet, but short and homophonic, as an operatic coro would be.

Hasse's second serenata, *Semele*, was probably written for the same patron as *Antonio*. As with the earlier work, there is no chorus, but a simple final trio. All fourteen arias are marked da capo. In all, there are two trios and three duets, which would lend a festive character to the work. It is divided into two parts, and plot development is again minimal. The title page calls it a "*drama per musica,*" but the mythological plot, including Giove, Giunone, and Semele, and the many ensembles suggest that this is more of a festa teatrale than a serenata.

Enea in Caonia, like the preceding two serenatas, opens with a three-part sinfonia. There are five singers, the plot is classical, there are no ensembles or choruses, and the work is divided into two parts: six arias in the first part, and nine in the second. In all respects, this fits the definition of a serenata.

"*Sei tu, Lidippe,*" probably written in 1734, may be, as the score states, a "cantata pastorale." The word cantata is immediately justified and qualified by the remainder of the title: "a più voci, per festeggiare il ritorno da Danzica della Maestà del Rè." The presence of multiple voices and the reason for performance both are arguments for its being considered a serenata. It is as long as *Antonio,* having eight da capo arias bracketed by a three-part sinfonia and a final coro, presumably intended only for the four singers. A predecessor of the many operas that Hasse was to write for important marriages, birthdays, and visits, it may well have been staged, though the lack of plot would have presented a problem. There is no reason why this cannot be considered a serenata.[20]

L'Asilo d'amore was Hasse's first true festa teatrale. The libretto is divided into neither scenes nor acts, but the music is a free succession of arias and choruses, recitativo semplice and obbligato. There are fifteen arias, all da capo, and the piece opens with a three-part sinfonia and closes with a true chorus. Several points differentiate this work from the usual opera seria, the most obvious being the choruses: all three of the choral sections in the body of the text include solo sections sung by the principal characters. Even the final chorus is divided by the librettist into sections for the full ensemble, for the soloists (all seven of whom are gods), and for the chorus alone.[21]

Il Natal di Giove is called an azione teatrale by Brunelli.[22] Hasse called it a serenata on the title page, and indeed it fits this category better: it has eleven arias and a cavatina, sung by five pastoral characters (Giove does not appear), bracketed by a three-part sinfonia and a final coro, probably sung by the soloists. Four relatively extended areas of recitativo obbligato increase the non-seria feeling of the work.

Alcide al bivio returns to the festa teatrale format seen in *L'Asilo.* It is long enough to need to be bound in three volumes, even though it has only twelve scenes in its one act. This is due to the complexities of the forms employed. It opens with a French ouverture, includes twelve da capo arias, four choruses, a quartet, three marches or short sinfonie, and seven pasages of recitativo obbligato. It is one of Hasse's most progressive works as far as new combinations of solo and chorus and use of obbligato recitative are concerned, and may well have influenced Gluck's *Orfeo,* produced two years later in the same city.[23]

Egeria, of 1764, follows in the path of *Alcide.* It is in one part, with no division into scenes. The autograph had to be bound in two volumes, even though it has only six arias and three choruses. It includes the first use of a half da capo aria in a festa teatrale, a long and complex final chorus, and five extended passages of obbligato recitative. The cast is made up of four gods and one mortal, also in the festa teatrale tradition.

Partenope is little different. Its two "parti" and their contents show its independence from the opera seria: a quartet closes the prima parte, and a slow-fast sinfonia opens the seconda parte. One trio, two choruses, and three non-da-capo arias are also to be found.

Hasse's penultimate dramatic work was *Piramo e Tisbe*, the intermezzo tragico commissioned by a dilettante and sung by her, her friend, and the librettist, Marco Coltellini. (See Chapter I, p. 32.) It has nothing in common with the intermezzo comico: it has an opening sinfonia; it was not performed with an opera seria; it has three singing parts; the leading couple are both sopranos; the subject is classical, not bourgeois. Yet it is not a serenata: there is too much plot emphasis and the ending is tragic. In form, it is unique in Hasse's opus.

As a late work, one might assume that some of the arias in *Piramo* would be half da capos or free forms and, indeed, this is the case. *Piramo* is Hasse's most modern opera, and of the nine arias, only one is a full da capo. One is in binary form, two are half da capos, and six are through-composed. The intermezzo also includes ten passages of recitativo obbligato, four duets (all through-composed), and a march. An innovative work in the light of Hasse's previous production, it had to remain an exercise, a sketch of what a full-scale opera, with all the modern forms, would have been like as composed by Hasse. We may well consider this work to demonstrate the sole example of Gluck's influence on Hasse.

These ten large-scale works are easily separated from the formal opera seria on one end of the sale and the small, intimate cantata on the other. While the earlier ones are distinguished by their size, the later ones also show a dependence on the chorus and the recitativo obbligato that is not found in either fixed genre. With the exception of *Piramo*, most of the difference is caused by the libretto used. These feste and serenate were not any more adventuresome than the opere serie in exploring new forms and methods of organization -- indeed, if anything, they were retrogressive in this respect. *Piramo* shows the only real experimentation with form that Hasse ever attempted, and even here, his originality stopped with his next work, *Ruggiero*, which returned to the conventions of opera seria.

CHAPTER III

HOW HASSE COMPOSED: THE EVIDENCE OF THE AUTOGRAPHS

At least thirty-four of Hasse's operas survive in the author's hand, more than have come down in autograph form from any other eighteenth-century master. These manuscripts range from the roughest of copies, full of corrections and changes, to final, relatively error-free fair copies. While no two autographs show the exact same patterns in their physical details, almost all follow the same general plan and appearance.

The majority of the autographs are to be found in the Conservatorio Giuseppe Verdi in Milan. They were not known to the early twentieth-century German scholars Rudolf Gerber, Carl Mennicke, and Albert Schatz, and are not listed by Eitner. Only persistent inquiry and research by Sven Hostrup Hansell identified these in 1965. Of thirty-two manuscripts numbered Mus. Tr. ms. 151-13 to 181-14 (two are bound together under one number), twenty-nine are wholly or mostly in Hasse's handwriting. Two, *Arminio IIb* and *L'Asilo d'amore*, are in several copyist's hands, with Hasse's corrections, and one, *Viriate*, is a professional, commercial copy.

Three more autographs are in the Conservatorio Benedetto Marcello in Venice (Ospedaletto XIX 323, XIX 325, XX 326). These have not previously been identified as autographs, but there is no doubt that they are in Hasse's hand. Another autograph, *La Sorella amante*, is in the Dresden Sächsische Landesbibliothek (Mus. 2477/f/98) under the title *Lavinia*, and yet another, the intermezzo *Don Tabarano*, is in the Deutsches Staatsbibliothek, in East Berlin (Ms. autogr. J. A. Hasse 4). The latter is exceptional, for it is only intermezzo that has survived in autograph. It is a fair copy, with no corrections, so its interest is minimal. Both German manuscripts are identified in card catalogues as autographs.

Similar to the *Arminio IIb* and *L'Asilo d'amore* scores mentioned above are several manuscripts in various libraries throughout Europe: a *Cajo Fabrizio b* in the Preussische Kulturbesitz in West Berlin, a *Tito Vespasiano Ib* in the Herzog August Bibliothek in Wolfenbüttel, a *Ciro riconosciuto* in the Bayerisches Staatsbibliothek in Munich. These are products of Dresden copyists, and include minor corrections made by Hasse.

Finally, in many of the European libraries, there are manuscripts produced by Dresden copyists. These were probably transcribed from Hasse's own copies. They are done with obvious care, and provide the most trustworthy source for operas whose autographs do not exist. Foremost in holdings is the Sächsische Landesbibliothek, the collection of which stems from the electoral libraries. The Bibliothèque Nationale in Paris also has many, whose bookplates from the *Menus plaisirs du Roi* give evidence to a surprising interest in Italian opera on the part of the French court in the 1750's.

In order to place the autographs in the context of Hasse's oeuvre, it is necessary to understand where they occur in his career. In Table III, which lists Hasse's opere serie, feste teatrali, and serenate in chronological order, works with autograph sources are starred. Those works of which no complete copies are to be found are identified with dashes. The works with Dresden copies available are indicated with a plus sign. It is unfortunate that so few of the early operas remain in autograph form, but it is still surprising that of the first eleven operas, three autographs survive, while two other operas are completely lost. Plates VIII-XI show early and late samples of Hasse's handwriting: from *Cajo Fabrizio a* (1732) and *La Clemenza de Tito II* (1759), demonstrating the remarkable consistency in handwriting over a period of twenty-seven years.

TABLE III

-*Antioco*	1721
Antonio e Cleopatra	1725
Sesostrate	1726
Semele, o sia la richiesta fatale	1726
Astarto	1726
Enea in Caonia	1727
*Gerone, tiranno di Siracusa	1728
Attalo, rè di Bitinia	1728
-*Ulderica*	1729
Tigrane (*Acts I and III)	1729
*La Sorella amante	1729
Artaserse Ia	1730
-*Dalisa*	1730
Arminio I	1730
Ezio I	1730
+*Cleofide I*	1731
-*Catone in Utica*	1731
*Cajo Fabrizio a	1732
Demetrio a	1732
Euristeo	1732

Issipile	1732
+*Siroe a*	1733
-*Artaserse Ib*	1734
Cajo Fabrizio b (*Act I, +Acts II and III)	1734
"Sei tu, Lidippe"	1734
Tito Vespasiano Ia	1735
Alessandro nell'Indie IIa	1736
Senocrita	1737
*Atalanta	1737
Asteria	1737
+*Tito Vespasiano Ib*	1738
Irene	1738
-*Alessandro nell'Indie IIb*	1738
Alfonso	1738
Viriate	1739
Artaserse Ic	1740
Demetrio b	1740
Numa (*Acts I & II) (+Act III)	1741
Lucio Papirio	1742
Didone abbandonata	1742
-*Alessandro nell'Indie IIc*	1743
+*L'Asilo d'amore*	1743
Antigono	1743
Ipermestra a	1744
*Semiramide a	1744
Arminio IIa	1745
La Spartana generosa, ovvero Archidamia	1747
*Semiramide b	1747
+*Leucippo a*	1747
-*Demetrio c*	1747
*Demofoonte Ia	1748
*Il Natal di Giove	1749
-*Demofoonte Ib*	1749
-*Leucippo*	1749
*Attilio Regolo	1750
*Ipermestra b	1751
*Ciro riconosciuto	1751
+*Leucippo c*	1751
*Adriano in Siria	1752
*Solimano	1753
+*Arminio IIb*	1753
*L'Eroe cinese	1753
*Artemisia	1754

*Ezio II	1755
*Il Rè pastore	1755
*L'Olimpiade a	1756
*Leucippo d	1756 (?)
Nitteti	1758
*Demofoonte II	1758
*Achille in Sciro	1759
*La Clemenza di Tito II	1759
*Artaserse II	1760
*Alcide al bivio	1760
*Zenobia	1761
*Il Trionfo di Clelia	1762
*Siroe b	1763
-Leucippo e	1763
*Egeria	1764
L'Olimpiade b (*partial)	1764
Romolo ed Ersilia	1765
*Partenope	1767
*Piramo e Tisbe a	1768
-Piramo e Tisbe b	1770
*Ruggiero, ovvero l'eroica gratitudine	1771

Most of the autographs are working copies; only a few show evidence that they were copied from rough drafts.[1]   Most show corrections in both recitative and aria that indicate that Hasse was still concerned with the composition of the music while the autographs were being written.   The autographs were meant to be and were in fact performing scores.   They are all in the oblong format for use at the keyboard, they are bound in volumes of usable thickness, and cuts in the music are either sewn up or sealed by wax.

The autographs also present evidence that Hasse composed in a specific and logical order, and kept to this order his entire life: he usually set all of the recitative at the same time, before he began to compose the arias.   The arias, in turn, were composed in order, from beginning to end of the opera.   Evidence for this is to be found in all of the autographs except for the three fair copies mentioned above.   A detailed list of the evidence would be appropriate in a complete edition; in this thesis, only typical examples will be provided.

Before turning to the evidence, we shall consider why the recitatives might be written before the arias.   Such a method makes sense in the highly dichotomized system of recitative and aria in opera seria.   One-third to one-half of the music in an opera, counted in measures, was recitative; the rest, with minor exceptions, was aria.   (The three or four

PLATES VIII AND IX

From *Cajo Fabrizio a* (1732), "In così lieto giorno," (I:1) (I-Mc, Part. Tr. ms. 157, v. 1, ff. 3 and 3′).

PLATE VIII

PLATE IX

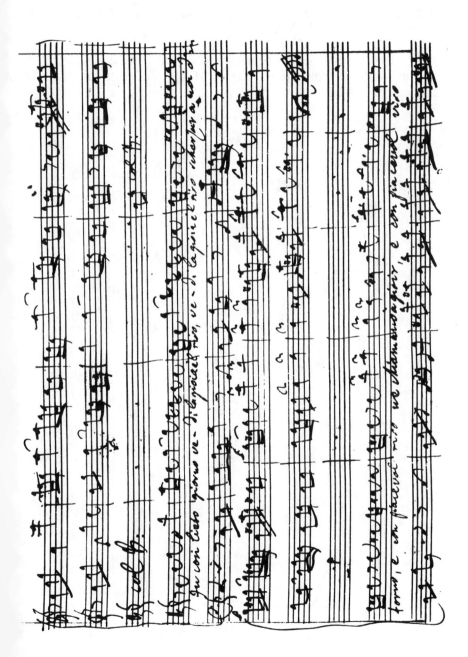

PLATES X AND XI

From *La Clemenza di Tito II* (1759), title page and sinfonia (I-Mc, Part. Tr. ms. 174, v. 1, ff. 1 and 1').

Despite the difference in time (27 years), Hasse's handwriting remains almost completely unchanged. Clefs and notes are virtually identical in manner of execution.

PLATE X

PLATE XI

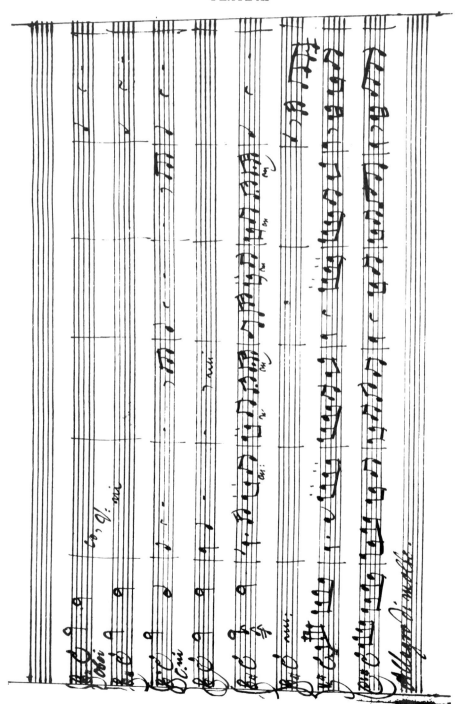

sections of recitativo obbligato and the one or two ensembles would be included with the arias.) Once the recitative and arias were composed, all of the important music was provided. The sinfonia and closing coro would be written shortly before the first performance. The recitativo semplice was easily separated from the rest of the libretto, and just as easily composed without reference to any other music that might be required, except for the immediate tonal connections with the surrounding arias.

It was probably easiest to compose the recitative all at one time. There was certainly no deep meaning attached to the music of the recitative; audiences needed to understand the plot, but they were anxious to hear the arias, too. The speed with which recitative was written would, if anything, enhance the feeling of "heightened" speech which it was attempting to create; the fluency with which Hasse set the recitative had as its natural result a great fluency in the sound of the music itself.

Technically, the recitative had to be set first, for it was the first music to be rehearsed. The words to the arias were certainly no trouble to learn; each singer had at most five arias, or fifty lines of poetry, and the music was usually cued to the singer by the opening ritornello of the aria. Clearly, the hardest part of the opera to memorize was the recitative.

Finally, the recitative did not have to fit the specific performers as closely as the arias, and could thus be set somewhat more easily without reference to the singers. While the coloratura and range of each aria were often closely matched to the abilities of the individual singer, this was not necessary with the recitative. It could be composed and sent on ahead of the composer, if he were writing in a different city, especially if the singers had not all been decided upon. Since most of Hasse's operas were written for cities with resident cappelle, this reason does not often apply.[2]

Hasse actually seems to have started work on the arias before the recitatives in many instances. This was the more creative task in composing an opera, and it is understandable that a composer might consider it the more rewarding and interesting. But at some point, shortly before rehearsals were to begin, he would have had to put aside the aria sketches and spend several days writing all the recitative so that the cast could start committing it to memory. With this out of the way, he could continue work on the arias.

Cajo Fabrizio a of 1732 is the first clear demonstration of this system. The autograph manuscript is made up of a series of gatherings or fascicles, consisting, for the most part, of one sheet per fascicle, folded once to provide two folios, or four pages (Diagram I). The assembly of

DIAGRAM I

1.

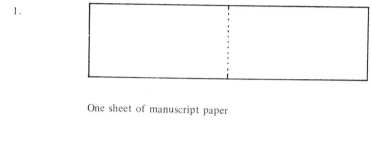

One sheet of manuscript paper

2.

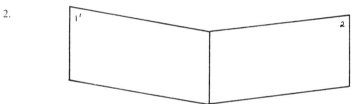

Folded into two folios, each with recto (1) and verso (1')

3.

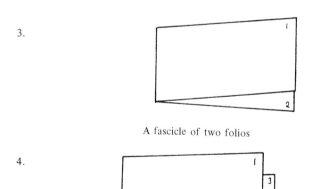

A fascicle of two folios

4.

fascicles into the manuscript is organized around the recitative, not around the arias. Every passage of recitative begins on a new fascicle. Normally, this means every scene opens on a new fascicle. Where a second scene follows a first without an aria intervening, the second scene follows directly and does not begin on a new fascicle. Where a scene ends in an aria, the aria often does not fill a fascicle to the end, but leaves several blank staves, possibly an entire blank page. The empty space is usually not used for recitative, but is left blank, and the next scene begins on a new fascicle.

The recitative itself rarely fills up exactly one fascicle, and there is almost always space left over at the end of a scene, on which the aria can be begun. This space is always used. If as few as three or four empty staves are left at the bottom of a page the aria begins in the available space. If only one or two staves remain, the aria begins on the top of the next page, whether or not it is the first page of a new fascicle. Additional fascicles are used to provide room for the completion of the aria.

Hasse kept a careful eye on music paper. He often squeezed an aria into the available space at the end of a fascicle, shortening the length of each bar drastically. In some cases, he may have even eliminated the B ritornello to save space, thus truncating a dal segno aria into a simple da capo. Evidence for this is only circumstantial. Hasse will also take advantage of a surplus of staves at the end of an aria, and with grand sweeps of the pen use an entire page for four or five bars and an expansive "dal segno."

There is much evidence that Hasse had at least a soprano and bass sketch of the aria before entering it into the manuscript, and that he knew exactly how many bars were necessary to finish an aria. In seven arias in *Cajo Fabrizio a*, he inserted half a sheet of paper in front of the following fascicle to accommodate the end of the preceding aria. The half-sheet becomes the first page of the following fascicle, and the recitative no longer begins the fascicle, but the stub of the half-sheet at the end of the fascicle clearly indicates what has happened (Diagram II).

After *Cajo Fabrizio a*, Hasse began using two-sheet fascicles in his autographs (Diagram III).

The addition of a page to accommodate an aria is also common in these manuscripts, but since only exceptionally long recitatives covered eight full pages, an added sheet could be wrapped around the entire fascicle, with the blank page used for the aria following the recitative (Diagram IV).

Occasionally, the problem of adding pages to complete an aria became even more complicated. If the following recitative extended for more than one fascicle, a sheet could not be wrapped around both succeeding fascicles because of difficulties in binding (Diagram V).

DIAGRAM II

1.

Insufficient space to finish aria on one fascicle.

2.

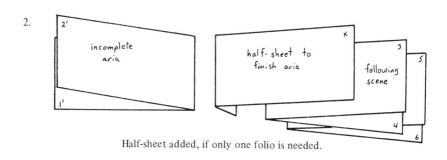

Half-sheet added, if only one folio is needed.

3.

Stub of half-sheet is placed between the
following two fascicles. In most cases, the following
recitative uses more than two folios. A whole sheet could not
be added since, if it were placed between the two fascicles, a
blank folio would interrupt the recitative, and if it were placed
after the second fascicle (assuming the recitative took up no
more than four folios) the fascicles could not be bound properly.

DIAGRAM III

1.

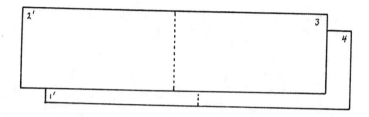

2.

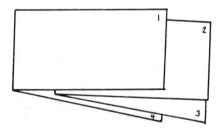

A standard two-sheet, four-folio fascicle.

DIAGRAM IV

1.

Insufficient room on first fascicle to complete aria. Recitative of following scene begins on first page of second fascicle.

2.

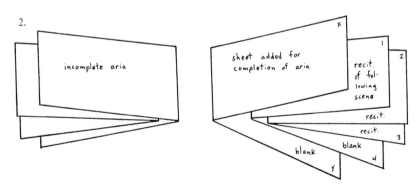

Sheet wrapped around second fascicle. Ff. x and x' used to complete aria. Ff. 4, 4', y, and y' later used to begin the following aria. F. 1 no longer opens fascicle.

DIAGRAM V

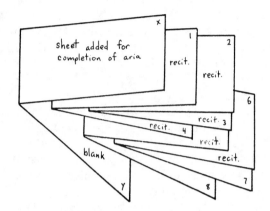

In this instance, the recitative covers ff. 1-6, extending over one complete fascicle and onto a second. When a sheet is needed to complete the preceding aria, it cannot be wrapped around both fascicles, as the diagram shows: the two spines of the two fascicles are now contained in the one spine of the added sheet, creating an awkward and difficult situation for the bookbinder. In later years, Hasse did not often cut folios off, leaving stubs, so a stub of folio y would not have been inserted between folios 4 and 5 or it would interrupt the order of the recitative. Another solution had to be found.

La Clemenza di Tito II offers an instance of how the problem was solved. Instead of adding a new sheet, the first sheet of the second fascicle was used. The last folio was turned backwards to become the first folio of the preceding fascicle, leaving the second sheet alone as the second fascicle (another sheet could be inserted) and making the first fascicle one of three sheets (Diagram VI). This provides exactly two pages for the completion of the preceding aria. If four pages had been needed, a one-sheet fascicle could have been added, or both final folios of the second fascicle could have been turned backwards, thus combining the two two-sheet fascicles into one of four sheets. The aria following the recitative, which ordinarily would have been entered on these blank sheets, can be copied on a new fascicle.

Most of the manuscripts show that at one time the great majority of recitatives were begun on the first pages of fascicles. This suggests that Hasse's method of composing them was to start with Act I, scene I, and to set recitative until he came to an aria. Then he would take a new fascicle, leaving the remainder of the old one blank, and begin with the next passage of recitative, composing until he again came to an aria. In this manner, the opera's recitative would be composed. The result would be a pile of fascicles, in order, with all of the arias missing. Hasse would then finish sketching the arias and enter them into their appropriate places, after the recitative passages that preceded them.

In itself, this does not suggest that the recitatives were composed hastily. There are other pieces of evidence that do support such a thesis. One of the most obvious is the presence of the handwriting of a copyist or copyists in the autograph scores. Hasse evidently would read a line of recitative, or have it read to him, set it to music, and immediately go on to the next line, without copying down the words. At a later time, the music was given to a copyist, who wrote in the dialogue. There can be no doubt that the music was entered first: where Hasse changed the text by repeating a word, or encountered a pair of syllables that might be given either one or two notes, he entered the word in the proper place himself, to eliminate doubt in the mind of the copyist. The rest of the words were filled in later by the copyist. In some cases, Hasse also inserted the words on either side of a cut in the text, suggesting that such editings may have been made spontaneously at times, and thus were not marked in the libretto.

Along with the music, Hasse entered the name of the character and his clef at every change of singer. Since he was very careful about using rests at every punctuation mark in the libretto, there was not much doubt possible for the copyist. At times, the copyist had to stretch words out, or cramp them together, in order to stay with the notes. The music always proceeds in an orderly fashion. (Plate XII).

DIAGRAM VI

1.

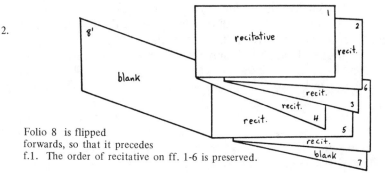

This is the solution to the dilemma
shown in Diagram V. Notice that folio 8 is blank.

2.

Folio 8 is flipped
forwards, so that it precedes
f.1. The order of recitative on ff. 1-6 is preserved.

3.

The recitative of f. 1 no longer
opens the fascicle. F. 5 no
longer opens the second fascicle; now it is the
last folio of the first fascicle. F. 8 now provides a blank folio for the
completion of the preceding aria. There are no binding problems.
A two-folio sheet can be inserted between ff. 6 and 7, making a four-
folio fascicle.

PLATE XII

From *La Clemenza di Tito II,* Act I, scene 1, end of scene (I-Mc, Part. Tr. ms. 174, v. 1, f. 19′).

All of the music on this page is in Hasse's hand. The words for the first system, and most of the second, are in the hand of a copyist. Notice that although the first five notes of the alto part are evenly spaced, the copyist has had to adjust the words "al grande addio" to insert them.

Furthermore, before the aria was inserted, Hasse crossed out the end of the original recitative, and changed it. The original music was obviously going to cadence in B♭, but when the aria was composed, Hasse decided instead to close on a phrygian cadence on E, since the aria was in A. Thus, the already-written portion of the music was reworked to cadence by "non e maturo" on G, much closer to the eventual goal.

The change in the melody at "e pur forse" was made to take the key into D, instead of d, again a change towards the sharp side of the circle of fifths, and away from the flat.

See also Plates XVIII and XX for examples of copyists' hands.

PLATE XII

The presence of the copyist also denies any possibility that the recitative was pre-composed on a rough copy and then entered into the performing score. If the recitative had been pre-composed, the copyist could have just as easily entered both words and music.[3] If time had been a factor, both Hasse and the copyist might have worked simultaneously on copying over the recitative, but certainly not on the same passages at the same time! Also, while mistakes are occasionally made, these are not the standard errors of copying, such as leaving out a bar, or misplacing the notes by a line. More commonly they are simply matters of incorrectly-accented words, or unmelodic lines. In *Semiramide b*, Hasse based the recitative on that used in *Semiramide a*, though the voices of the singers were different. The manuscript abounds in mistakes such as putting an alto clef where a soprano clef is necessary, and vice versa.

Many of Hasse's manuscripts seem to begin quite leisurely, with the first act and perhaps part of the second being written with recitative and aria following one another continuously, with no break or sign of haste. Perhaps the first few arias were sketched out first, then entered in the performance score one by one, with the recitative being filled in as it was needed.

Attilio Regolo was one of Metastasio's most prized librettos, and Hasse took special pains with it. In Act I, only scenes 7 and 11 might have originally begun fascicles. In the manuscript as it appears today, the recitative is no longer on the first page of the gatherings. In Act II, only scene 3 and 9 begin fascicles, possibly only because the preceding arias happened to end on the last page of a fascicle. In Act III, the method changes. Scenes 1-2 open the act;[4] 3, 4 and 5 seem to have originally begun fascicles, but are no longer on the first page of their respective gatherings. (Added sheets have been wrapped around them, making six-folio fascicles.) Scenes 7, 8, and 9-10 all begin on new fascicles. Yet the overall appearance of care is apparent even here, for no copyist's hand is to be found anywhere on the manuscript. We may assume that Hasse had most of the earlier arias set by the time he had to start on the recitative, and still not being pressed for time, was able to insert them as the recitative was composed.

Ciro riconosciuto is an example of a more typical manuscript. In Act I, only scenes 1, 5, 6-7, and 11 begin fascicles; 2-3, 4, 8, 9, 10, 12, and 13 do not. In Act II, the balance changes: scenes 1, 2-3-4-5, 7, 8, 9, 10 and 11 begin fascicles; only 6 and 12 are sandwiched between arias. Scene 6 has only nine lines of text, scene 12 has four; setting such short passages separately would have been a waste of time and paper. Act III follows the pattern of Act II. Furthermore, a copyist was employed for the recitative beginning in II:2 and continuing through the second and third acts.

Once the recitative was completed, Hasse could again work on the arias if, indeed, he had already begun to write them. There is a variety of evidence suggesting that the succeeding arias had not yet been written. Most convincingly, the final cadences of the recitatives were often left incomplete, and were filled in when the arias were entered at a later time. When the recitative was written, the key of the following aria had not been decided, so the cadence could not be completed. This is most obvious where a copyist aided in writing, for five or six lines before the end of the recitative, the copyist's hand stops and Hasse's hand completes the words and music. Sometimes the difference in ink and pen makes it obvious that the change was made at a later time. Sometimes the ink and pen match that used in the following aria, showing that the two were inserted at the same time. In most cases, there is ample room for tonal maneuvering; at times, previously-written recitative will be crossed out to provide more opportunity for modulation, when the key in which the recitative had paused was too far from the eventual goal. (Plates XIII-XV)

Yet there are manuscripts written in the "separate aria and recitative" system that have no evidence for the cadence being withheld until the aria was inserted. This fact seems to support the contention that at times, many or all of the arias must have been sketched out before the pressures of rehearsal made the writing of the recitative necessary. It is also possible that Hasse could have had firm notions about the keys of some arias, based on conventions and the theory of affects, while other arias suggested no such obvious feelings to him.

Even where no copyist was used, evidence can sometimes be found to suggest that the cadences were added later. In *Artaserse II*, which is completely in Hasse's hand, small crosses over the recitative towards the end of each scene probably served as quick guides to show where the music had not yet been entered. If these crosses were only for Hasse's use, they appear superfluous. Hasse may have entered the words beyond this point, and given the entire scene to a copyist for transcription for the singer's rehearsal copies. In this case he might well have entered the crosses as a signal to the copyist not to continue the recitative past that point. In *Semiramide b* he writes "fin qui solamente," and "sin qui," both meaning "up to here," and serving the same purpose. (Plate XVI)

PLATES XIII-XV

From *Ipermestra b*, Act I, scene 1, end of scene (I-Mc, Part. Tr. ms 167, v. 1, ff. 18'-19').

In this case, both words and music are copied, both presumably from the lost *Ipermestra a* autograph. Hasse did not have the copyist finish the scene, but, probably at a later time, completed it himself. Enough recitative was left unset to enable him to cadence in any key he wished, although the eventual cadence was on A, a fifth away from the close of the copied section. Ordinarily, a cadence on B would have been expected, for the following aria is in E. In *Ipermestra a,* the scene had cadenced on E, preparing for an aria in A.

PLATE XIII

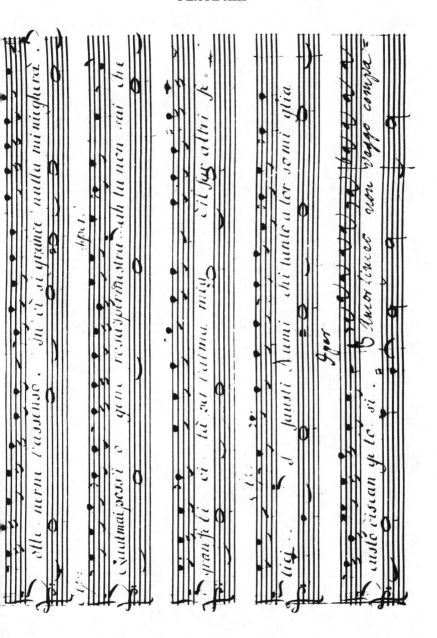

PLATE XIV

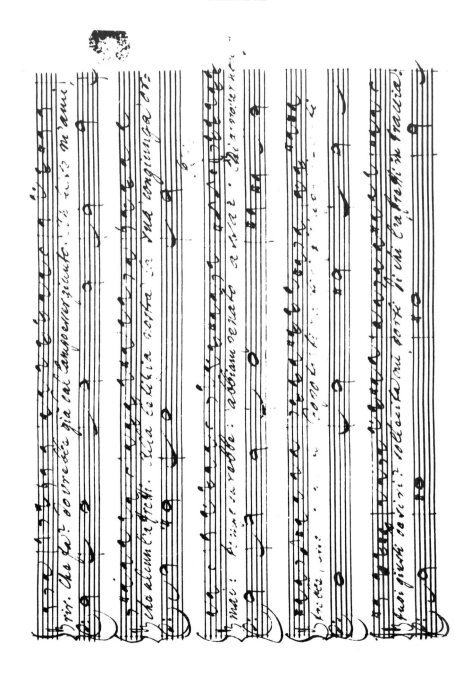

PLATE XV

PLATE XVI

From *Semiramide b,* Act II, scene 11, end of scene (I-Vc, Ospedaletto XX 326, v. 2, fasc. 15, f. 4′).

Note, besides "fin qui solamente" on the top of the page, the revised recitative melody on the first three notes. The aria is squeezed into the available four staves at the bottom of the page, an example of Hasse's economical use of paper. The corrections on bars four and five of the aria were probably made at the time of writing the aria, and not later, judging from the similarity of ink.

PLATE XVI

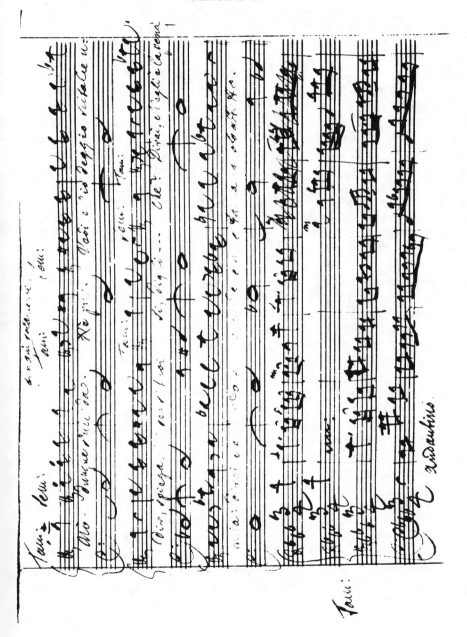

Sometimes, as in *Artemisia,* Hasse wrote in the words, but not the music, up to the cadence; other times, as in *Adriano in Siria,* he left out both; in both cases, he had been using a blunt pen for the music and a sharp one for the words, but the cadential progression was completed with a third pen, one that matches the following aria.

As a rule, once the copyist was finished with the recitatives, he was not employed again. It did occasionally happen that Hasse would use the copyist in the course of inserting the arias. *Tigrane,* an early opera (1729), had several of these exceptions to the rule: in II:8 the recitativo obbligato was entered after an aria (II:7). This is usual, but in this case it was followed chronologically by recitativo semplice; and both passages of recitative used a copyist to write in the words. While *Tigrane* uses separate fascicles for the recitative for the most part, this instance seems to suggest that Hasse had not quite settled completely into his later pattern of composition. Obbligato recitative, like arias, rarely shows a copyist's hand.

More surprising is the case of Act I, scene 3, in *La Clemenza di Tito II* (1759). This scene was written while the arias were being entered into the manuscript, which would suggest a scoring totally in Hasse's hand. Yet the copyist was employed to enter the words. Taken on its own, it shows only that Hasse considered the recitative too short to compose beforehand (it is only thirteen lines long), yet long enough to warrant using the copyist once the music was written. In the body of Hasse's autographs, the situation is quite rare.

A third exception, but one with opposite implications, is the autograph to *Atalanta.* This opera was written in 37 days (see Chapter I, p. 18). For the most part, the recitatives were composed before the arias. But in a unique situation, Hasse considered one of the arias minor enough to be composed along with the recitative, just as short passages of recitative seem to have been composed with the arias. The piece is a cavatina, "Sul viver nostro Die," (III:2). Furthermore, it is one of the only true three-part songs written by Hasse, scored simply for violin, bass voice, and separate continuo. If Hasse ever wrote an aria down without first drafting it, the occasion may have been here.

One final exceptional instance should be mentioned. Hasse appears to have composed the serenata *Il Natal de Giove,* with an abundance of time at his disposal. The work is one act long, and is preceded by a sinfonia and prologue and followed by a licenza. Each of the four sections begins a fascicle; once begun, each section is written straight through. No copyist is used. It is tempting to postulate that the body of Metastasio's poem was composed first, while the prologue and licenza (by an anonymous poet, probably Pasquini) followed later. The sinfonia would have been composed after the rest of the opera. There is no internal evidence for this in the manuscript.

Though Hasse was probably proficient enough as a composer to compose arias in his head and set them down in the performing score without major corrections, it is more likely that he resorted to skeleton scores as rough drafts, composing melody and bass first, and completing the orchestration later. These sketches would of course have been discarded after the completion of the aria. Most of the manuscripts show clearly that the soprano and bass were entered at the same time, the soprano consisting of the first violin in the ritornellos and the vocal line in the texted sections. These were followed within a short time by the violins, then later by the violas, and finally, sometimes much later, by the winds. Horn and flute parts are usually accommodated in the score, but obbligato oboe parts were often late afterthoughts, squeezed into the vocal staff in the ritornellos, and various empty staves in the texted sections.

Most corrections made in the course of copying the aria involve only the voice, or the voice and continuo; the rest of the staves are blank. It is difficult to say if a specific correction was made before or after the entire aria was thought out; most changes are of the most minor rhythmic or melodic alterations. Occasionally, as in *Il Rè pastore*, act I, scene 4, "Per me rispondete," copying errors can be observed.[5] In this instance, an entire measure was omitted, and was discovered only when the words were being written in, after several measures of vocal line and continuo had been copied down. This pattern of copying a few measures of music and then inserting the words is demonstrated in the second stanza, where the music was copied through the fermata of the cadenza, and then the words were copied in. When the actual cadence was inserted, along with its continuation in the B ritornello, Hasse forgot that he had not completed the vocal line. The last note and syllable of the voice, the "-tà" of "libertà," are not in the autograph.

The aria "Se la frode" from *Artemisia*, act II scene 7, shows an extensive correction, one of the longest among the autographs, where the first nine measures of the aria are crossed out and replaced:

While this at first suggests that Hasse was in the process of composing the aria at this point, closer examination reveals that he carefully retained the bass line, so that the revised melody could be accommodated throughout the aria. Thus the aria had already been composed at this point, and was just being subjected to a last-minute revision.

Another interesting example is from *Siroe b*, Act II, scene 1, in the aria "Mi lagnerò tacendo." In this aria, Hasse originally wrote a B ritornello that provided a bridge to the opening of A_1. He then changed his mind, crossed out the ritornello, and wrote in one that went to A_2, making the aria a half da capo. (Plate XVII) He had already written in the dal segno (§) in the B ritornello, and had to cross it out, but there is no § at the appropriate place in A_1. If he had been copying from a completely orchestrated rough draft, the original § probably would have been entered in the body of the aria. If, as is more probable, he was copying from a sketch of the melody and continuo, it is hard to imagine that a minor detail such as the § would have been inserted in the rough draft, and thus it would not have found its way into the finished copy. The B ritornello may not have even been included in the rough draft. (If the performance copy were the first and only draft, the sign also would not be present in the A_1 stanza.)

The physical evidence of the autographs does provide much of interest about Hasse's compositions. Hasse himself asserted that it took six months to compose a good opera.[6] We might assume that he would start composing his October opera some time in February, near the close of Carnival. The Carnival opera might be started in June or July, put aside in September and early October, and finished in November and December. Usually, the pace would be leisurely at first, with arias carefully planned and perhaps copied down along with the stretches of recitative connecting them. One or two months before the premiere, it would become necessary to have all of the recitative ready for preliminary rehearsals, and toward this end he may have worked steadily for several days, composing all of the longer passages in order, leaving the ends blank for the eventual insertion of cadences, and inserting arias that had been completed.

Composition of the arias would then continue. Some later ones might have been composed already, if he had been interested in writing all of Faustina's or Annibali's arias at one time, but they would not have been inserted in the proper place between the recitative passages. The passages could be completed through the final cadence in such cases, since the key of the aria would have been known.

After all of the arias were sketched out, the rest of the recitatives could be completed in the appropriate keys, and the arias could be copied into the performance score and orchestrated. Finally, a licenza, chorus, and sinfonia would be composed and rehearsed, perhaps only days before the premiere, and the new opera would be ready to perform.

The autographs provide other sorts of information. Occasionally, they give evidence of last-minute addition and removal of arias. While

PLATE XVII

From *Siroe b* "Mi lagnerò tacendo," (II:1), (I-Mc, Part. Tr. ms. 178, v. 2, f. 5').

The cancelled measure was to have been harmonized as the dominant of B♭, the key of the aria.

PLATE XVII

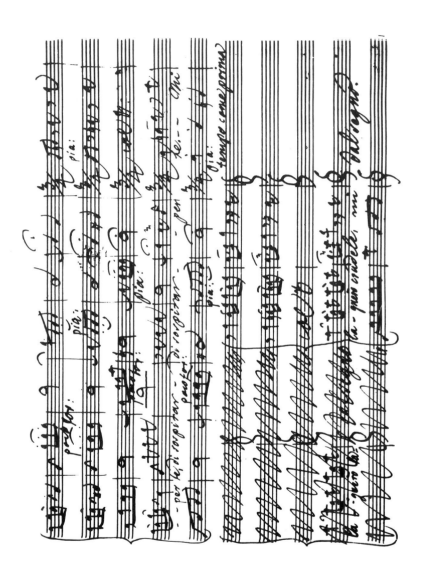

such information is not as a whole significant, it does provide a sidelight on the requirements of opera production.

One example provides an indication of rehearsal practice and the trustworthiness of librettos. In *Cajo Fabrizio a,* Act III, scene 6, the recitative is followed by the notation "l'aria." The rest of the page is blank; the aria was never written, or at least never inserted into the autograph. The libretto has the aria of Volusio, "Tinta la fronte, e il volto" at this point; there seems to have been no time even to insert an appendix in the libretto to the effect that this aria would not be sung. Hasse was presumably in Turin on 26 December 1731 for the first performance of his *Catone in Utica,* and if he stayed for the first week of performances and then spent four days travelling as quickly as possible to Rome, he would have had a week to supervise rehearsals before the premiere of *Cajo Fabrizio* on 12 January 1732. If "Tinta la fronte" had not been sent ahead to Rome, there may well not have been time to write and rehearse it, even though the libretto was already printed with the aria included. Stage politics certainly also played a part, for Volusio was the secondo uomo, and with "Tinta la fronte" he would have had five arias, the same number as the first couple and the king. The seconda donna had only three arias.

A slightly different circumstance turns up in *La Clemenza di Tito II.* In Act I, scene 9, an aria was added after the recitative had been composed. Tito's aria, "Ah se fosse," found in the original Metastasian libretto, was apparently originally intended to be cut, but at a later time was inserted. No copies of the libretto are to be found so it cannot be determined whether the aria was added very close to the premiere, or even for a later performance. The circumstances of its addition are worth noting (Diagram VII). The added aria fits very neatly on a fascicle of two sheets, and since most of scene 9 was on the left side of the middle of a fascicle, there was very little problem in inserting the aria. (Plates XVIII-XX)

La Clemenza de Tito II also provides evidence that Hasse originally planned to set Publio's aria at Act II, scene 4, "Sia lontano ogni cimento," and cut his aria at Act III, scene 1, "Tardi s'avvede." After the recitative was written, the former was cut and the latter was set. The cue "Aria di Publio" at the end of Act II, scene 4 was crossed out and a short scene 5 was added, in Hasse's hand completely, without the aid of a copyist as in II:4, ending with an aria for Servilia.[7] At Act III, scene 1 the scene very conveniently ended at the bottom of the left-hand side of the middle of a fascicle, so a sheet of paper with Publio's aria was inserted without even the necessity of copying over any recitative. All that was required was a V-I cadence (originally a V-VI, but in the proper key, luckily) at the end of the scene.

DIAGRAM VII

1.

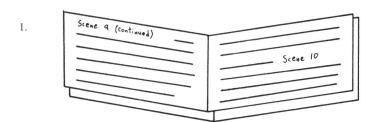

No aria between scenes 9 and 10.

2.

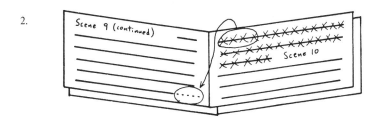

Decision made to add aria after scene 9. It will fit neatly in center of fascicle. Recitative of scene 9 on second half of fascicle is crossed out, partially rewritten on last page of first half. (See circles in diagram above.)

3.

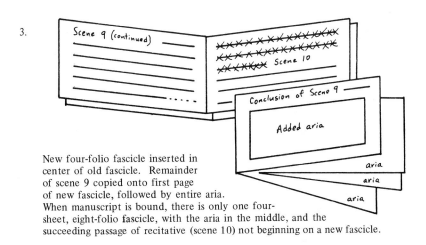

New four-folio fascicle inserted in center of old fascicle. Remainder of scene 9 copied onto first page of new fascicle, followed by entire aria. When manuscript is bound, there is only one four-sheet, eight-folio fascicle, with the aria in the middle, and the succeeding passage of recitative (scene 10) not beginning on a new fascicle.

PLATES XVIII-XX

From *La Clemenza di Tito II*, Act I, scene 9, end of scene, beginning of aria, "Ah se fosse intorno al trono," (*op. cit.*, v. 1, ff. 58', 59, and 63).

All of the music on Plates XVIII and XIX is in Hasse's hand. On Plate XVIII, Hasse squeezed in "come il grato mio" at the end of the page, in his own hand. On Plate XIX, "cor" is also in Hasse's hand. The rest of the text, beginning with "se grata. . ." is in the hand of a second copyist.

Plate XX explains what has happened. Hasse had originally not intended an aria at scene 9. When it was inserted, at a later time, the recitative had to be changed to cadence on G, for the added aria was in C. The old recitative, on f. 63, became superfluous and was cancelled.

PLATE XVIII

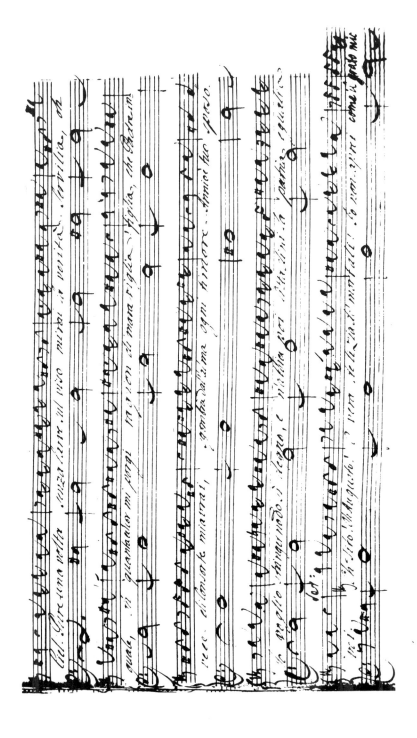

PLATE XIX

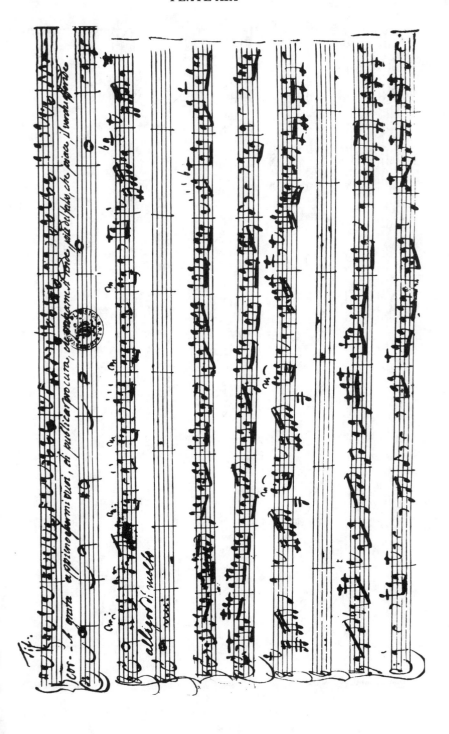

PLATE XX

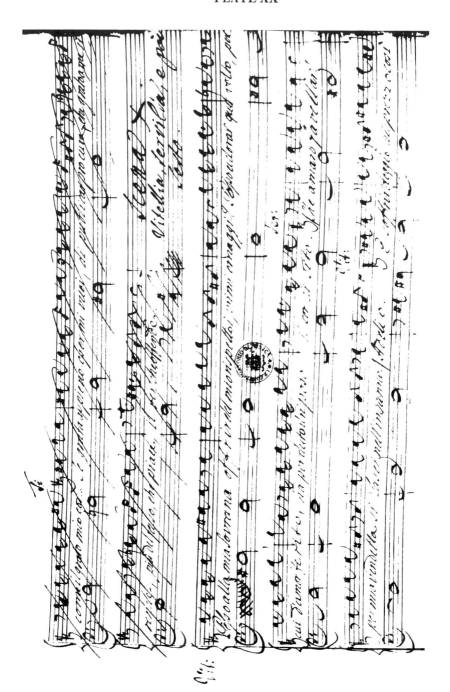

Very rarely is a change made that improves the music to any great extent. Changes in the accompaniment or in the rhythm of the voice part of an aria, repetition of a measure--these are the sort of corrections in which the autographs abound. Corrections never show a new or different way of thinking about the music. Even in the few cases where a change makes an obvious improvement in the music, the music itself does not become more startling or original.

Hasse was continually rethinking his music, as even the minor corrections show. For him the temptation to revise was not strong when the performance copy was first being put together; it became greater when the opera itself was being considered for a second or third production. It is this situation that becomes the most fruitful in terms of corrections made to change and improve the music. Though such corrections can be observed by comparison of copies of different versions, the autographs themselves provide fascinating insights into the very process of revision. The subject of revision in Hasse's operas is the concern of Chapter IV.

CHAPTER IV

HASSE'S REVISIONS

A: Introduction

What Constitutes a Revision

In 1772, Hasse told Charles Burney that "he had set all of the operas of Metastasio except *Temistocle*; some of them three or four times over, and almost all of them twice."[1] To the student of Hasse's operas, this statement raises several serious questions. The primary one is how to define "setting." What is the difference between a libretto set a second time, and an opera revised to a greater or lesser extent? Are there indeed any librettos which can be considered to be set a second time, as a completely new opera, and thus justify Hasse's claim? If this is found to be a rare situation, then should a revision be considered a second, completely new, setting? When an opera is revised only superficially, should it be distinguished from heavily-altered versions? These are all questions of definitions, and this chapter will attempt to provide workable answers.

The problem of identifying revisions has always plagued historians. The proliferation of scores which differ from the autograph or libretto in multiple respects thus raises the further question of "pasticci," or works altered by the addition of music by other composers.[2]

The first duty of the researcher is to separate the operas which Hasse is known to have written and revised, from those which seem to have been produced by others, with or without his permission or acquiescence, but, with alterations that are probably not Hasse's. Literally hundreds of libretti exist which list Hasse as the composer of the music, but which differ in small respects from the original settings, name another composer (or several) as contributing, are based on libretti which Hasse is not known to have set, or originate in cities which Hasse never visited.

The second and third of these instances are quite clear examples of pasticci, and do not need further definition. The fourth instance, however, often becomes the deciding factor in determining whether or not an opera is a pasticcio, and thus whether or not the "small differences" of the first instance were made by Hasse or by some other composer.

Hasse's circle of activity was quite narrow. His career was centered on a limited group of theatres:

1. Wolfenbüttel, 1721
2. Naples, 1725-1732 (San Bartolomeo and private theatres)
3. Dresden, 1731-1763
4. Venice, 1730-1749 (San Giovanni Grisostomo and San Samuele)
5. Lesser, isolated Italian theatres, 1730-1735 (Milan, 1730, Turin, 1731, Rome, 1732, Bologna, 1733, Pesaro, 1735)
6. Naples, 1758-1760 (San Carlo) and Venice, 1758 (San Benedetto)
7. Warsaw, 1759-1763 (and perhaps 1754)
8. Vienna, 1760-1770 (and an isolated instance in 1744)
9. Lesser, isolated Italian theatres, 1765-1771 (Turin, 1765, Milan, 1771)

Several of the operas within this circle may have been revised by Hasse but performed in his absence (*Alessandro IIc*, Venice, 1743, and *Artaserse Ib*, Venice, 1734), and isolated examples outside of this group may have been supervised by him (*Arminio IIa*, Vienna, 1747). Otherwise, operas presented outside of this circle seem to have been pasticci, and operas presented within it are almost certainly either first productions or authorized revisions.

This sharp limitation of the scope of Hasse's career is not only correlated by what we know of his life, but also by two circumstantial situations. First, the libretti outside of this circle all have arias which do not appear in first productions or later revisions, and, second, the music to these new arias does not survive, either in complete scores or as loose arias.[3]

There are actually four categories of operas that can be said to have been supervised by Hasse. The first, and most obvious, is the first setting by Hasse of music to a specific libretto. The second is the revival or repetition by Hasse of an old opera, but without any music being changed or added.[4] The third category is the repetition, with revisions, but using much of the original music. The last, and smallest, is the complete rewriting of an opera, using a libretto already set at one time. Hasse seems to have done the latter only five times, and at least twice some music from the earlier version was eventually incorporated.

The pasticci also fall into four groups. The category closest to the original opera includes those works attributed to Hasse, and usually following his libretto closely, but with arias added which were not set in the original. The second category includes operas whose libretti quite clearly state that some of the music is not by Hasse, whether or not the added music is by the local maestro di cappella or by a better known composer. The third includes operas on libretti never set by Hasse, but attributed to him, presumably for publicity reasons, whether or not some of the music was taken from his operas. And the last consists of admitted pasticci, with a libretto written or borrowed for the occasion, and the music taken from a wide selection of the popular composers of the time, at times all named and given specific credit. These four groups lie outside the scope of this dissertation. They are listed in Appendices B, C, and D.

Hasse revised fourteen of his operas, seven of them more than once. Twenty-one operas were repeated unchanged, in either Dresden or Warsaw, counting operas repeated within a year, but for a different season. Table IV is a chronological list of the operas which were either repeated intact, revised, or completely rewritten. Column I consists of first performances and revisions, and column II is repeated operas. Roman numerals refer to different settings of the same libretto, and letters refer to different revisions of the same opera. Versions in parentheses do not survive intact.

TABLE IV

			I	II
1.	*Artaserse*	*Ia*	Venice, 1730	
		(Ib)	Venice, 1734	
		Ic	Dresden, 1740	
		II	Naples, 1760	Warsaw, 1760
2.	*Arminio*	*I*[5]	Milan, 1730	
		IIa[6]	Dresden, 1745	
		IIb	Dresden, 1753	Warsaw, 1761
3.	*Ezio*	*I*	Naples, 1730	
		II	Dresden, 1755	Dresden, 1756
4.	*Cleofide*	*I*[7]	Dresden, 1731	
	Alessandro	*IIa*	Venice, 1736	
		(IIb)	Venice, 1738	
		(IIc)	Venice, 1743	
5.	*Cajo Fabrizio*	*a*	Rome, 1732	
		b	Dresden, 1734	
6.	*Demetrio*	*a*	Venice, 1732	
		b	Dresden, 1740	
		(c)	Venice, 1747	

TABLE IV (continued)

7.	*Siroe*	a	Bologna, 1733	
		b	Warsaw, 1763	Dresden, 1763
8.	*Tito Vespasiano*	Ia	Pesaro, 1735	
		Ib	Dresden, 1738	Dresden, 1740
	La Clemenza di Tito	II	Naples, 1759	
9.	*Asteria*		Dresden, Aug. 1737	Hubertusburg, Oct. 1737
10.	*Numa*		Hubertusburg, 1741	Dresden, 1743
11.	*Didone abbandonata*		Hubertusburg, 1742	Dresden, 1743
12.	*Ipermestra*	a	Vienna, 1744	
		b	Hubertusberg, 1751	Dresden, 1752
13.	*Semiramide*	a	Venice, 1744	
		b	Dresden, 1747	Warsaw, 1760
14.	*La Spartana generosa*		Dresden, 1747	Dresden, 1748
15.	*Leucippo*	a	Hubertusburg, 1747	
		(b)	Venice, 1749	
		c	Dresden, 1751	
		d	Dresden, 1756? (planned)	
		(e)?[8]	Dresden, 1763 (planned)	
16.	*Demofoonte*	Ia	Dresden, 1748	
		(Ib)	Venice, 1749	
		II	Naples, 1758	Warsaw, 1759
17.	*Ciro riconosciuto*		Dresden, 1751	Warsaw, 1762
18.	*Solimano*		Dresden, 1753	Dresden, 1754
19.	*L'Eroe cinese*		Dresden, 1753	Warsaw, 1754[9]
20.	*Artemisia*		Dresden, 1754	Dresden, 1755

TABLE IV (continued)

21.	*Il Rè pastore*		Hubertusburg, 1755	Dresden, 1756
				Warsaw, 1762
22.	*L'Olimpiade*	*a*	Dresden, 1756	Warsaw, 1761
		b	Turin, 1765	
23.	*Nitteti*		Venice, 1758	Warsaw, 1759
24.	*Zenobia*		Vienna, 1761	Warsaw, 1761
25.	*Il Trionfo di Clelia*		Vienna, 1762	Warsaw, 1762
26.	*Piramo e Tisbe a*		Vienna, 1768	
	(b)		Vienna, 1770	

Of the eighty-three operas listed in Chapter III, Table III (pp. 56-58), nineteen are revisions and five are second settings of an old libretto. Of the 106 distinct productions and revivals that Hasse supervised during his lifetime, sixty-nine concerned operas that had been or would be revised or revived. This is quite a significant percentage of his total output, and emphasizes that, not even considering pasticci, Hasse was writing works that would not be discarded after one season. The remainder of this chapter is concerned with the fourteen operas that Hasse would revise a total of twenty-four times between 1730 and 1770.

Reasons for the Revisions

The purpose of a revision was to provide new music for new singers in a new city. If, during the course of revising an opera, an improvement could be made easily, Hasse was not averse to doing so. Yet, usually more hard-headed sentiments ruled his actions. Aesthetic concerns do not seem to have been a major reason for his revisions.

No opera was revived in a different city without being altered in some way.[10] The presence of the different singers, some with voice ranges different from those of the original interpreters, often made revision unavoidable. Many times, the prima donna or the primo uomo was the primary recipient of revisions, suggesting that the reports of the enormous influence they held over composers in the eighteenth century were not exaggerated in the case of Hasse.

Hasse used many strategies when revising an opera. Sometimes all the music was replaced, as with *La Clemenza di Tito II* or *Demofoonte II*. The opera could be rewritten almost completely, with only a few favorite arias retained, as with *Alessandro nell'Indie IIa*, or *Artaserse II*. Individual arias could be replaced by others, leaving the recitative intact. The new arias could be written to either new or old texts, or indeed, could be contrafacta or parodies: new texts written to conform to the libretto, but set to pre-existing music. Old music could be revised; the instrumentation could be increased; coloratura shortened, lengthened, or rewritten; repeated measures cut; ritornelli shortened. The whole aria could simply be transposed, or specific high and low notes changed. New arias could be added where none were previously. Old arias could be cut without being replaced. Recitative could be shortened, transposed, or rewritten.

Yet the plot was never altered by these changes. The very process of giving a character one less aria, or one more, changes his importance, and shifts the emphasis of the plot, but there is no evidence that this was done for dramatic reasons.[11]

Circumstances of the Revisions

A list of the revisions by city emphasizes how often a change of location influenced the decision to rework the music, and how limited the possibilities were in Hasse's career.

TABLE V

Operas for Italian cities, revised for Dresden:

Artaserse Ia, Venice 1730	*Ic*, Dresden, 1740
Cajo Fabrizio a, Rome 1732	*b*, Dresden, 1734
Demetrio a, Venice, 1732	*b*, Dresden, 1740
Siroe a, Bologna, 1733	*b*, Warsaw, 1763
Tito Ia, Pesaro, 1735	*Ib*, Dresden, 1738
Semiramide a, Venice, 1744	*b*, Dresden, 1747

Operas for Dresden, revised for Venice:

Demetrio b, Dresden, 1740	*c*, Venice, 1749
Leucippo a, Dresden, 1747	*b*, Venice, 1749
Demofoonte Ia, Dresden, 1748	*Ib*, Venice, 1749

Miscellaneous revisions for new cities:

Ipermestra a, Vienna, 1744	*b*, Dresden, 1751
L'Olimpiade a, Dresden, 1756	*b*, Turin, 1765

Only four operas were revised for later performance in the same city in which they were originally produced:

TABLE VI

Artaserse Ia, Venice, 1730	*Ib,* Venice, 1734
Alessandro IIa, Venice, 1736	*IIb,* Venice, 1738
	IIc, Venice, 1743
Arminio IIa, Dresden, 1745	*IIb,* Dresden, 1751
Leucippo a, Dresden, 1747	*c,* Dresden, 1751
	d, Dresden, 1756
	e, Dresden, 1763

For the sake of comparison, it should be noted that all five of the completely rewritten operas were intended for new cities:

TABLE VII

Artaserse Ia, Venice 1730	
Ic, Dresden, 1740	*II,* Naples, 1760
Ezio I, Naples, 1731	*II,* Dresden, 1755
Cleofide I, Dresden, 1731	*IIa,* Venice, 1736
Tito Ia, Pesaro, 1735	
Ib, Dresden, 1738	*II,* Naples, 1759
Demofoonte Ia, Dresden, 1748	
Ib, Venice, 1749	*II,* Naples, 1758

The next frequent justification for revision was the necessity of providing new music for a different primo uomo or prima donna. In ten of the seventeen revisions for which music survives, at least one of the important characters had more than half of his arias replaced by new ones:

TABLE VIII

Opera	Total # new arias	Character	# of new arias
Leucippo c	5	Primo uomo (title)	5
Cajo Fabrizio b	6	Prima donna	5
Artaserse Ic	10	Prima donna	5
Siroe b	14	Primo uomo (title)	4
Arminio IIb	9	Title role	4

TABLE VIII (continued)

Opera	Total # new arias	Character	# of new arias
Semiramide b	8	Prima donna (title)	3
Demofoonte Ib	9	Prima donna	3
		Primo uomo (title)	3
L'Olimpiade b	7	Primo uomo	3
Alessandro IIb	6	Title role	3
Alessandro IIc	7	Title role	3

In these nine operas, more than half of the seventy-five new arias were intended for the one (or two) most important singers.

In several operas, a lack of time may have determined the extent and scope of revisions. In some instances, all of the revised or replaced arias are found in the first half of the opera, suggesting that Hasse did not have time to finish the process of revision. In two revisions, the new arias are in the second half, implying that Hasse was originally pressed to finish the first version, and did not have time to polish the second half to his satisfaction, but was able to do so when an opportunity came to revive it:[12]

TABLE IX

Operas written in haste:

	First half old arias	new arias	Second half old arias	new arias
Tito Ia/Ib	12	2	2	10
Demetrio a/b	5	10	0	13

Operas revised in haste:

	First half old arias	new arias	Second half old arias	new arias
Semiramide a/b	7	8	11	0
Siroe a/b	0	11	7	3

Demetrio a/b does not show any special interest in writing new arias for leading characters, giving further credence to the idea that it was revised at least partly to improve the music. In both of the operas revised in haste, Hasse made sure that the important singers received new arias in *both* halves of the new version, again suggesting that these were the primary concern in many revisions.

Substitute texts and contrafacta or parodies present specific problems. Both circumstances occur throughout Hasse's career, and are not limited to revisions of operas. Both forms of substitution actually usually contain revisions themselves: key, tempo, or coloratura passages are the most common forms of change. The two forms of substitution are equally apt to be found, and are usually found in the same operas. An opera written in haste, or revised in haste, will make use of both time-saving devices.

Substitute texts can be described as all those which are not found in the original libretto. These separate themselves into two types: texts taken from other operas, and texts which seem to be written specifically for the new opera. In the latter case, it is highly likely that the aria is also a contrafactum, that the text was written to fit both an old aria and a new libretto. Often, it is not possible to locate the original source of the music, and it must be considered possible that some substitute texts are added solely to improve the libretto. Substitute texts from earlier operas are relatively simple to isolate, through alphabetical list of aria texts.

Contrafacta also separate themselves into two types: those set to texts taken from the libretto of the new opera, and those set to new texts, specially written for the occasion. The first type entails finding a pre-composed aria that matches in its poetical meter and musical affect the new text. The second type suggests that an especially good aria was made useable a second time by the writing of a new text. This form of parody is synonymous with the second type of substitute aria mentioned in the preceding paragraph.

Contrafacta are extremely difficult to trace. The music is not always taken from immediately adjacent operas. In some cases, it may be twenty years older than the rest of the production. One contrafactum from *Demetrio c* (1747) originated with *La Sorella amante* (1729). An orderly catalogue of aria incipits, a much more difficult project than alphabetizing titles, is necessary for a complete indentification of contrafacta. The present study cannot claim to have found all of the examples of contrafacta in Hasse's operatic opus; this must remain a project for future research. In this study, concerned primarily with differences between versions of the same opera, the presence of contrafacta does not change any of the basic conclusions.[12a]

Substituting a few arias was an easy way of revising an opera for another city. The three operas given by Hasse in Venice in 1747 and 1749 demonstrate this. When *Demetrio c* was revised in 1747, eleven substitute arias were inserted, five of which were taken, textually, from earlier Hasse operas. Since the music is not available, it is not possible to determine if the other six are contrafacta, a likely possibility. *Leucippo b* of 1749 had two, one of which was from an earlier opera, and *Demofoonte Ib,* of the same year, had eight substitutes, two from other operas.[13]

The two other revisions staged in Venice also present problems with substitute texts. *Artaserse Ib* of 1734 does not have Hasse's name on the libretto, and has nine arias not found in the 1730 version. Two of these are from the original Metastasian libretto, early evidence of Hasse's desire to replace substitutes with originals when he had the opportunity. Two are from *Siroe a,* which Hasse had set the preceding year. A sixth is an aria which was used again later that year in the revision of *Cajo Fabrizio* produced in Dresden by Hasse. This is a certain connection between the two productions. Hasse was in Venice until the first week of January, 1734, so he certainly would have been able to preside at the premiere if *Artaserse* were one of the first operas of the season.

The *Alessandro IIb* of 1738 is based on Hasse's production of 1736, and the two substitute texts, plus four others, are found in the rather ambivalently-titled collection of "Arie: della nova Aggiunta dell'Opera del Sigr. Gio: Hasse Dal Teatro in San Giov. Grisostomo, 1738."[14]   The *Alessandro IIc* of the Carnival season of 1743 has seven substitute texts, one taken from Hasse's *Demetrio a* of 1732, also produced in Venice.[15]   Another is from the libretto of *Semiramide,* not set by Hasse until the Carnival season of 1745. It is conceivable, though unlikely, that Hasse had received a contract for the 1745 Carnival and had already started to set this opera in 1742. It is not even sure that Hasse was in Venice in 1743. This revision must therefore be considered doubtful.

When new singers had voice ranges different from the original interpreters of the roles, adjustments were essential. Rather than just transposing the parts, Hasse often seems happier revising them completely, often with a greater frequency than the parts that remained unchanged. This is caused to some extent by the lack of flexibility in choosing the important singers: the impresario was far more likely to hire the prima donna on the basis of her fame and ability than on her range.   The lesser parts could then be shuffled to some extent, to minimize the necessity of revisions. At least six operas show a strong preference for revising arias for the singers with different ranges.

A rare reason for revision was a drastic change in the ability of the singer holding a specific role. When *Tito Ia* was revised in 1738, the

TABLE X

Opera	Roles with Changed Ranges # of Old Arias / # of New		Roles with the Same Range # of Old / # of New	
Ipermestra a/b	1	5	10	7
Demetrio a/b	0	12	5	6
Siroe a/b	2	9	4	5

In the following operas, only one voice, that of the primo uomo (*L'Olimpiade*), the title role (*Arminio*), or the prima donna (*Semiramide*) was changed, and this skews the figures to an even greater extent:

L'Olimpiade a/b	2	3	11	5
Arminio IIa/IIb	2	4	15	5
Semiramide a/b	2	3	16	5

part of Publio was taken by Antonio Campioli. He was an alto, like Giacomo Peruzzi, who had sung it at Pesaro, in 1735. But while Peruzzi was, to judge from the music, quite good at coloratura, his range was only slightly over an octave. Campioli, on the other hand, had a range of almost two octaves, but no ability for coloratura. Thus it was essential that his two arias be completely rewritten.

A different instance occurred in *Demetrio a* and *b*, where the part of Olinto was sung in 1732 by Giuseppe Appiani, *detto* Appianino. Appiani was twenty years old and had made his debut only one year before; he was to become one of the most famous singers of Europe by the time of his premature death in 1742, but Hasse trusted him with nothing complicated.[15a] In 1740, Rochetti received the part, and besides having the three original arias replaced with much more difficult ones, he was given two additional ones to exploit his superior technique.

After all of the above exigencies had been considered, Hasse could devote his efforts in revision to creating better music. In fact, it is rare that a revision consists simply of replacing a badly-written aria by a better one.

The following table lists the fourteen revised operas, along with ten further revisions, with which the remainder of this chapter is concerned. Also listed are the sources used for the various revisions, the number of new arias, and other points that might have a bearing on the energy, the effort, the time that was put into a specific revision.

TABLE XI

1. *Artaserse Ib*, Venice 1734
   No score; information
   from libretto

   A makeshift refurbishing of
   Venice, 1730 production

   9 new arias: 1/3 new.
   (2 from *Siroe a*, 1 also in
   Cajo Fabrizio b, 2 added
   from original libretto,
   4 other substitute texts)

2. *Cajo Fabrizio b*, Dresden, 1734
   Autograph of Act I;
   Dresden copy of remainder

   A revision for Faustina

   6 new arias: 1/5 new.
   (2 substitute texts, 4
   arias rewritten; 5 of the
   new arias for Faustina)

3. *Alessandro nell'Indie IIa*, Venice, 1736
   Venetian copy

   A completely new opera, salvaging
   several pieces from *Cleofide I*, but
   having no recitative in common

   20 new arias: 9/10 new.
   New recitative.
   (1 aria, 1 march, 1 duet-
   cavatina kept; 2 arias and
   1 cavatina revised greatly)

4. *Tito Vespasiano Ib*, Dresden, 1738
   Dresden copy

   Act I and first half of
   Act II: minor changes;
   second half of Act II and
   Act III, heavily revised

   13 new arias.

5. *Alessandro nell'Indie IIb*, Venice, 1738
   Venice score of 6 arias

   A refurbishing of 1736
   production: evenly distributed

   6 new arias: 1/4 new.
   (3 for Alessandro; 2
   substitute texts)

6. *Artaserse Ic*, Dresden, 1740
   Dresden copy

   A revision for Faustina,
   keeping almost all the
   original substitute texts

   10 new arias: 1/3 new.
   (7 substitute texts
   rewritten, 1 Metastasian
   text added; 5 new arias
   for Faustina)

TABLE XI (continued)

7. *Demetrio b*, Dresden, 1740
    Dresden copy

    An extensive revision of a
    hastily-written opera

22 new arias: 3/4 new.
Recitative mostly revised
from 1732 version.
(5 arias kept from 1732,
7 substitute texts replaced
by Metastasian texts, but
2 substitutes added)

8. *Alessandro nell'Indie IIc*, Venice, 1743
    No scores

    Perhaps not connected with
    Hasse. A refurbishing of
    1738 production

7 new arias: 1/3 new.
(4 substitute texts added,
1 substitute from 1736 and
2 from 1738 replaced by
new substitutes; 1
substitute taken from
Demetrio a of 1732, 1 from
libretto of *Semiramide*)

9. *Semiramide b*, Dresden, 1747
    Autograph score

    A hasty revision of 1745
    production

8 new arias: 1/3 new.
(1 of 3 substitute texts
replaced; all new arias
from first 2/3 of opera)

10. *Demetrio c*, Venice, 1747
    Dresden score of 2
    arias

    A makeshift refurbishing of
    1732 and 1740 versions

11 new arias: 1/2 new.
(6 arias cut, leaving 22;
3 substitute texts, from
*Antigono, Didone
abbandonata,* and
Ipermestra a; and a paraphrase of one from *La
Sorella amante*)

11. *Demofoonte Ib,* Venice, 1749
    Italian copy of 21
    loose arias

    A refurbishing of original
    Dresden production of 1748

9 new arias: 1/3 new
(all are substitute texts;
2 from *La Spartana
generosa,* 1 from *Siroe a;*
6 for prima donna and
primo uomo)

TABLE XI (continued)

12. *Leucippo b*, Venice, 1749
    no scores

    A slight refurbishing of
    Dresden production of 1747

2 new arias.
(both are substitutes;
1 from *Didone abban-
donata*)

13. *Ipermestra b*, Dresden, 1751
    Autograph

    Unhurried revision of
    Viennese production of 1744

12 new arias: 1/2 new.
(5 substitute texts added)
(1744 version had used
uncut Metastasian libretto)

14. *Leucippo c*, Dresden, 1751
    Dresden score

    A revision for Salimbeni's
    debut in Dresden

5 new arias: 1/5 new.
(all for primo uomo)

15. *Arminio IIb*, Dresden, 1753
    Dresden score

    A revision primarily for
    Monticelli's debut in
    Dresden

10 new arias: 2/5 new.
(9 substitute texts added;
4 new arias for title
role)

16. *Ezio II*, Dresden, 1753
    Autograph

    Probably completely new

Presumably 100% new.
(*Ezio I*, of 1730,
unavailable; 1/2 of arias
on new texts)

17. *Leucippo d*, Dresden, 1756?
    Autograph

    Probably never performed.
    Hurried revision for Dresden
    or perhaps Warsaw

3 new arias, compared to
Leucippo a.
(1 substitute from
Leucippo c, 1 from *Attilio
Regolo*)

18. *Demofoonte II*, Naples, 1758
    Autograph

    Completely new opera

100% new. (1 substitute
text, taken from *La
Spartana generosa,* but
with new music)

TABLE XI (continued)

19. *La Clemenza di Tito II, Naples, 1759*
   Autograph

   Completely different
and
   from *Tito Ia* and *Ib*

   100% new.
   (1 substitute text and
   10 contrafacta from
   L'Olimpiade a, Ezio II,

   Il Rè pastore)

20. *Artaserse II,* Naples, 1760
   Autograph
   Almost totally new opera

   20 new arias; only 3 from
   1740; all recitative new.

21. *Siroe b,* Dresden, 1763
   Autograph

   Intended to be completely
   new, but forced by pressure
   of time to borrow from
   1733 version

   14 new arias: 3/4 new;
   all new recitative.
   (3 substitute texts replaced,
   1 kept, 1 replaced by
   another, 1 added; 5 new
   arias for primo uomo)

22. *Leucippo e,* Dresden, 1763
   no score
   no libretto
   Described by Fürstenau.
   Never performed

   ?
   (perhaps same as
   Leucippo a or c)

23. *L'Olimpiade b,* Turin, 1765
   Autograph fragments
   Italian copy of arias

   Revised for new production
   in Turin, but no record of
   commission survives

   7 new arias: 1/3 new.
   Recitative lost.
   (3 new arias for primo
   uomo)

24. *Piramo e Tisbe b,* Vienna, 1770
   no score
   no libretto
   Described by Hasse as a revision

   ?

The major part of this chapter is concerned with the observation of several of the revisions in detail. It is not necessary to cover all of the operas listed above, since most of them have points in common. The selected operas have been chosen as good examples of specific problems or approaches to the process of revision, progressing at the same time from a revision with only a few new arias to one that was set again from the beginning.

1. *Leucippo a, c,* and *d.* The five new arias in *Leucippo c* were all for one new singer. *Leucippo d* shows what happens when an opera is revived with virtually no changes in the music.

2. *Semiramide a* and *b.* The autograph shows how the process of revision took place, and the results of a lack of time upon the revision.

3. *Demetrio a* and *b.* This is an opera written in haste, and revised at leisure, so that almost none of the original remained.

4. *Ipermestra a* and *b.* In the second version, half the arias are revised, scattered evenly throughout the opera, suggesting that both the original and the revision were carefully planned and completed.

5. *Siroe a* and *b.* The second version begins as if a completely new opera had been planned, but apparently pressures of time forced the abandonment of the plan, and Hasse reverted to following the original version.

6. *Tito Vespasiano Ib* and *La Clemenza di Tito II.* The presence of the second version has never been generally acknowledged. Yet the latter is a good example of the complete re-setting of an old libretto, along with a liberal use of contrafacta.

B. Six revised operas

1: Leucippo

Leucippo a was composed in 1747. It was one of Hasse's most successful operas on a Pasquini libretto: performances took place in Brunswick the same year, Salzthal in 1748, Venice in 1749, Prague in 1752, Frankfurt in 1754, Mannheim in 1757, Pressburg in 1759, Berlin in 1765, and again in Brunswick in 1765.[16] Of these, the only production connected with Hasse was that of Venice. In later years the opera was altered two or three times for Dresden, in 1751, 1756, and perhaps 1763.[17]

The 1749 Venetian production does not survive in any score. The libretto is almost identical to the 1747 opera, with one aria added for Clistene, the seconda donna, and one of Nunte's arias replaced by an aria from *Didone abbandonata*, presumably from Hasse's setting. As in Dresden, Carestini sang the title role, and his arias were probably unchanged.

In 1751 the famous castrato Felice Salimbeni came to join the Dresden company. In honor of this occasion, Hasse rewrote all of the arias for the title role of *Leucippo*. Scores of this version survive, showing that no other part was altered at all. One score, by a Dresden copyist, has the five new arias in the back, preceded, when necessary, by alternative recitative passages to cadence in keys relative to the new arias.[18] Three of Leucippo's arias were rewritten on the original texts, and two others were given new words. Analogous situations are almost nonexistent, the closest being the 1734 revision of *Cajo Fabrizio* that gave five of six new arias to Faustina.

Carestini's arias show that the singer had no problems of range or execution. He may have tired easily: while his first arias have a range of F$^\sharp$ to f$^\sharp$', the last two only go as low as G (in the penultimate aria) and A (in the last aria), and as high as d'. Still, the last aria, "Voler che in vita," (III:5), is a 3/8 time più tosto allegro, and was probably quite rapid. Carestini's coloratura emphasized stepwise, rather than disjunct, passages. "Così geloso il cane," (I:9), a brilliant showpiece, demonstrates his abilities to their best advantage:

Salimbeni's range was much higher than Carestini's (from B to c"), and at the very least his part would have had to have been transposed. While he, too, was highly skilled as a singer, he was given less coloratura; the oramental parts of the arias do not intrude as greatly as in Carestini's. His coloratura inclined slightly more to leaps than to stepwise passages, and his range expanded as the opera progressed, with the high c" coming in his last aria, "Voler che in vita," (III:5), a 3/8 allegretto e con spirito piece. "Per me vivi," on the other hand, is a lento love aria, with nothing difficult in the written part, though the improvised repeat of the da capo was probably quite spectacular. His second aria, "Non ti sovvien," (I:9), is his most important piece, the only one to be scored for horns and oboes, and serves as a good example of Salimbeni's technique:

The rest of the 1751 cast was probably very much like that of 1747. All but one of the singers was still active; the exception was Denner, who last sang in 1747, and by 1751 had been replaced by Mingotti.[19]   Hasse would not have been eager to give Mingotti any special attention, in any event.   (See Chapter I, pp. 22-26.)

The autograph of *Leucippo* represents neither of these versions. It is yet another revision, probably that of the opera planned for 7 October 1756. Hasse was in the process of rehearsing an unknown opera for Dresden in 1756 when the outbreak of the Seven Years War caused the cancellation of the planned performance. The autograph fits this date and place; the handwriting includes Hasse's and that of three copyists all associated with Dresden manuscripts. It can safely be assumed that the opera in question was intended for Dresden performance, or at least was prepared in Dresden.

Two substituted arias are found in this version of the opera. One of these, "Da voi cari lumi," (I:5), is taken from *Attilio Regolo*, performed in Dresden in 1750. The other is "Ah che da lei lontano," (II:2), one of the substitute arias from the 1751 version of the opera. Thus, the opera can be dated as after 1750 and probably after 1751, especially since these arias are both in the hand of a copyist, suggesting that the originals had already been composed and that these arias were copied from another manuscript. The most decisive argument for dating

s that in the years 1753 to 1756, and at no other time, the cappella
included five sopranos and a bass. With the retirement of Annibali, an
alto, in 1752, and his replacement by Monticelli, a mezzo-soprano, the
opera would have been cast with Albuzzi as Dafne, the prima donna,
Pilaja as Climene, the seconda donna, Monticelli as Leucippo, Belli as
Delio, and Führich as Nunte. (Schuster seems to have been inactive
after 1753.) Rochetti, who had not sung between 1753 and 1755, began
to participate again in the latter year, so it was probably he who was to
have taken the part of Celinda, a transposed version of Amorevoli's
Narete.

Several factors suggest that this may not have been the case. It
was quite rare for Hasse to include substitute arias that had once been
performed in Dresden, in operas revised for Dresden. The October
opera had up to then been a new work, not a revision. And there is no
information on why Amorevoli would not have been able to sing the part
of Narete as it was originally set. Hasse never kept strictly to precedent:
Leucippo had already been revised once for Dresden, and during the
years that followed, the October opera was always a revival, never a
premiere. Perhaps this opera was intended for production in Warsaw.

The most interesting change made for this fourth version was the
transposition of the tenor part of Narete to the soprano clef. Hasse was
not in the habit of giving his tenors parts written in soprano clef, and
this was not his intent in this case. Since it was not usually considered
appropriate for a soprano to sing the part of a father, Narete was
transformed into Celinda, the confidant of Leucippo.[20] This required
many minor changes in the libretto, to eliminate such references as "oh
padre." One aria also required a textual change, Narete's "Quando
penso, figlio amato" becoming Celinda's "Quando penso, sventurato."
However, Leucippo's first aria, "Nel lasciarti, o Padre amato," was not
changed!

It does seem as though time may have again played a factor in
this last revision of *Leucippo*. There is only one totally new aria. The
only other changes from 1747 are the two substitute arias mentioned
above. In actuality, *Leucippo d* was revised considerably, but with only
small amounts of truly new music being written. Many of the arias are
copied, even though they are transposed if necessary. But only five of
the first thirteen are copied, while seven of the last ten are.

The arias of Celinda/Narete fit in well with this theory: the first
aria is revised and transposed, the second is completely new, though on
the original text, and the last is copied and transposed only. That
Celinda received the only new aria suggests that the singer was someone
of importance.

Pilaja needed much revision in her arias: all three were revised,
the first only in insignificant respects (though it was transposed), the last

two quite considerably. Two of Leucippo's five arias were copied unchanged, one being the new aria from 1751. Two others were transposed, and three were revised in minor details. The three middle arias were copied, but since the first was revised slightly, it suggests that Hasse made changes on the original autograph, and then had the time to have the aria copied over. Leucippo's last aria was also revised and transposed, but it is found in Hasse's hand in the performing score. This suggests that, rather than correcting the original, Hasse transposed the aria himself, and, to save time, revised the music simultaneously.

Albuzzi seems to have been quite able to handle Faustina's coloratura: only one aria was revised, though all five were transposed up a major second or third. Führich and Rochetti had no trouble with their roles either; Rochetti was probably singing his original part, and Hasse's bass arias are never very demanding. The five arias assigned to these singers are indeed the only ones copied unchanged from the 1747 version.

Tonal reordering due to transpositions does not seem to have bothered Hasse. Act II had ended with arias in D, C, and B♭ in 1747, but in 1756 this was changed to D, F, and B♭. And Act III, ending originally in D, E♭, and F, was changed to G, F, and F. The opera also begins in F, and this penultimate piece, changed to F in 1756, serves as an attempt to round off the opera tonally, to a greater degree than originally.

Leucippo d illustrates what may have been done with other operas whose revised forms do not survive. Of all the revisions, only *Leucippo b* has fewer new arias (two). But the libretto of *Leucippo d* (if a libretto was indeed printed) would have shown only the two of the three new arias which had new texts. This corroborates the information provided by the loose arias of *Demofoonte Ib* (see above, p. 303, note 13). Very few of the arias with old texts can be expected to have new music written for them, especially if the revision is not a major one. *Leucippo d* demonstrates to what degree Hasse was willing to transpose and borrow in order to avoid major revisions, when he copied over an opera for a new production.

2: *Semiramide*

Semiramide is the only Hasse autograph that survives as a working copy for a revision. Much of the score is from the 1745 version, but all of the changes for the 1747 production are incorporated into the manuscript in Hasse's handwriting. It is known that Hasse was pressed for time while he was revising this opera; the manuscript shows this lack of time in many ways (see Chapter I, p. 22). That a clean copy does not survive provides the greatest evidence: this very untidy manuscript was probably used in the performance, and, unlike *Ipermestra b*, *Leucippo d*, and *Arminio IIb*, was not copied over by copyists before the performance. The autographs for *Ipermestra a*, *Leucippo a*, and *Arminio IIa* do not survive; they would have been reduced to scrap in the same way that *Semiramide a* was, and once they were recopied, the original would have been discarded.

An exact listing of which parts of the autograph stem from 1745 and which are from 1747 is given in Table XII. This does not include the recitative, almost all of which is from 1745. The parts of Semiramide and Tamiri, both sung by altos in 1745, were taken by sopranos in 1747. Hasse merely entered stemless notes above the recitative, keeping the same bass, but raising the tessitura in necessary places, in order to keep the amount of recopying to a minimum. (Plate XXI) Exceptions to this have obvious explanations. In Act I, scene 11, it was necessary because of the removal of a fascicle to recopy the recitative at the end of the scene in 1747. Hasse kept the alto clef for the part of Semiramide, in order to conform to the rest of the scene, but the tessitura was raised, and the revised stemless voice part is not present. In Act II, scene 6, copied over for the same reason in 1747, Semiramide was given a soprano clef, changing from alto on f. 32' (retained from 1745) to soprano on f. 33.

The part of Scitalce, written in soprano clef in 1745, was sung by an alto in 1747. But the 1745 soprano, Carestini, had by that point in his career lost the top notes of his range, and gained several in his lower register, and the alto, Annibali, had no trouble with the part as it was written, untransposed and, for the most part, unaltered.

In several cases, the manuscript shows where a 1745 aria was replaced by a new one in 1747. The first time this occurs is in Act I, scene 3. Here, the opening of Semiramide's 1745 aria, "Non so se più t'accendi," is crossed out, and a fascicle of two folios is inserted with the replacement aria, on the same text. The preceding recitative had cadenced on A, since the original aria had been in D. The new aria was in F, but the third-relation, though less common, was still acceptable, so the recitative did not have to be altered.

The Act I, scene 8 aria, "Come alle amiche arene," was also replaced, but the cadence on D certainly could not be used for the new aria, which was in C. The cadence was rewritten. (Plates XXII and XXIII)

The 1745 libretto does not match the scores of the first version.[21] Two arias, "Ei d'amore," (I:12), and "Sentirsi dire," (III:11), are not listed in the libretto, but are found in the scores. A third, "In braccio," (III:4), is listed in the libretto, but was apparently never set. The autograph passes from scene 4 to scene 5 without a sign that an aria was ever considered for that scene.   Act III, scene 11, in contrast, is a completely separate fascicle, for both recitative and aria, ending with three blank pages, thus showing that the aria was added after the 1745 libretto was printed, but before the opera was finished.[22]

TABLE XII

Sinfonia:		b (1747)
		b
		a (1745)
I:3		b
:4		a
:5		a
:7		a
:8		b
:11		b
:13		b
:14		b
:15		b
II:2	(coro)	b
:2	(aria)	a & b
:3		a
:4		a & b
:6		b
:8		b
:9		a
:11		a
:12		b
:13		a & b
III:3		a
:5		a
:7		b
:9		a & b
:10		a
:11		a
:14		a

PLATE XXI

Semiramide b (*op. cit.*), v. 1, fasc. 1, f. 4′ (I:1,2)

Corrections are visible at the top of the page. Stemless notes are present on the last two systems, generally keeping Semiramide's range above middle C.

PLATE XXI

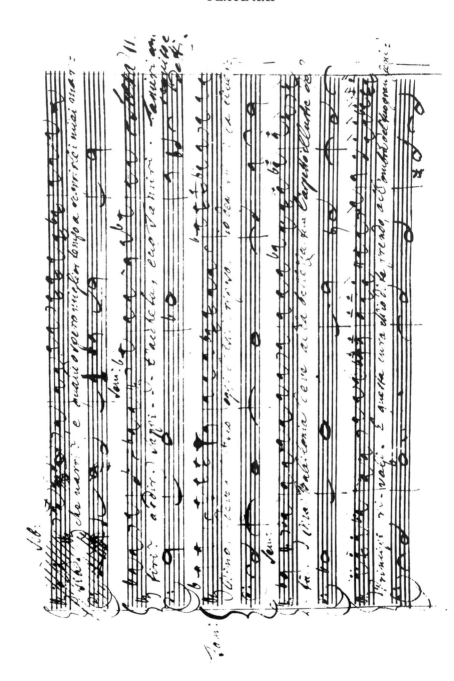

PLATES XXII AND XXIII

Semiramide b (*op. cit.*) v. 1, fasc. 10, f. 4; fasc. 11, f. 1. (I:8, recitative and "Come alle ameche arene," both versions.)

It did not take much to change this cadence from D to g. The crossed-out aria is from 1745, the new one from 1747.

PLATE XXII

PLATE XXIII

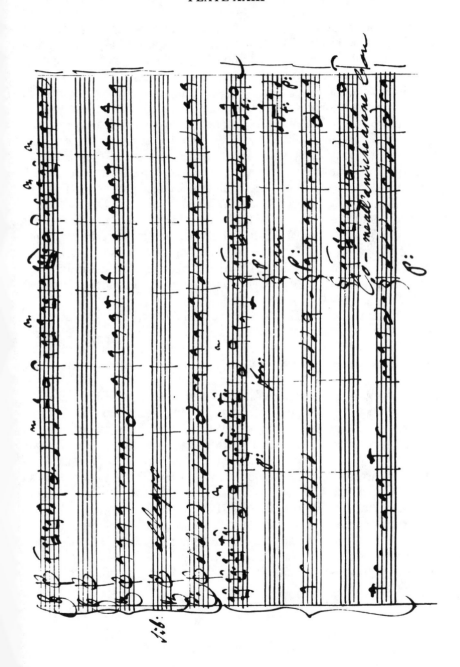

The haste with which the revision was made not only prevented Hasse from having a fair copy made, but also limited the amount of revision that could be done. Only eight pieces of music, including a chorus, are new to the 1747 production. All eight of these are found in the first fifteen musical numbers, though Hasse found time to copy over two arias that were transposed, from the last eleven numbers. Parts of four arias were copied over in 1747, with various revisions, and fitted in neatly with the remnants of the 1745 arias. One complete aria, "Talor se il vento freme," (I:14), revised in several respects, was also copied over.

The placement of the revised and copied arias suggests that Hasse revised as he composed: from beginning to end of the opera. As he ran out of time, be became less and less concerned with revision. A schematic drawing (Table XIII) illustrates this process. Ten X's (XXXXXXXXXX) indicate a new 1747 aria. Eight X's (XXXXXXXX) indicate an aria copied over in 1747, but based on 1745 music. Six X's (XXXXXX) represent a 1745 aria with some pages recopied in 1747, with changes. Four X's (XXXX) represent a 1745 aria with some corrections added to the manuscript in 1747: dynamics, cancellations, instruments added, and the like. (Plate XXIV) Two X's (XX) represent an aria left untouched in 1747.

From Table XIII, it is clear that no rewriting took place after II:8. A diminishing of revision is even discernible at II:2. This diminution of effort occurs for all of the singers, and does not spare the prima donna or primo uomo, though efforts to counter this trend are visible.

Vittoria Tesi sang the role of Semiramide in 1745. In 1747, Faustina sang it. Tesi, in 1745, was forty-five years old, and Faustina probably forty-seven, but the vocal powers of Faustina were much greater than those of Tesi, to judge from the music written for the two. Tesi may well have been superior in beauty of tone or in quality of sustained notes. Despite the difference in clef, both singers had an effective range in 1745 of c to f', an eleventh, though Faustina does receive one a', in "Voi non sapete," (I:13). Faustina was more effective in the upper fifth of her range, while Tesi sang best in the middle fifth of this eleventh, if we can trust Hasse's settings. Tesi's arias also lack coloratura sections; they avoid slow tempos, with the two slowest arias being a rather brisk andante and allegretto. Faustina's arias are also all fast, ignoring the eighteenth-century convention that each singer be given a selection of different aria-types. All but one are in common time.

TABLE XIII

Sinfonia:	XXXXXXXXXX
	XXXXXXXXXX
	XX
I:3	XXXXXXXXXX
:4	XX
:5	XXXX
:7	XXXX
:8	XXXXXXXXXX
:11	XXXXXXXXXX
:13	XXXXXXXXXX
:14	XXXXXXXX
:15	XXXXXXXX
II:2	XXXXXXXXXX
:2	XXXXXX
:3	XXXX
:4	XXXXXX
:6	XXXXXXXXXX
:8	XXXXXXXXXX
:9	XXXX
:11	XXXX
:12	XXXXXXXX
:13	XXXXXX
III:3	XX
:5	XX
:7	XXXXXXXX
:9	XXXXXX
:10	XX
:11	XX
:14	XXXX

PLATE XXIV

Semiramide b (*op. cit.*) from "Vorrei spiegar l'affanno," (I:5). v. 1, fasc. 6, f. 1'

This shows the addition of the viola line to the aria, several melodic changes in the violin part, readjustment of the dynamics, and the addition of two measures of coloratura (one on the following page). This is a great amount of revision, and seems to have been done for the second production.

PLATE XXIV

Faustina received three new arias in 1747. No other singer had more than one new aria given to him. That Hasse would have given Faustina five new arias if he had had the time is beyond question. The fourth of the five arias is considerably reworked in the accompaniment, but the fifth is different only in the most minor details. Neither has any sort of coloratura, even though both were copied completely in 1747. Perhaps this gave Faustina a chance to rest from the tiring vocal calisthenics that the Dresden audience expected from her.

Hasse did use the opportunity of recopying "Tradita, sprezzata," (II:12), to improve areas within it. The opening, with its dominant seventh added in the second instead of the third measure, is slightly better, and the addition of thirds to the harmony shows a greater care in orchestration:

The minor change in the melody at m. 3 of the opening ritornello was probably made so that Faustina could avoid having to leap up to e' at the equivalent place in the A_1 stanza.

The end of the A$_2$ stanza is also altered to be more dramatic:

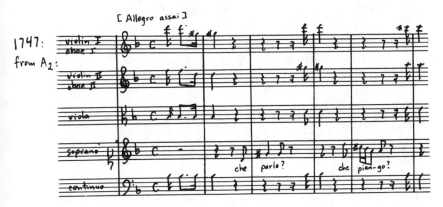

The recitative idiom within the aria may have been a cliché even in 1747, but it is rare for Hasse to use such a device.

The 1745 version of "Tradita" includes a crescendo, starting at "piano" and continuing "forte a poco a poco" beneath a rising melodic scale in the violins. In the 1747 version, the only indication at this point is "poco forte" which suggests either that the Dresden orchestra did not need the indication for the crescendo or that the device was not used at all in Dresden.

Scitalce, the primo uomo, was sung by Carestini in Venice and by Annibali in Dresden. Carestini was the superior singer. Hasse did try to rewrite for Annibali, who, as mentioned above, shared Carestini's range. But almost nothing was changed. Only one new aria was written, "Se intende si poco," (I:10), which replaced "Ardo per te." The latter was a substitute aria, and may have been inserted by Hasse as a contrafactum, but in general there is no sign that the 1745 version was rushed in any way, and the possibility remains that "Ardo per te" was a favorite aria of Carestini's from one of his previous roles. "Se intende" includes a leap from d' to A, the two extremes of Annibali's range, showing that he still retained his vocal. control. Of the other four arias, two were revised on the 1745 autograph, one was recopied totally, and the fourth had only the middle of the aria recopied. The last two arias show some evidence that Annibali tired more easily than Carestini, for large sections of coloratura are cut from both, which otherwise remained almost totally unchanged. In "Passaggier che sulla sponda" (II:13), several low F's and G's were eliminated in 1747, since they were below Annibali's range. Carestini's mezzo-soprano voice, as shown in the 1735 *Tito Vespasiano*, had a range of A - g', while by 1745 (in *Semiramide*) it had dropped to F - e'.

The less-important roles have only occasional changes. That of Mirteo, sung in Venice by Ghirardi and in Dresden by Rochetti, was not changed much: even though the two were not evenly matched, there was no time to revise. One aria, "Rondinella, in cui rapita," (I:15), was greatly revised, not for vocal reasons, but apparently to improve the aria. The headmotive was completely rewritten, and this necessitated changing much of the interior sections of the aria:

The revision of the ritornelli shows the care that Hasse could put into revision when he wished, and had the opportunity. Not only do all four ritornelli use the headmotive in 1747, but a minor motive [x], used three times and then abandoned in the 1745 A ritornello, becomes the motive for the spinning-out of the ritornelli in 1747.

Ircane's part, sung by Ottavio Albuzzi in 1745, and by Amorevoli in 1747, was altered to the greatest extent in the aria "Tu sei lieto, io vivo in pene," (II:8). This was completely rewritten, and although the second version includes a much more spectacular section of coloratura, the aria itself is not much better than the workable 1745 version. "Talor se il vento freme," (I:14), was one of the arias with a middle section copied over in 1747. The difference is visible in the ink and in the fact that the inserted fascicle no longer matches the Venetian copy. Perhaps

the original had had too many alterations made in it, for there are no musical differences between this and the 1745 aria.

Even though Denner, a mezzo-soprano, took the place of the alto Giacometti as the singer of Tamiri's role, her arias were not changed to any extent. Some coloratura is cut from "Non so se sdegno sia," (II:11) and from "Tu mi disprezzi, ingrato," (II:2), and the aria added at a late date in 1745, "Ei d'amore," (I:12), is cut. None of the four arias is transposed from the alto clef.

One of the most obvious examples of the pressure of time is found in the arias of Sibari, sung by Perini in Venice and Bindi in Dresden. Perini was evidently a poor singer, for his aria "Come alle amiche arene," (I:8) has short, simple runs and a range of an eleventh, from d to g'. Since this fell in the first act, Hasse could rewrite it, so that the completely new 1747 aria is filled with long, spectacular sections of coloratura taking full advantage of Bindi's range of nearly two octaves, from C to b♭'. The melody is also improved immeasurably:

Yet there was no time to do the same for "Quando un fallo e strada al regno," in Act III, scene 5, so Bindi had to make do with Perini's limited range and abilities, so limited in fact that in 1745 Hasse had cut the aria to a simple cavatina, without even the opportunity to embellish the da capo!

As with *Leucippo,* the frequency of transposition of arias in the revised version suggests comparison of key structures for evidence that Hasse considered any kind of tonal structure in his operas. The transpositions at the end of Act II do seem to provide more coherence:

> 1745: b,   B♭, E♭, c,   D
>
> 1747: F,   B♭, E♭, d,   D

Hasse sometimes prefers stepwise motion between numbers to the fourth or fifth relationships that become prevalent with later composers. The first five arias of Act I in 1745 combine the two relationships; in 1747 the first set change, after the fourth aria, is taken into consideration, with the first four arias making a neat tonal package:

> 1745: D E♭ B♭ F / G
>
> 1747: F E♭ B♭ F / C

The first set change of Act II also becomes a tonal unit, beginning and ending in the same key, opening with a fifth-relationship and closing with stepwise motion, in 1747. The sequence had been rather aimless in 1745:

> 1745: D D B♭ A F
>
> 1747: G D B♭ A G

But such structures were of secondary importance to Hasse; the second set of Act I was changed from a nice mirror-image idea to a less organized group, though the end pair of arias remained the same:

1745: G D E C D G

1747: C D   F D G

The Dresden libretto does not match its version of the opera either, listing six arias that were not ever set, but this is certainly because Hasse did not have time to set all the arias that he had hoped. The reasons for eliminating "Ei d'amore" are unknown, as has been mentioned. In 1760, when the opera was produced for the court in exile in Poland, the libretto finally caught up with the score, since it matches it with only one exception, Sibari's aria, "Vieni che poi sereno," intended for Act II, scene 7.[23] At the appropriate point in the autograph, Hasse added a note: "N.B: Qui viene l'aria di Sibari." This note is squeezed in, obviously a second thought; it is then crossed out. Evidently Hasse intended to expand Bindi's small part with another aria. For some reason, this aria was again eliminated after the libretto was printed, if indeed it was written at all.

    Semiramide provides a view into how the process of revision took shape in the autograph score, and how the exigencies of time and pressure influenced the revision. *Demetrio* demonstrates the reverse situation: a first version that is hurriedly done, and a revision so leisurely that almost nothing remains of the original by the time the process is complete.

3: *Demetrio*

    1732 was a busy year for Hasse: he had to write five completely new operas from Carnival to fall: *Catone in Utica* for Turin, *Cajo Fabrizio* for Rome, and *Demetrio* for Venice, all for the Carnival season, *Euristeo* for Venice at Ascension, and *Issipile* for Naples, probably in the fall. The first three of these show some haste in their composition, with substitute texts becoming more and more frequent towards the end of the operas, a situation present also in the two operas of 1731, *Cleofide* and *Dalisa*. In 1740, with more time available, Hasse revised *Demetrio* completely for performance during the Dresden Carnival. This, too, was not unusual; the same process was followed in 1738 with *Tito Vespasiano* (originally set in 1735 in Pesaro) and in 1740 with *Artaserse* (originally set in 1730 and revised in 1734, in Venice).

    The process of revision was much more thorough in the case of *Demetrio* than with the two other operas revised for Dresden around this time. This was to a large degree a function of the hasty composition visible in the first version of the work. While very few revised operas lose more than half of their original arias, *Demetrio* lost all but five of the twenty-four pieces of music of the Venetian version. Despite this drastic effort, *Demetrio* may still be considered a revision, not an entirely new setting, for much of the recitative, the framework of the opera, was retained. Though three of the roles were taken in 1740 by singers with different tessituras, Hasse kept as much of the old recitative as he could, though often only the basic outline remained:

Demetrio a used seven substitute texts, more than any original opera but *Cleofide*. Also, at least three arias are contrafacta, and the sinfonia was borrowed from *Gerone*. This suggests that *Demetrio* was intended for late in the season, and was staged after *Catone in Utica* and *Cajo Fabrizio*. Indeed, four of the five arias that are definitely from other operas are taken from these two.[24] Further, the opera has only twenty-four pieces of music, not counting the sinfonia and a march; a chorus, a duet, and five arias are cut from the Metastasian libretto.

In 1740, Hasse kept five of the arias, all of them from the first half of the 1732 version and none of them contrafacta or substitute texts. He also expanded the musical substance, adding the chorus and three arias. A fourth aria seems to have been added under pressure or extra-musical motives, for where Metastasio had intended an aria for the seconda donna, Hasse instead wrote, on a substitute text, one for the royal retainer. The primo uomo participates in a duet, where he formerly had a solo aria; another of his arias is cut and replaced at a later point with a Metastasian aria cut in 1732. The duet of the penultimate scene is still not set, but its function is taken at a more appropriate and dramatic point with the duet mentioned above, which is found in the middle of Act II, at the end of a long scene where Cleonice tearfully asks Demetrio to leave her for the good of the nation.

Demetrio b has twenty-eight numbers: twenty-five arias, two choruses, and a duet. This increase in the number of set pieces is consistent with other operas Hasse set for Dresden around 1740. *Artaserse Ic* of 1740 and *Tito Ib* of 1738 both have twenty-seven numbers. Venetian operas of the period around 1732 usually had somewhat fewer. *Artaserse Ia* of 1730 had twenty-seven, but *Artaserse Ib* of 1734 had twenty-five. *Euristeo* (1732) had twenty-one, and *Alessandro IIa* and *IIb*, of 1736 and 1738, both had twenty-five.

As with the two versions of *Tito*, Faustina sang the role of the prima donna in both versions of *Demetrio*. Also like *Tito*, three of the other parts changed ranges: Olinto, Mitrane, and Barsene were sung in 1740 by sopranos instead of the altos who had the parts in 1732. The balance of importance among the characters shifted between the two versions, and the number of arias of each demonstrates this:

TABLE XIV

	1732	1740
Cleonice: prima donna	5	6^x
Demetrio (Alceste): primo uomo	5	5^x
Barsene: seconda donna	4	4

TABLE XIV (continued)

1732   1740

	1732	1740
Olinto: secondo uomo	3	5
Fenicio: royal retainer	3	4
Mitrane: general	3	3

ᕁOne of these is a duet

All three of Olinto's 1732 arias were contrafacta. In 1740, Hasse had the time to replace these; also, Rochetti was a much more seasoned singer than Appiani (see p. 107), and could easily handle the greater load of five arias. The equalization of the parts of Barsene and Fenicio, with Barsene's demotion below the level of Olinto, her lover, is also due to extra-musical considerations: the first two were sung by Caterina and Filippo Giorgi, visitors to the court, and tact or politics seems to have required roles of equal importance.

The five arias that were retained were all for characters whose ranges did not change: Cleonice (one aria), Alceste/Demetrio (three arias), and Fenicio (one aria). The three arias for Alceste are well-crafted and interesting pieces of music, but this reversal of the usual trend of writing new music for the main singers is otherwise hard to explain.[25] All three come from the first half of the opera, and their composition was probably not rushed, in any case. Faustina retained only one of her five arias, a more usual situation, although she had sung the role in 1732 also. Three of the arias had been on substitute texts in the first version, and their replacement by the original Metastasian arias would have been a matter of course.

Faustina's first aria, in both versions, was the Metastasian "Fra tanti pensieri," (I:3). This was completely rewritten in 1740, and in the second version is more appropriate for an opening aria of the prima donna. The first version is più tosto andante, a moderate tempo, as indicated also by the note values: the rhythm is the syncopated ♩ ♩ ♩ that is found in many of Hasse's arias. The second version is an unequivocal allegro, with the note values halved, though the same rhythm predominates: ♪♩ ♩♪. Much more coloratura is present, with a two-measure run in A_1 being replaced by one of ten measures in 1740. Faustina also may have lost some of her facility in her upper range: this aria rises only to f', though the 1732 version had gone to g'[26].

Faustina's second aria was replaced on the general principle of replacing substitute texts. The original "Se non posso," (I:8), is quite a good aria, replaced by a slightly more florid "Se libera non sono." The

Act II, scene 7 aria, "Nacque agli affanni," was kept in its entirety; not even the high g' was eliminated. The duet "Dal mio ben," (II:12), is a substitute text, but it is a welcome addition to the opera, both in the change of texture it provides, and in its dramatic function. It is rather experimental in its harmonies, at one point modulating from B to E through an unusual excursion: B - e - A - G$^{\#7}$ - C$^{\#7}$ - F$^{\#7}$ - B^7 - E^7 - A - V/E - E.

"Non ho più core" was replaced by the Metastasian "Manca sollecità", (II:13), but the second aria is also a musical improvement: it is a charming 3/8 allegro set for the most part for a trio of flute and two violins, without the basso continuo (except at the ends of sections). It is in e, Hasse's only minor-key aria in 1740.[27]

The last of Faustina's arias seems to revert to the reasoning of her second one. "So ben anch'io," (III:3), a substitute text, was replaced by the Metastasian "Io so qual pena sia," which, like the 1732 aria, is an undistinguished andante. The range is only to f' instead of a': perhaps Faustina tired mored easily in 1740.

The first three of Alceste's arias were retained. The fourth was replaced by the duet, "Dal mio ben." But the fifth is a puzzle. "Quel labbro adorato," (III:4) was replaced later in the act, at scene 10, by "Se tutti i miei pensieri." Both texts are Metastasian. Neither aria is especially interesting musically, the 1732 aria being especially dull, but "Quel labbro adorato" is more effective dramatically, as a love song to Cleonice, while the second is a negative response to Barsene's romantic overtures to him. Perhaps the addition of the love duet made the first aria superfluous, and in compensation Alceste was given a piece that was closer to the end of the opera: "Se tutti" is the penultimate aria of the drama.

The other characters, being less important, are less interesting in the reasons for changes. The part of Olinto, as has been mentioned, was taken by a much more effective singer in 1740, and this is reflected in the arias: two are added, and the replacements for the three contrafacta all show much more coloratura. "Non fidi al mar," (II:8), is altogether written on a grander scale, including horns in 1740, and "Più non sembra," (III:5) is more adventuresome, having a B stanza in a contrasting tempo. The latter replaces "Non sembra ardito e fiero," which, though based loosely on the Metastasian original, is ridiculous in its imagery, with a consequent loss of seriousness in the music. The Metastasian A stanza is:

Più non sembra ardito e fiero
Quel leon, che, prigioniero,
A soffrir la sua catena
Lungamente s'avvezzò.

(No longer bold and proud seems
That lion, which, emprisoned,
Has slowly accustomed himself
To endure his chains.)

This, in 1732, became, because of the necessity of fitting the pre-composed music:

Non sembra ardito e fiero
Leon che prigioniero
In grazie, in scherzi, in gioco
Anche in catena e stretto
Si vede a dilettar.

(Not bold and proud seems
The imprisoned lion who
Amuses himself in games and jokes,
Although he is chained
And caged.)

The aria from which the music was taken, "Sara vezzosa," (*Cajo Fabrizio* III:1) includes a little joking figure between the strings and the singer on the words "le grazie, il gioco, il riso" (games, play, laughter). When this is included in the new text, any remnant of seriousness that might have remained from the original Metastasian text is destroyed:

Even the range of the 1732 singer is rather small: c - e'.

Two of Barsene's four arias were taken from earlier operas, so it is logical that these would be replaced in 1740. But two others were rewritten on the same Metastasian texts used in 1732: "Misero, tu non sei," (I:4) and "Vorrei da' lacci tuoi," (I:15). Neither of the arias is strikingly good or bad, so one must assume that they were rewritten only because the tessitura of the singer had changed. The role of Mitrane, like that of Olinto, was taken by a much more skillful singer in the person of Bindi in 1740. Catterina della Parte had received three arias in 1732, all syllabic, with runs being short or nonexistent; in 1740 Hasse gave Bindi all new arias, much more florid, though the range was still roughly an eleventh. A comparison of the coloratura passages in "Alma grande," (I:6), shows the typical difference:

The part of Fenicio was sung by a tenor in both versions, though Filippo Giorgi received four arias in 1740, in contrast to Barbieri's three in 1732. Neither singer was good at coloratura, but Giorgi had a high c′ which Hasse gave him in one aria. Otherwise, the arias are very similar, and there is no obvious reason for revision.

To sum up, there were twenty-eight pieces of music in the 1740 opera. Four had been added, five had been retained, and nine were replacements for substitute texts and contrafacta. A duet replaced an aria, and the final chorus had been expanded. Simple consideration for the singers must have dictated the replacement of the remaining eight arias by eight new ones on the same texts. Two for Mitrane were caused by the differing abilities of the singers. Two for Barsene were instigated by the change in voice range. There is thus no "factual" reason for rewriting the last four arias of the 1740 version, and though the other arias were often improvements, it can only be answered that Hasse rewrote these four for personal, musical, considerations. Four of twenty-eight is a small percentage.

Taking the process involved with *Demetrio* one step further results in the situation of *Cleofide I* (Dresden, 1731) and *Alessandro nell'Indie IIa* (Venice, 1736). *Cleofide*, like *Demetrio a*, included a great many substitute texts, probably all contrafacta, all of which were eliminated when the opera was revised in 1736. Six pieces were retained in 1736 from the old opera. But of these six, only one is a full aria that is not revised. One is a march, and one is a cavatina of nine measures. The other three include a cavatina, "Se mai più," (I:7), an aria, "Se mai turbo," (I:8), and a duet, "Se mai più," (I:17), which duplicates the text of the first two pieces. These three all use the melodies from 1731, but are otherwise almost totally changed. Furthermore, they make a unit that is one of the most striking aspects of the Metastasian libretto, and may well have been kept as the most successful feature of the 1731 production.

The text had been heavily revised by the poet Michelangelo Boccardi from Metastasio's original, to make the piece serve more as a vehicle for Faustina's Dresden debut, with the result that her role is rather lopsided, with six arias, a duet, and a cavatina-duet. The many changes in the text of the recitative, added to the fact that three of the singers' tessiture changed, made it not worthwhile to retain any of the original recitative. Only four scenes with singers of unchanged tessitura remained in the 1736 version; six other scenes that would have included these three singers were changed or eliminated by reverting to the Metastasian libretto.

This completely new recitative makes it more logical to call *Alessandro nell'Indie IIa* a completely new opera. With only one entire aria kept between the two versions, *Cleofide I* is in the same situation as *Artaserse Ia*, which kept three arias when it was rewritten as *Artaserse II*. But it should be realized that in the former case, the new opera was composed with the old one serving as a model, not, as with *Artaserse*, beginning with the precept of writing a completely new opera and eventually using parts of the old one.

No singers were the same in the two productions of *Cleofide* and *Alessandro*; even Faustina was replaced by Tesi in Venice. And only thirteen of the texts used in 1731 were, in any case, used again in 1736.[28] The reduction in the length of the opera by five arias in 1736 was not a matter of lack of time or of a general shift in taste, but probably more of a Venetian preference for shorter operas mentioned above (p. 135).

Alessandro IIa itself served as the original opera from which two revisions were derived. In 1738, when *Alessandro* was again presented in Venice, possibly under Hasse's auspices, two arias were cut, and six arias were replaced with substitutes and in 1743, again possibly under Hasse's guidance, seven texts were replaced with substitutes, though the number and distribution of arias remained the same.

4: *Ipermestra*

It is rare to find an instance where the libretto of an opera matches the score perfectly. Yet this is the case for both *Ipermestra a* and *b:* the first version, performed in Vienna in 1744, and the revised opera, produced in Dresden in 1751. Almost exactly half the arias were rewritten for the second version, and it seems that *Ipermestra* is an example of what Hasse would have done with *Semiramide*, if he had had the time.

While it was Hasse's practice to use substitute texts when he was pressed for time, and replace them when the opera was revised, *Ipermestra* reverses the procedure. The first setting was the premiere of the libretto. This was a great honor for Hasse, and it was obligatory that the libretto be set in its untouched form. In 1751, however, Hasse had the freedom to change what he wanted to, and he substituted five new texts for original Metastasian arias. There is no indication of a lack of time; the arias do not appear to come from earlier operas, and it may be presumed that they were written by Migliavacca, the Dresden court poet, for the occasion. Even in 1751 the recitative was not cut.

In 1751 only two of the characters had different ranges from the original interpreters. Danao, the king, was sung in Vienna by a bass, and in Dresden by Amorevoli, a tenor.[29] Plistene, the secondo uomo, was sung in Vienna by a tenor, in Dresden by Annibali, an alto.[30] These two characters have the highest percentage of rewritten arias: of a total of six arias, only one of Plistene's is not new, but is merely transposed. On the other hand, Adrasto, the confidant, sung by tenors in both versions, had both of his arias transposed, one down a major second and the other down a minor third. Even though this part is technically also for a singer of a different tessitura, Hasse did not consider him important enough to write new arias.[31]

The other three characters, Ipermestra, the prima donna, Linceo, the primo uomo, and Elpinice, the seconda donna, have a total of seven new arias and eight old ones. There is no sign of haste in the distribution of these new arias: five of the nine arias in Act I are new, five of the eight in Act II, and two of the six in Act III.

The autograph is quite similar in appearance to that of *Leucippo*. It includes a variety of handwriting and a sometimes haphazard arrangement of fascicles. If *Semiramide* had been revised at leisure, it too would have looked like this autograph. A description of the makeup of the autograph demonstrates what happens when a performing copy is made for a revised opera, presumably from the autograph of the first version:

TABLE XV

Act I

Sinfonia: A new sinfonia was written for the 1751 version, and this is in Hasse's hand.

Scene 1: Most of this scene is in the hand of a copyist. While the first line uses new music, the rest is identical to the 1744 version. At the last speech, Hasse begins to write in the words and music: the end of this speech differs from the 1744 version, and it is followed by an additional line, set to original music. The aria is also on a substitute text, and its music is new: this also appears in Hasse's hand. Hasse had instructed the copyist to stop at the above-mentioned point, so that he could insert the new cadence and aria himself.[32]

Scene 2: This opens with a speech by Ipermestra, identical to the 1744 version. After this speech, Danao enters. Since this part was sung by a tenor in 1751, his music had to be transposed. The following dialogue between Impermestra and Danao took much from the 1744 version, but all was rather freely adapted. Clearly it was not worth the time for a copyist to copy just the first speech. The whole scene and following aria (again on a new text) are in Hasse's hand.

Scene 3: This scene, for Ipermestra and Linceo, and its closing aria for Ipermestra, are identical to that of 1744, including a section of accompanied recitative. They are entirely in the hand of the copyist.

Scene 4: As with scene 1, this scene opens with a new line of music, followed by 1744 music. This line is a slight improvement over the original:

It was probably changed by Hasse on the 1744 autograph, for the first three speeches are in the hand of a copyist. At this point, Plistene enters, and since his part had to be transposed, Hasse finished the scene. The aria that follows is revised in respect to the coloratura, but it is completely in Hasse's hand.

Scenes 5-9: These include either Plistene or Danao. The arias are new; the recitatives are all based to some extent on the 1744 version. Everything is in Hasse's hand, including the aria closing scene 7, which is transposed and revised in minor details.

Scene 10:   Although this is a completely new scene, it is copied by a copyist different from the one used throughout the rest of the manuscript. The scene may have been rewritten by Hasse and then copied over later for legibility. Since this scene is on the same fascicle as the preceding aria, we may assume that it had been completed before the aria, and copied in when Hasse completed entering the aria into the score. The aria that follows this scene is simply transposed from the 1744 version, and is in the hand of the original copyist. It is on a new fascicle, and may well have been composed before the preceding scene.

Act II

Scene 1:   The pressing issue of time seems to have arisen at this point, at least as far as preparing recitative for rehearsal was concerned.   Here, Hasse wrote in the music to the recitatives, and a copyist entered the words later.   This technique is employed rather inconsistently through the rest of the opera.   Since scene 1 includes Danao, it could not be copied exactly from the 1744 manuscript, but to save time, Hasse only wrote in the new music.

Scene 2:   This is again in the hands of Hasse (for the music) and a copyist (for the words).   A passage of recitativo obbligato, copied from the 1744 version, was entered solely by Hasse, even though there was only one change made from the original version.   The alternative would have been to have the entire passage copied, impossible in its position within a scene that had to be extensively rewritten.   The recitative does not end with a sentence or two completely in Hasse's hand, suggesting that at this specific point, Hasse knew what key the following aria was in, and that this aria (new in 1751) was thus already written or sketched out.

Scene 3:   This follows the same pattern as scenes one and two.   Again, the recitative goes right up to the aria without a break.

Scenes 4-7:   These scenes are an integral part of the manuscript, following the aria of scene 3 without starting on a new fascicle.   However, they are completely in Hasse's hand. Perhaps he had the time to put in the words to the recitatives himself; the method used in scenes 1 and 2 may have become too cumbersome.   This section was not composed before the preceding scenes.   Scenes 4-6 include Plistene, and had to be rewritten, but scene 7 is a solo for Elpinice, exactly the same as in 1744.   As if it took Hasse several minutes to realize this, the following aria, also taken intact from 1744, is totally in the copyist's hand.   Again, it seems as though the arias were already planned out, and Hasse was revising from the autograph as he went along the recitatives.   This was done at top speed, for he revised scene 6 and copied scene 7 completely before he realized that he had wished to insert an aria based on the last two lines of scene 6 at that point.   He then had to cross out both scenes, (since scene 6 ended in the middle of the page), recopy scene 6 up to the cadence (it was only four lines of music), insert the new aria, and recopy scene 7.   Hasse actually copied down the exact same scene 7 twice, even though it was the same as the 1744 version, before turning over the manuscript to his copyist for the job of entering the aria.   This aria, incidentally, is on a new fascicle, and may well have been copied before the recitative was completed.   This would help explain why Hasse copied scene 7 himself.

Scenes 8-9:   These again are in Hasse's hand, along with the scene 9 aria.

Scene 10:   This scene, between Ipermestra and Linceo, is taken completely from the 1744 version, along with its concluding duet. It is copied in its entirety.

Act III

This follows the general patterns of the first two acts. Scenes 1 and 2 are in a copyist's hand, scenes 3 through 6 are in Hasse's hand,. scenes 7 and 8 are in both Hasse's and a copyist's hand. The opening of the scene 8 aria (borrowed from 1744) is in Hasse's hand, but it is completed by the copyist; the two scenes following are in Hasse's hand alone. (Plates XXV - XXVII) There is only one break in the otherwise continuous makeup of the manuscript: scene 7 begins on a new fascicle. All other new fascicles fall in the middle of scenes or arias.

This act seems to be following a highly specific approach to each scene, depending on whether the music was newly composed or not. It seems especially likely that the music to scenes 7 and 8 was begun by Hasse while the copyist was working on scene 1, and then, part way into the scene 8 aria, Hasse traded with the copyist, so that the copyist could enter the words to the recitative and finish copying the aria (which is from 1744), while Hasse finished scenes 3 through 6.   Diagram VIII illustrates this process. While this hypothesis is perhaps fanciful, it does provide an explanation for the confusing proliferation of methods used in piecing the manuscript together, and suggests some of the events that may well have occurred during the course of writing or revising an opera.

As with *Semiramide*, Hasse concerned himself only in the most general way with key affects or relationships between arias. Linceo's passionate aria, "Io non pretendo," (I:10), for example, is transposed from the "affective" key of E♭ to F without hesitation, partly because Ipermestra had been given a completely new aria, "Se pietà da voi," (I:9), immediately preceding, also in E♭. The result is that Act I closes with arias in the keys of C, D, E♭, and F, instead of B♭, C, f, and E♭. Act III, similarly, closes D, E♭, F, G, instead of F, G, F, G. Act II has no apparent pattern: in 1744 it closed D, B♭, c, A, and in 1751 the first aria was replaced with one in E♭. There is only the vaguest overall tonal plan to both versions of the opera:

	Sinfonia	Act I	Act II	Act III
1744:	D	A--E♭	A----A	G----G
1751:	C	E---F	C----A	G----G

As with most of Hasse's revisions, arias were changed most ofte because of the singers.   Danao was a much more skilled singer i

PLATES XXV · XXVII

Ipermestra b (*op. cit.*) v. 3, ff. 32′ - 33′. (III:8), "Ah non mi dir così."

The end of scene 8 is in Hasse's hand for the music, a copyist's for the words. The aria, borrowed from the earlier version, begins in Hasse's hand, and continues in that of the copyist, both for words and music. In his haste, Hasse recopied the last two measures on f. 33 when he turned the page, and had to cross out the duplicated music.

PLATE XXV

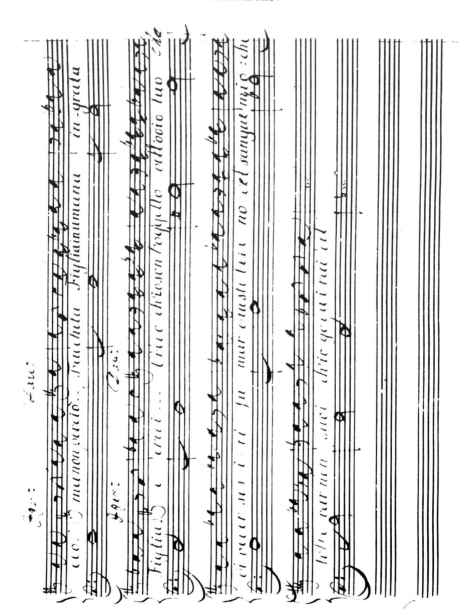

PLATE XXVI

PLATE XXVII

DIAGRAM VIII

Order of composition of *Ipermestra b*, Act III:

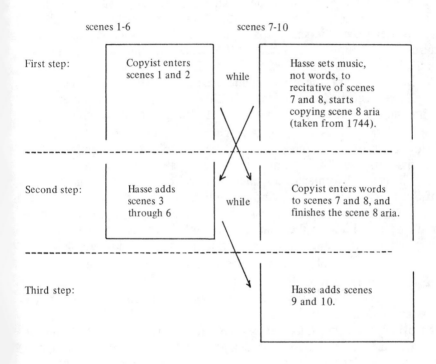

scenes 1-6   scenes 7-10

First step: Copyist enters   Hasse sets music,
                   scenes 1 and 2   while   not words, to
                                                        recitative of scenes
                                                        7 and 8, starts
                                                        copying scene 8 aria
                                                        (taken from 1744).

Second step: Hasse adds   Copyist enters words
                   scenes 3   while   to scenes 7 and 8, and
                   through 6   finishes the scene 8 aria.

Third step: Hasse adds scenes
                                                        9 and 10.

Dresden, so all three of his arias were rewritten, this time with long and difficult coloratura passages, which had been simple or nonexistent in 1744.

Plistene's voice range also changed, but the capabilities of the Viennese singer seem well-matched with those of Annibali. The first aria was rewritten on the same text, but this seems more a matter of sensibility than skill: the new aria is an andante with flute accompaniment, written with somewhat more care than the 1744 version. The second aria of Plistene in 1751, "Tornerò," (II:6), was probably added because of the stature of Annibali in the Dresden cappella. The third aria, "Vuoi ch'io lasci," (III:5), was transposed only, though individual figures and rhythms were altered slightly.

Ipermestra, the prima donna, received only two new arias. This may have been because of Hasse's dislike of Mingotti, who became the prima donna of the cappella in 1751. Her range closely matched that of the Viennese singer (a high note of g' or bᵇ', a low one of Bᵇ, a fourth below the e of the Viennese singer); the runs of "Ah non parlar," (I:3), her first aria, and "Ah non mi dir," (III:8), her last, a cavatina, show that the Viennese performer could sing rapid and difficult coloratura. Three of the four middle arias (including a duet) are all very simple, yet they were retained by a second version. The second aria upsets any theory that might be built on these facts: "Se pietà da voi," (I:9), was rewritten completely, and changed from an allegretto aria in f with simple, lyrical runs, to a bravura, fiery piece, allegro di molto, in Eᵇ, with an enormous range of two octaves, between Bᵇ and bᵇ'!

Linceo, the primo uomo, was sung by Rochetti, who only rarely was given such an important part, while Annibali, who usually received the primo uomo position, was relegated to secondo, possibly so that the former part could remain in the soprano clef; it was easier to change Plistene's smaller part to an alto tessitura. The small amount of attention given to Linceo's part bears witness to this theory. Of his four arias and duet, two arias and the duet remained substantially unchanged. One run in "Di pena si forte," (I:4), was improved:

Two other arias were completely rewritten: "Gonfio tu vedi," (II:5), which was made much more difficult, and "Tremo per l'idol mio," (III:4), which had its upper range expanded from e' to b♭', but beyond this is a much better aria, with a more distinctive theme and more cohesive phrasing:

The revisions of the two minor characters that remain were done for obvious reasons. Elpinice, sung by Albuzzi, was given three new, much harder arias, and kept only one of the more pleasant, facile 1744 ones. And Adriano, the confidant, received no new arias, but the two from the 1744 version were merely transposed upwards to fit the range of the visiting tenor, Cornelius.

This opera raises several interesting problems. In the first version, why does Ipermestra herself have such widely-differing arias, as far as technique is concerned?[33] Why do both versions have the extraordinary number of three parts for natural male voices? Why was Annibali relegated to a minor role? Why did Rochetti become the primo uomo?

Most puzzling is the question of whether this revision was done in haste or not. At first glance, the substitute texts might suggest this, but they all seem to have been written specifically for this revision, suggesting the opposite. The manuscript is not put together in the "separate recitative" manner that usually suggests that the dialogue was done separately and in a hurry. The presence of the copyist's hand for the words in several places does suggest as much, but this system is not used with enough consistency to suggest a great lack of time. Another sign of haste: Plistene's last aria is his only one not to be rewritten, but is merely transposed; Ipermestra's last three pieces are all copied from the 1744 version. But the only aria that shows a sign of being written after the recitative is the very first, of Elpinice, where the recitative was finished only when the aria was entered. All of the other recitative sections run right up to the cadences before the aria without stopping, suggesting that Hasse already knew what keys the arias were in.

Perhaps the best answer is that the revision was not done in haste, but that time-saving devices were, nevertheless, used at times. Hasse's favorite singers were the ones who received the most new arias: Annibali, Amorevoli, and Albuzzi (eight out of ten); Rochetti, Mingotti, and Cornelius received the fewest (four out of thirteen). But if it were a matter of favoritism, surely Annibali would have been given a better role. The question cannot be answered at this time.

5: *Siroe*

Like *Ipermestra, Siroe* was approximately half revised when Hasse prepared the Bologna production of 1733 for a Warsaw debut in 1763. But this revision was not evenly done. Originally, the new production was intended to be a completely new opera on a previously set libretto, as *Artaserse, Demofoonte,* and *La Clemenza di Tito* of the 1758 to 1760 seasons in Naples had been. Accordingly, the recitative was all completely rewritten, without reference to the earlier version. Time must have been somewhat at a premium, for Hasse probably did not begin writing the arias until most of the recitative was written.

Siroe provides the most conclusive evidence that Hasse usually set the arias in order from beginning to end. Half-way through the opera, he evidently realized he did not have enough time for the completion of the opera as he had planned it. Up to that point all of the arias had been entirely new, but starting with Cosroe's aria, "Tu di pietà," (II:12), Hasse began to use arias taken from the 1733 setting.

Coinciding with this point is an interesting event in the autograph. At "Tu di pietà," Hasse's handwriting suddenly becomes crabbed and cramped in the manner that is associated with the attacks of gout that became more and more frequent towards the end of his life. Perhaps Hasse had refrained from composing the second half because of such an attack, hoping that he would recover; with time growing short, he had to continue, and resorted to the expedient of finishing the opera with arias from the earlier version.   Plate XXVIII illustrates the difference between the two hands.

Because of the many arias (seven of twenty-one) taken from the earlier version, *Siroe* is better considered as two versions of the same opera, not as two different settings of the same libretto.   It is listed in Table III as *Siroe a* and *Siroe b* for this reason.

As a result of this forced change in plans, the first eleven arias are new, but of the last ten, only three are new.   The 1733 opera had seven substitute arias, but, although all but one were replaced, four others were added.   In the last half of the opera, however, two of the substitute arias of 1733 were dropped and not replaced, a third was replaced by the Metastasian text (becoming one of the three new arias in this half), and the last was kept intact.   The second of the three new arias in the second half is in fact one of the four new substitute texts, and was either a contrafactum, or, perhaps, planned and sketched before the necessity of completing the opera became too immediate.   The first and last of the three are both for *Siroe*, the title character and primo uomo, who, despite all pressures, received no 1733 arias in the revised opera.

Hasse seems to have taken the most pains with the role of Siroe. This part was sung in 1763 by Pasquale Bruscolini, and he was one of two singers to receive all new arias.

Since the two versions lie so far apart in Hasse's career, a comparison of the two has wider implications than just the revision process.   The changes in his style between 1733 and 1763 are most visible.   Many of these differences have already been discussed in Chapter II; to recapitulate:

1: *Siroe a* has no half da capo arias. *Siroe b* has three of these.

2: In *Siroe a*, only two arias use instruments other than strings. (While oboes may have been used *ad libitum*, there is no indication of where this might have happened; the two arias use horns.)   In *Siroe b*, nineteen of the twenty-one pieces of music, not counting the sinfonia, use some obbligato wind instrumentation: oboes six times; horns and oboes five times; oboes, flutes and horns three times; oboes and flutes once; flutes alone, once, along with muted strings for the only time.

3: *Siroe a* has three passages of recitative obbligato; *Siroe b* has five.

4: *Siroe a* has approximately 1200 lines of recitativo semplice. *Siroe b* has only 800 lines; or about 2/3 the amount.

Changes in harmonic practice are extremely hard to pinpoint. There seems to be a very small increase in the use of strange tonalities for color: diminished seventh and augmented sixth chords, parallel and relative minors in quick excursions.   More specific differences are:

PLATE XXVIII

Siroe b, (I-Mc, Part. Tr. ms. 178), v. 2, f. 5. (I:4) "Contente non siete."

The original end of the B ritornello, and the opening of A, ("Contente non") are in a hand that is firm and decisive. The second B ritornello, added later to make the aria into a half da capo, is crabbed and awkward; the stems of the notes are thin and shaky. (Notice the oboe parts, probably crossed out after their individual score was copied.)

PLATE XXVIII

5: *Siroe a* uses accidentals in the head-motives (up to the modulation to the dominant) in only one aria. *Siroe b* has six arias with head-motives using chromatic notes.

6: Three arias in *Siroe a* move to a key other than the dominant or relative major at the end of the A_1 stanza: all move to supertonic. Six arias in *Siroe b* move to a different key: five to the supertonic, one to the minor dominant. This, however, is exceptional for both operas. Usually, Hasse only has one or two arias that have such a key sequence in any one opera, and this holds true throughout his career.

7: In both *Siroe a* and *b*, only one aria is in a minor key: this is one aspect that does not change in the thirty intervening years.

Relatively minor structural changes in the da capo aria are also visible:

8: Seven arias in *Siroe a* have a B section starting in the tonic of the aria, and then moving to another key. In *Siroe b*, thirteen arias do this.

9: Only one aria in *Siroe a* has a B section in a contrasting meter and tempo, while six arias in *Siroe b* have this. (Two of these are from *Siroe a*, purposely recomposed in stanza B.) These six would naturally not need to modulate from the tonic of the aria, and thus lower the number that might otherwise be counted in item 8 above.

10: Ten arias in *Siroe b* have a B ritornello that begins in the tonic, and thus have no modulatory bridge. In *Siroe b*, only one aria (one of the seven from *Siroe a*) lacks this modulatory bridge.

The most remarkable facet of composition seen in these two revisions is the almost total lack of general stylistic change. That there was a style change at all is certainly to be expected; Hasse was not isolated from artistic developments, and even if he had been, it is inconceivable that he would not have changed on his own over a period of thirty years. Indeed, one can often see a simplification and clarification of a melodic line, a change from straightforward melodic fomulae, ornamented by rhythmic figures to more sophisticated and long-winded phrases, made more interesting by unexpected excursions and melodic turns. But this stylistic change is quite subtle and hard to perceive. Gerber did not notice it, nor, for that matter, did Hasse, as he, apparently heedlessly, combined music from 1733 with other pieces written in the more modern idiom of 1763.

In the 1763 version, two characters received all new arias. That Siroe, the primo uomo, should be one is not surprising. But the second was Arasse, the general, who was given the third of the three new arias of the second half of the opera. It is most interesting that Arasse also received three of the four substitute texts in the opera. Antonio Pio

Fabri, who sang the role, was new to the Dresden cappella, and may have brought his favorite arias with him.

Both he and Siroe had different tessiture than the original interpreters. Yet it is doubtful that voice ranges had anything to do with which arias were revised. Emira, the third character to have a new range, received two arias in the second half of the opera that were merely transposed to fit her soprano voice.

MUSICAL EXAMPLE I

MUSICAL EXAMPLE II

Some of the new arias are obvious improvements on the originals. A case in point is "Fra l'orror della tempesta," (I:17), which is much more lively, with its added flutes, horns, and oboes, and a constant sixteenth-note motion in the violins, when compared to the original. Even the head-motive is more dramatic, with its octave leap and dotted rhythm, compared with the 1733 leap of a fifth and quarter-note motion. The style change mentioned above is also visible in the more sophisticated melody of the second version. The "volto imbruna" uses the same melodic idea in both versions; it serves in 1733 as a starting-off point for a melody that has been emphasizing the tonic for eight measures; in 1763 it serves as the first firm tonic cadence of the melody. (Musical Examples I and II).

On the other hand, the two versions of "La sorte mia tiranna," (I:13) are not so easily judged as to superiority. The second version is certainly patterned after the first, but it is so changed that it is new music in all respects. Whether it is better is another question. The second version does have a more memorable melody, though it is less original in its obvious derivation from the triad. The first version is well-shaped, with its opening leap, the filling-in of the interval with stepwise motion downward, and the leap up again on "tiranna." The second version ties all three phrases together very smoothly: the second phrase repeats the ornament of the first, and the third is in the same rhythm as the second. The E♯ in measure three also adds interest to the line:

"Gelido in ogni vena," (III:5), was one of the seven arias that were retained in 1763. The vocal line underwent minor revision that is not really typical for arias that were retained from version to version. Instead, with a few small changes, Hasse greatly improved the shape of the melody, showing how he could improve an aria when he had no other reason for revising it.

The first version has a top note in A_1 of e, reached some thirteen times in the course of the melody. A_2 is better, reaching g three times before a climax on a is attained near the cadence. In 1763, the melodic line in A_1 was much better organized: d in measure 1, e in measure 3, f in measure 5, g in measure 12, and a in measure 13, immediately preceding the cadence. A_2 is more arch-shaped, with its climax, b, coming in measure 24, and the more usual g's and a's coming near the cadence. The elimination of the third and fourth measures also tightens up the progress of the line, besides making the opening less of a formula.

"Tu di pietà," (II:12), another of Cosroe's arias, also shows that Amorevoli, the Dresden singer, was, even at an advanced age, a better tenor than Filippo Giorgi, who had sung the role in Bologna. Hasse makes much use of his high a in the opening bars of the A_2 stanza in 1763, although the rest of the aria is taken from 1733.

Also in "Tu di pietà" is a typical example of Hasse's contrapuntal technique. The second version is an apparently effortless increase in motion with the imitation added in the bass line. This change, which thickens the texture to great advantage, indicates no

rebirth of interest in counterpoint: the imitation is taken from the B
stanza of the 1733 version: (Musical Example III).

MUSICAL EXAMPLE III

One of the greatest advances formally and musically in 1763 is the recitativo obbligato that follows Medarse's aria "Tu decidi," (II:6). In this aria, Medarse has sworn fidelity to Cosroe, his and Siroe's father, after telling Cosroe that Siroe is guilty of treason. The following scene (II:7) was originally set with the rest of the simple recitative, and is found in the autograph on the first page of a fascicle. But when Hasse was writing the arias, he decided to set this solo scene again. The recitative is inserted into the final ritornello of the preceding aria, "Tu decidi." In the monologue, Cosroe reacts to Medarse's statement. Since Siroe is his favorite son, Cosroe is very hurt, but he cannot bring himself to condemn his son to death. In the recitative, Cosroe gives his thoughts between isolated measures of the ritornello melody of Medarse's aria, a melody used for the line "per te solo, o padre amato," "only for thee, beloved father." This has one meaning for Cosroe and another for the audience, which is aware that it is Medarse who is actually the traitor. After the monologue ends, the interrupted ritornello is allowed to come to its close. (Musical Example IV)

MUSICAL EXAMPLE IV

MUSICAL EXAMPLE IV (continued)

MUSICAL EXAMPLE IV (continued)

MUSICAL EXAMPLE IV (continued)

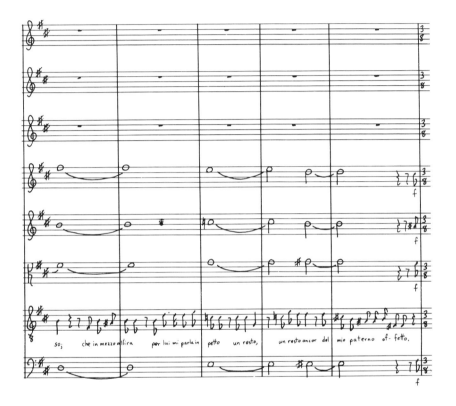

MUSICAL EXAMPLE IV (continued)

MUSICAL EXAMPLE IV (continued)

The recitativo obbligato of II:15 is almost the same in both versions, though that of *Siroe b* starts three lines earlier. This provides added evidence, if any is needed, that Hasse thought of the orchestrally accompanied recitatives as larger pieces of music, to be composed carefully, with the arias, and not as simply expanded versions of simple recitative, to be dashed off with the rest of the dialogue. At the end ofthe scene, however, Hasse makes several changes which make the 1763 version much more effective, especially because of its word and motivic repetition and its cadence into the following aria (Musical Example V).

The new arias on substitute texts do not show much in the way of improvement. Strangely, most new texts do not have the same affect as the ones they replace. The only one that does, "Tu decidi," is, uniquely, a replacement for another substitute text. Both it and the replaced text, "Ebbi da te," paraphrase the Metastasian original, "Deggio a te," and "Tu decidi" in fact uses the second stanza of "Deggio a te." "Ebbi da te" is in a moderato 3/4 time, and "Tu decidi" is an andantino 3/8.

At several times, a replaced aria has a different affect because of the surrounding arias. In 1733, "Ancor io," (I:5), was a fast aria (with an exceptional slow opening) between two slow ones. In 1763, both the preceding and following arias were cut, and when "Ancor io," a substitute text, was replaced by the Metastasian original, Hasse took the opportunity to make the new aria, "D'ogni amator," a slow one, since it was now found between two allegro arias, "Se il mio paterno," (I:1), and "O placido il mare," (I:8). As we shall see in the following section on *Tito*, Hasse had a strong tendency to keep the same affect when the text remained the same, even though the music might be completely new.

The unique circumstances surrounding the revision of *Siroe* thus yield conclusions that do not coincide with those of other revisions. Yet this revision provides much primary evidence on how Hasse composed, if not on how he revised; in either case, he was always interested in improving his own music.

6: *Tito Vespasiano Ib* and *La Clemenza di Tito II*

We have already discussed briefly the circumstances of the composition of *Tito Vespasiano Ia* for Pesaro in 1735, including the rapid completion of the third act by the use of contrafacta and substitute arias. It is logical to assume that the revision of *Tito Vespasiano* for Dresden in 1738, which eliminated the substitutions, represents more accurately the composer's intentions concerning the libretto. In 1759, Hasse used the libretto once again, this time titling the opera *La Clemenza di Tito*, but not using any of the music previously composed in 1735 and 1738. An equivalent situation had occurred or would occur with several other

MUSICAL EXAMPLE V

opera libretti, but several factors make *Tito* especially worthwhile as an object of study. The two settings of *Cleofide I/Alessandro IIa* are only four years apart; those of *Demofoonte Ia* and *II* only ten years apart. The versions of *Artaserse* have been known and discussed since the beginning of this century. The earlier version of *Ezio* was not identified as such until 1976 and could not be utilized in this study.

The Naples version of *Tito,* on the other hand, was separated from its predecessor by twenty-one years, and has never been identified as a different opera from that of Pesaro or Dresden. Furthermore, *Tito II* contains a very large number of contrafacta, presenting yet another aspect of revision that has not yet been dealt with in detail.[34]

The first step in a comparison is an aria-by-aria tabulation of meter, tempo, and key; contrafacta are indicated by brackets.

TABLE XVI

Scene	Singer	Aria	1738	1759
I:2	Vit.	Deh se piacer	3/8 allegretto Bb	3/8 allegro A
I:3	Annio	Io sento	¢ allegretto* G	C allegro, ma non troppo F
I:4	Sesto	Opprimete	2/4 allegro D	C allegro, ma non troppo 3/8 andantino C
I:5	Coro	Serbate	3/8 allegro G	3/8 allegro, e con spirito, ma non presto C
I:5	Tito	Del più sublime	3/8 più tosto allegro B♭	[3/8 allegretto F]
I:6	Annio	Ah! perdono	3/4 poco moderato G	CUT

TABLE XVI (continued)

Scene	Singer	Aria	1738	1759
I:7	Serv.	Amo te solo	3/4 allegro A	C allegro A
I:9	Tito	Ah! se fosse	₵ allegro ma non troppo C	⎡C allegro di⎤ ⎢molto ⎥ ⎣ C ⎦
I:10	Serv.	Non ti lagnar	₵ allegro* E	CUT
I:11	Sesto	Parto, ma tu	₵ un poco andante G	3/4 un poco lento C allegretto G
I:13	Vit.	Quando sarà	C adagio 3/8 Allegretto* B♭	⎡(Perchè la calma)⎤ ⎢C andante ⎥ ⎣ F ⎦
II:4	Publio	Sia lontano	3/8 allegretto G	CUT
II:5	Serv.	Almen, se non	3/4 amoroso C	⎡(Cari affetti) ⎤ ⎢3/8 comodetto⎥ ⎢C allegro ⎥ ⎣ C ⎦
II:6	Vit.	Come potesti	₵ presto 3/8 larghetto G/g	⎡(Tu me da me ⎤ ⎢dividi) 3/4 ⎥ ⎢allegro assai⎥ ⎣ B♭ ⎦
II:7	Sesto	Fra stupido	₵ più tosto allegro E♭	C andante E♭
II:9	Tito	Tu, infedel	3/8 allegro di molto E	C allegro di molto D

TABLE XVI (continued)

Scene	Singer	Aria	1738	1759
II:12	Serv.	Non odo	₵ allegro assai C	CUT
II:13	Annio	Ch'io parto	₵ allegro ma non troppo B♭	3/8 andante ma non troppo E
II:15	Sesto	Se mai senti	3/8 un poco lento c	C lento 3/8 allegretto D
II:16	Vit.	Tremo fra	C allegro ma non troppo E♭	⎡(Fra dubbiosi)⎤ 3/8 allegro e con spirito ⎣ G ⎦
III:1	Publio	Tardi s'avvede	₵ allegro D	⎡C allegro⎤ ⎣ A ⎦
III:3	Annio	Pietà, signor	3/8 un poco lento G	⎡(Ah, pietà,⎤ signor) 3/8 andante amoroso ⎣ D ⎦
III:6	Sesto	Vo disperato	3/8 allegro ma non presto 3/8 adagio d	3/8 allegro 3/8 adagio f
III:8	Tito	Se all'impero	₵ moderato 3/8 allegretto e piano assai D	⎡₵ maestoso,⎤ ma non troppo lento 3/8 andantino ⎣ D ⎦

TABLE XVI (continued)

Scene	Singer	Aria	1738	1759
III:9	Serv.	Se altro	C allegro ma non troppo A	C allegro F
III:10	Vit.	Getta il nocchier	3/8 allegro ma troppo F	⌈(Se per serbarmi) 3/8 allegro ⌊ G ⌋
III:11	Coro	Che del ciel	3/8 allegretto A	⌈(Del nostro Cesare) C allegro e con spirito ⌊ D ⌋

---

*These tempi are from D-Mbs, mus. mss. 6312. The Dresden copy (D-Dl, Mus. 2477/F/22) has no tempo markings in these instances.

The location and use of the contrafacta immediately produce several conclusions. Primarily, this seems to be a result of a general desire to lessen the amount of work and to make use of good material not yet heard in Naples. Of the twenty-two arias and choruses of *Tito II*, more than half, twelve, are from *Ezio II* (1755), *Il Rè pastore* (1755), and *L'Olimpiade a* (1756), his last three operas composed for Dresden. Table XVII is a list of the borrowed arias, their sources, and the singers. (The Naples cast is not known.)

TABLE XVII

Contrafactum	Source
I:5 Del più sublime soglio (Metastasio) Tito (tenor)	So che fanciullo Amore *L'Olimpiade*, II:7 Amorevoli (tenor)
I:9 Ah, se fosse intorno al trono (Metastasio) Tito (tenor)	Il nocchier, che si figura *Ezio*, I:5 Amorevoli (tenor)

TABLE XVII (continued)

Contrafactum	Source

I:13 Perchè la calma
(Metastasian paraphrase)
Vitellia (soprano)

Se un bel ardire
Ezio, I:6
Belli (soprano)

II:5 Cari affetti del cor mio
(Metastasian paraphrase)
Servilia (soprano)

Quanto mai felice siete
Ezio, I:7
Pilaja (soprano)

II:6 Tu me da me dividi
(Metastasio: from *L'Olimpiade*)
Vitellia (soprano)

Tu me da me dividi
L'Olimpiade, II:11
Albuzzi (soprano)

II:11 Tu, infedel, non hai difese
(Metastasio)
Tito (tenor)

Quel destrier, che all'albergo
L'Olimpiade, I:3
Belli (soprano)

II:16 Fra dubbiosi affetti miei
(Metastasian paraphrase)
Vitellia (soprano)

Alla selva, al prato, al fonte
Il Rè pastore, I:1
Albuzzi (soprano)

III:1 Tardi s'avvede
(Metastasio)
Publio (soprano)

No, la speranza
L'Olimpiade, II:12
Pilaja (soprano)

III:3 Ah, pietà, signor, di lui
(Metastasian paraphrase)
Annio (alto)

L'amerò, sarò constante
Il Rè pastore, III:1
Monticelli (soprano)

III:8 Se all'impero amici dei
(Metastasio)
Tito (tenor)

Voi, che fausti ognor donate
Il Rè pastore, III:7
Bruscolini (alto)

III:11 Se per serbarmi fede
(paraphrase of parodied text)
Vitellia (soprano)

Se tu di me fai dono
Il Rè pastore, III:5
Pilaja (soprano)

III:13 Del nostro Cesare
(Paraphrase of parodied text)
Coro (SATB)

Del forte Licida
L'Olimpiade, II:6
Coro (SATB)

All of the arias for Tito (four), Vitellia (four), and Publio (one) are replaced by contrafacta, along with one each for Servilia and Annio, and the final coro. This certainly coincides with Hasse's general desire to provide new music for the leading characters, but it should also be remembered that, compared with the earlier versions of *Tito*, all of the singers received new music; indeed, the leading singers are almost the only ones to receive second-hand music in this instance. The cast for the Naples production is not known, but it does not seem especially likely that any of the Dresden singers participated in the 1759 production. If, for example, all of Tito's arias had been sung by Amorevoli in various roles in Dresden, we might assume that Amorevoli also took the role of Tito in Naples. But only two of Tito's arias were sung by Amorevoli originally; the others were written for Belli and Bruscolini. A more likely possibility is that the singers who took the roles of Tito and Vitellia were hired shortly before the performance, and Hasse was too pressed for time to write individually-tailored arias for them. Another likely explanation is that these two singers were colleagues who did not mind singing contrafacta.

The time element is also an obvious factor. *Tito* was Hasse's second opera for the season in Naples, and he may not have expected to be asked to provide it. The opera shows a distinct trend towards the use of contrafacta as it continues: six of the nine numbers of the first act are new, but only three of the seven numbers of the second act, and only two of the seven of the third act. Looking at these another way, and ignoring the arias for Tito and Vitellia, we find no contrafacta in Act I one in Act II, and three in Act III. But the choices seem to be due at least in part to mere chance. It is worth noting that, with some overlapping, the arias from *Ezio* come first, followed by those from *L'Olimpiade*, and ending with those from *Il Rè pastore*. The three arias of *Ezio*, furthermore, are consecutive ones, both in the original opera and on the list of contrafacta in *Tito*. It is as if Hasse flipped through the score at random, in search of suitable arias. As we shall see below chance seems to be as good an explanation as musical or poetical content.

The contrafacta texts are of four types. First are those which belong to the libretto of *Tito*, and are adapted to the pre-existent music. There are five of these. Next, there are those which are paraphrases of the *Tito* texts, rewritten to fit the poetic meter and structure of the borrowed music: four fit into this category. One is rather exceptional "Se per serbarmi fede" is a paraphrase of the text "Se tu di me fa dono," from which the music was taken. This will be discussed below.[3] The last aria is not technically a contrafactum, but rather a substituted o borrowed aria, included in the above list for the sake of completeness "Tu me da me dividi."

Musical changes in parodied arias are usually minor: the key is changed in one case, the singer's clef (and range) in three cases, the tempo in five cases, the instrumentation in six. Tempo is never radically changed; indeed it sometimes seems to be a matter of Neapolitan versus Dresden convention. Two times, the marking "allegro assai" is changed to "allegro di molto," although "Tu me da me dividi" remains at allegro assai. Instrumentation, too, seems to be due to a distaste in Naples for wind instruments: flutes are eliminated three times, and oboes twice, never from the same aria, however. This is not a matter of the Neapolitan oboist doubling on flute, for two arias include both pairs of winds. Horns are added to one aria.

It is not rare for minor melodic changes to be made to accomodate the new text. Often, the sections of coloratura are revised, as Hasse often did when revising arias between versions of the same opera, to tailor the piece to the capacities of a new singer. Several times, the end of a stanza will be completely rewritten, from the coloratura section on, as Hasse apparently becomes carried away by the process of revision as he begins to make changes. Interesting is the complete rewriting of the B stanza of "Cari affetti." Although the meter changes to C in both, the tempo is altered from allegro to allegretto. After the first two notes, the second version departs from the first, keeping to the same harmonic pattern, cadencing in the same key, and being identified as a very rare (by 1759) simple da capo aria, without B ritornello, as is its model.

The final coro has one of the clearest examples of pragmatism in revision in Hasse's entire opus. The last three measures of the coro are cut, not to tighten the musical structure, but for the simple fact that to include them would have meant going over onto another page of valuable manuscript paper.

Reinhard Strohm has said, of another contrafactum, "One might even say: it is not the content or even the affect of these two texts that, in their correspondence, permit the parody, but actually the disinterest in content and the absence of affect."[36] This statement holds true for the ten contrafacta in *Tito*; it is not in the least an overstatement. Hasse finds it possible to use the music of "Alla selva, al prato, al fonte," for "Fra dubbiosi affetti miei":

Alla selva, al prato, al fonte
Io n'andro col gregge amato;
E alla selva, al fonte, al prato
L'idol mio con me verrà.

(To the woods, the meadow, the spring,
I will go with my loving flock;
And to the woods, the meadow, the spring,
My beloved will come with me.)

Fra dubbiosi affetti miei
Che ho nel seno uniti insieme
Sono oppressa, non ho speme,
E non fo che palpitar.

(Amid my dubious feelings
That are united in my breast
I am oppressed, I have no hope
And I can only tremble.)

This of course could not take place, had the music been especially descriptive of either affect. This is not the case, the music is pleasant and undistinguished:

The text is an average sample of a Metastasian paraphrase. The original aria is clearly superior, in its incisive imagery, to the anonymous strophe created in 1759. The original Metastasian aria reads:

> Tremo fra dubbi miei;
> Pavento i rai del giorno
> L'aure, che ascolto intorno
> Mi fanno palpitar.

> (I tremble amid my doubts;
> I fear the light of day.
> The breezes, which I hear around me
> Make me tremble.)

Another interesting text is that of "Quel destrier," whose music is set to the words "Tu infedel." While the general emotions are similar, the difference in poetic structure would ordinarily seem to make a contrafactum out of the question. The original is written in endecasillabo, the replacement in ottenario:

> Quel destrier, che all'albergo è vicino,
> Più veloce s'affretta nel corso:
> Non l'arresta l'angustia del morso,
> Non la voce che legge gli da.

> (That steed, which approaches shelter
> Hurries even faster in its course:
> The pain of the bit does not stop it,
> Nor does the voice of its master.)

> Tu, infedel, non hai difese.
> E palese il tradimento
> Io pavento d'oltraggiarti
> Nel chiamarti traditor.

> (You, unfaithful one, do not have a defense.
> Your treachery is revealed.
> Yet I am afraid of insulting you
> In calling you "traitor.")

The adjustments are quite simply done, and the opening motive actually seems to fit the new text better than the old:

Other forms of adjustment have to take place when the new text
has more lines of poetry than the old one.   The B stanza of "No, la
speranza" is only four lines long.   When Hasse took this music and set it
to "Tardi, S'avvede," he had to write new music for the last two lines of
the six-line stanza.   Since in the original setting, lines 3 and 4 had been
repeated, the new version turns out to be no longer than the old, though
the music of the conclusion is completely rewritten.

In "Del più sublime soglio," whose B stanza has six lines as compared to the three lines (the first line of the original four-line stanza is not set by Hasse) of "So ch'è fanciullo Amore," the opposite is true. The first seventeen measures of the B stanza are completely new, setting lines 1 through 5 and replacing the eight measures of the original which set lines 1 and 2. The last fourteen measures, dealing with the last line and its repeats, are exactly the same in both versions.

A final example of text replacement is seen in the last aria of the opera. The Metastasian text at this point is:

Getta il nocchier talora
Pur qui tesori all'onde
Che da remote sponde
Per tanto mar portò;

E, giunto al lido amico
Gli dei ringrazia ancora,
Che ritornò mendico
Ma salvo ritornò.

(Sometimes the helmsman must jettison
Even treasures into the sea,
That from remote shores,
Over broad seas, he has brought.

And, landing on the friendly shore
He still thanks the gods
That he has returned poor,
But has returned safely.)

The music chosen for this location was obviously picked for its text, which must have struck an especially dramatic chord in Hasse's sensibilities:

Se tu di me fai dono,
Se vuoi che d'altri io sia,
Perchè la colpa e mia?
Perchè son io crudel?

La mia dolcezza imita:
L'abbandonata io sono
E non t'insulto ardita,
Chiamandoti infedel.

(If you give me away,
If you wish that I become someone else's,
Why is it my fault?
Why am I guilty?

You mock my weakness:
I am the abandoned one
And it is not a grave insult
For me to call you "unfaithful.")

The question of abandonment and guilt is crucial at this point in the libretto of *Tito Vespasiano*. Vitellia, the singer, has caused the death sentence of Sesto, who loves her and has tried to assassinate Tito for her. Of course, in *Tito*, it is Vitellia who is actually guilty, and must decide whether to reveal her own guilt and save Sesto. The original text is not dramatically effective in its imagery, which has only the vaguest connection to the action. In 1735, Hasse seems to have replaced this with a terzetto, though it was set as written in 1738. In 1759, the replacement text serves as the only example of a contrafactum that was not only chosen on the basis of the fitness of the original text and music, but, at the same time, strengthens the dramatic character of the work:

Se per serbarmi fede
Si perde chi m'adora
Perchè la colpa mia
Perchè non palesar?

Una meglior mercede
Chi reo per me si fece
E di morir non cura
Da me dovea sperar.

(If to serve me faithfully
Means ruin to him who loves me,
Why do I not
Reveal my guilt?

He who becomes a traitor for me
And who dies willingly for me
Should have hoped for
A better reward from me.)

"Getta il nocchier," with the exact poetic structure of "Se tu di me fai dono," could have been used as a substitute text itself, were it not for dramatic considerations. The contrafactum and its model are dealing with the same emotions of confusion and doubt, although the perspective is from opposite sides: the singer is now the guilty party, not the wronged one.

The new arias and the parodied arias behave in roughly the same ways when compared to the 1738 version of *Tito*. The parodies would not be expected to be reminiscent of the 1738 version, but, like the newly-composed arias, they stay remarkably close to the general affects of the earlier arias. Of the ten newly-composed pieces, only four do not keep the original duple or triple meter of the 1738 version. Yet only four of the eleven contrafacta or substitutes change meter, and one of these was an aria that changed affect with the substituted text.

Key was not as important as meter. Of the two minor-key arias of 1738, one, "Se mai senti," became major, and the other, "Vo disperato," remained in a minor key. The latter, incidentally, is a two-tempo aria in both versions, meter and tempi remain the same: a very close coincidence. Six other arias keep the same key as in the earlier version; this includes three contrafacta, none of which changed affect. It may also be worth noting that six other arias and choruses (five of which are contrafacta) are in a key only a fifth removed from the original; this may be a result only of the limited selection of keys available to Hasse.

The third correlation, tempo, is a harder one to make, because of the great variation in indications that are possible. Specifically, andante tempos of various sorts are the most ambiguous. An extreme example of this ambiguity is Vitellia's aria, "Come potesti," (II:6), of 1738, which, in different manuscripts is marked larghetto, andante, and adagio, in the order of their trustworthiness.[37] And Sesto's "Fra stupido," (II:7) of 1738 is marked either più tosto allegro, poco andante, or giusto allegro. On the other hand, Sesto's "Parto, ma tu, ben mio," (I:11), is either un poco andante, or adagio. The Dresden andante, the first one, must have been rather slower than the Italian tempo. Hasse himself may have considered the term to be ambiguous, for he used it only these three times in 1738.

We might hazard the following arrangement of tempos, taken from both versions of *Tito*:

TABLE XVIII

presto
allegro di molto
allegro assai
allegro, e con spirito
allegro, e con spirito ma non presto
allegro
più tosto allegro
allegro ma non presto
allegro ma non troppo
allegretto

andante
andante, ma non troppo
un poco andante

andante amoroso
andantino
comodetto
amoroso
moderato
poco moderato
maestoso, ma non troppo lento

larghetto
un poco lento
lento
adagio

Each version has fifteen possible tempo markings: quite a selection. A comparison of tempo markings shows that only three arias have exactly the same tempo from version to version: these use allegro and allegro di molto. One of these, "Tu, infedel," is a contrafactum, changed from allegro assai in its *L'Olimpiade* version to allegro di molto, to match the 1738 tempo indication.

Yet few arias differ greatly. "Fra stupido," (II:7) goes from più tosto allegro in 1738 to andante in 1759; "Ch'io parto reo," (II:13), changes from allegro ma non troppo to andante ma non troppo. "Quando sarà," (I:13), marked adagio, is replaced by the contrafactum "Perchè la calma," (andante); "Pietà, signor," (III:3), (un poco lento), is replaced by "Ah, pietà, signor," (andante amoroso). These are the greatest changes, and all are mitigated by the ambiguity of the term "andante." Indeed, the 1738 version of "Fra stupido" does exist in a copy marked poco andante. The remainder of the arias stay within the general tempo of the original, considering the three basic speeds to be: allegro/allegretto, andante/moderato, and lento/adagio.

Thus, meter and tempo seem to be the most closely allied to text. It might well be possible to demonstrate how all arias in D have the same general character, and how a 3/8 allegro aria in A has a slightly different feeling, one closer to other arias in A, from a 3/8 allegro aria in B♭ on the same text. Hasse may well have had specific feelings for certain keys, and at times combined key with meter and tempo when it was convenient. But tonality was never, as such, a large concern of his.

Specific melodic reminiscences are not common in the 1759 version. Rhythmic similarities may be accidental, caused by the necessity of accenting the same words in the same places. Yet a few specific similarities, all from newly-composed arias, are striking enough to be mentioned.

The very first aria, "Deh se piacer," (I:2), shows the 1759 version adopting the striking five-bar phrase of the 1738 opening:

Further on, both arias use a diminished chord on the exceptionally-accented "alletta" in the second stanza:

"Io sento," (I:3), the second aria, also reflects the 1738 version, though both rhythm and phrasing are stereotypical patterns:

The rhythm of "Amo te solo," (I:7), in the A_2 stanza, was clearly adopted by Hasse in 1759, to use to begin the aria:

·And the octave drop of "Parto, ma tu, ben mio," (I:11), also from A_2, was borrowed in 1759:

"Fra stupido," (II:7), also takes from 1738 the off-beat "dubbio," but it is raised in 1759 to a much more expressive level with the use of the flatted seventh degree:

And perhaps the most interesting is "Vo disperato," (III:6), in which the 1759 head-motive is a contraction of the 1738 opening. The sustained note on "costanza" is perhaps too obvious word-painting, but the 1759 version does show a better use of the raised fourth, taken from 1738 but used rather prosaically in the earlier aria on a minor piece of coloratura:

It seems most likely that these are not memories, but results of looking at the original music, and deciding to improve upon it. Hasse wrote in 1757 that he was sending for the scores he had left in Dresden when the Seven Years War began. The circumstances of *Demofoonte II*, *La Clemenza di Tito II*, and *Artaserse II* provide some sort of evidence that in 1758 he received the scores, that they were not destroyed in the bombardment of Dresden. They also seem to suggest strongly that Hasse himself considered them to be final, up-to-date versions.

As with *Siroe*, the stylistic changes in *Tito II* are small. While *Tito Ib* has five arias with obbligato instruments (two with flutes, two with horns, and one with theorbo and bassoon), *Tito II* has eight: one with oboe, four with oboe and horn, one with oboe, flute, horn and muted strings, one with oboe and flute, and one exceptional bravura aria (a contrafactum), Tito's "Se all'impero, amici dei," (III:8), with trumpets, timpani, oboes, and horns; exceptional because not even the overture uses trumpets and timpani.

As far as key structure within the aria is concerned, two of the 1738 arias move to the supertonic at the end of A_1. A third has an experimental structure, still built into the da capo idea: Vitellia's "Come potesti," (II:6). The A_1 stanza opens with a cut-time presto, in G, and then goes to a 3/8 larghetto, in g, which modulates to B♭. A_2 begins in B♭, but again in a ₵ presto, and returns to g before the 3/8 larghetto returns and cadences in G. The A_2 ritornello, like the opening one, is again presto. The B section is structured the same way: opening in ₵ presto, but in e, and then moving to the 3/8 larghetto, in E, before cadencing in A. There is no B ritornello. There are, incidentally, five arias without B ritornelli in *Tito Ib*.

In Tito II, there are no arias which do not go to the dominant or the relative major, and none that have an unusual structure. Three arias lack B ritornelli. A fourth, Vitellia's opening "Deh se piacer," (I:3), was originally without B ritornello, but sometime after it was written, Hasse altered it to a dal segno. The only aria that is a half da capo is the coro (I:5), "Serbate, o Dei custodi," which also was changed after being inserted into the score.

While *Tito Ib* has three arias with a new tempo and meter for the B stanza, *Tito II* has five, not much of an increase. It has already been pointed out that *Tito Ib* has two arias in minor keys, while *Tito II* has only one. All of this shows how little Neapolitan taste had changed in twenty-one years.

The revisions of *Tito* lead to the same conclusion as those concerning *Siroe*. Yet with *Siroe*, it is known that Hasse had a copy of the old opera with him, and presumable that he consulted it while he was writing the new version. With *Tito*, this fact can also be assumed, and suggests another conclusion about this opera, along with *Artaserse* and *Demofoonte*: that he knew the older works were imperfect examples of his younger days, and that it was possible to rewrite them in a more nearly perfect form.

In the cases of *Tito*, however, the issue was complicated both by lack of time and by the desire to make use of previously-composed pieces. It is clear that, for Hasse as for most eighteenth-century composers, an opera was never considered to be a perfect, polished work of art, but rather a work whose purpose was entertainment, and which was to be written in the most direct way possible to fulfill this function.

Tito also supports other conclusions derived from *Siroe*: that while there is a definite stylistic change that occurs in Hasse's music in his later years, he remains overwhelmingly conservative in his retention of the forms and conventions of his formative years as a composer; that he largely considers himself to be refining the techniques he had learned years earlier, polishing the style which he himself, to a great extent, was responsible for creating.

C: Summary

Hasse revised his operas for a variety of reasons. The circumstances of original composition greatly affected the extent to which they were revised, and the reasons for revision. It should be clear that pragmatism was the primary concern of the composer. No one consideration was supreme. Many factors decided what was to stay and what was to be changed.

In a delicate balance were considerations of who was singing the individual roles, how well they could perform the part that was already present, how much of the original opera did not belong in a "finished" production, whether the original librettist would be insulted, what the revising poet thought concerning the display of his own talent, what the tastes of the city in which the opera would be produced were concerning the length of the opera, the number and origin of permissible pre-composed substitutes, and possibly even how much coloratura would be written out, and how much improvised. Always a factor was the amount of time available in which to make the required, recommended, and possible changes. Along with these, probably always in his mind, but never the primary factor, was how the music could be improved.

All of these factors, ever in flux, determined that *Cajo Fabrizio* would be given six new arias, five of them for Faustina, that *Ipermestra* would only keep eleven arias, that *Alessandro* would be completely different from *Cleofide*, that the revision of *Semiramide* would itself be unfinished, but that the revision of *Demetrio* would polish the many rough edges of the original composition.

A great part of Hasse's energy was expended in revising operas: twenty-four of his eighty-three operas are revisions, or complete rewritings, almost one-third of his output. In order to understand his life and his career, it is necessary that these be untangled and explicated, so that the true amount of energy and work which he put into his production can become clear.

Two basic kinds of revisions emerge from this chapter: those intended to freshen a work as quickly as possible, and those seriously meant to improve the opera. Yet even with the latter, it is most difficult to tell where necessities stop and improvements begin, except with the five operas that were obviously intended to supercede completely the old versions.

But no two sets of circumstances surrounding the revision of an opera were ever the same. Consequently, no two revisions were ever made for exactly the same reasons.

CHAPTER V

HASSE AND THE NEAPOLITANS

In the seventeenth and eighteenth centuries, opera developed along lines that related to its dramatic purpose. This means that it was nearly always in the vanguard of what was "modern." The necessity of emphasizing the vocal line and keeping the accompaniment separate and unconfusing led opera to approach what we might consider a "classical" style, of homophony, slow and regular harmonic rhythm, and emphasis on tonic and dominant tonalities (to the almost total exclusion of mediant and submediant), decades before these became common in instrumental music.

These aspects could all be seen in the operas of Alessandro Scarlatti, as well as in works of composers of the late "Venetian" school, by the first decade of the Eighteenth Century. An extremely early example of this simplified kind of music can be found in Scarlatti's *Gerone, tiranno di Siracusa* (Naples, 1693). (Musical Example VI) In this aria, the only example of the thicker-textured "old-fashioned" counterpoint is the slight attempt at imitation at the opening of the second stanza, and at its repeat. Even though the second stanza modulates freely through D minor and B minor before cadencing in C$^{\sharp}$ minor, it keeps primarily to tonic and dominant harmonies within the new keys.

Other elements of the new style, which appear in operas of the first and second decades of the new century, show the changing relationship between the orchestra and the voice. The accompaniment no longer alternates with the voice, as its equal. Instead, it only introduces the tune and then either follows the voice in unison, or provides a simple rhythmic and harmonic background, while the text is being sung. Arias accompanied solely by continuo begin to disappear. The habit of introducing the vocal part with a "motto," isolated from the rest of the aria, also becomes much rarer. Instances of a "question-response" alternation of voice and orchestra are suppressed in favor of a continuous, unbroken vocal line which cedes position to the orchestra only at clearly defined ritornelli.

These changes also appear at the turn of the century, and slowly become the norm instead of the exception. In instrumental music, the equivalent harmonic and textural changes began to occur around 1720; the coincidence of the style in the two genres can be considered as the start of the new era, whether it is called "galant," "rococo," "pre-classic," or "classic."[1]

MUSICAL EXAMPLE VI

Alessandro Scarlatti:

"Se amor ti dice," (I:5) from *Gerone, tiranno di Siracusa*, Naples, 1693. (GB-Och, MS. 990)

MUSICAL EXAMPLE VI (continued)

Along with musical changes, another set of changes took place in opera, quite suddenly, between 1715 and 1720. The so-called "Arcadian" reform of opera libretti had to do with "classicism" in its literary sense. Among its changes were the elimination of comic characters and scenes from opera seria, the placement of most arias at the ends of scenes, the reduction of the number of arias in an opera from 40 or 50 to 20 or 30, the reduction of the number of characters to six or seven, and the sharp decrease in subsidiary plots, unnecessary complications, and mistaken or hidden identities. Begun by Apostolo Zeno, these reforms were codified by Pietro Trapassi, known as Metastasio.

The musical changes that occurred in conjunction with the operatic ones were equally distinctive and sudden: the da capo aria that had been the standard form since the end of the seventeenth century changed shape. Instead of having a short first stanza, often not modulatory, a long second stanza with several tonalities (and a cadence on each), and a return to the first stanza (ABA form), the first stanza was expanded so that the words were sung twice, the first time cadencing on the dominant, and the second returning to the tonic; and the second stanza was reduced to one that modulated once or twice, but usually cadenced only at the end, in a key that was neither the tonic nor the one used at the opening of the B stanza ($A_1 A_2 B A_1 A_2$ form, or five-part da capo aria).

The new type of libretto, combined with the new aria form, and the new styles of harmonic and instrumental accompaniment, coalesced and triumphed at Naples by 1720, with works of Leonardo Leo, Francesco Feo, and others. Niccolò Porpora, often mentioned as an originator of the style, seems to be more of a follower. His *Flavio Anicio Olibrio*, performed in Naples in 1711, was revised in 1722 for performance in Rome, but nevertheless it still demonstrates an intermediate stage between the old and new styles.[2] (Musical Examples VII and VIII) Both "Sdegno amore" and "Perchè ad amarmi?" have the perfunctory A_1 ritornello, which is merely a short pause, and the two-part B stanza. "Sdegno" lacks a B ritornello, and "Perchè" includes a ritornello that is obviously Venetian in style, separate from the body of the aria and utilizing the entire string section for the only time. More to the point here are the older techniques of using the orchestra only at points of emphasis in "Sdegno,"[3] and the concertato violoncello with its imitative entries in "Perchè." The key-consciousness of the five-part aria is also rudimentary, with, in "Sdegno," the sequence being:

$$A_1 \text{ stanza}, \quad A_2 \text{ stanza}$$
$$\text{I} \qquad\qquad \text{V-I}$$

and, in "Perchè":

$$A_1 \text{ stanza}, \quad A_2 \text{ stanza}.$$
$$\text{i-III} \qquad\quad \text{i}$$

Flavio also includes such standard seventeenth-century types as motto arias and continuo arias.

Feo's *Siface, rè di Numidia* was produced in Naples in 1723, at the height of his career. Faustina was one of the performers, and Hasse undoubtedly was well-acquainted with the score. "Affetti mi prometti," which opens the opera (I:2), shows the most modern techniques in aria construction at that time: (Musical Example IX).

It has more extensive A stanzas, with a true ritornello separating them, a new practice of not using the continuo at all while the performer was singing (indicated by "senza bassi"), and a B section in only one continuous melody, with one full cadence at the end. More conservative is the lack of written-out coloratura and the placement of cadenzas on rests instead of on the penultimate syllable of the aria. The key sequence uses the rare alternative modulation, to supertonic, that survived in Hasse's operas for the next fifty years. In its sound and effect, this is a true "protoclassical" aria.

Siface also has arias that are reminiscent of the old style, such as "Rendimi i lacci miei" (II:12), with its motto opening, and "Fiume che torbido" (II:13), which uses continuo accompaniment for half of the aria. These are exceptions; the new style is otherwise dominant. A very modern feature is the presence in more than half the arias of a B ritornello, though this does not serve the purpose of modulating to the

MUSICAL EXAMPLE VII

Niccolò Porpora:
"Sdegno amore," (I:4), from *Flavio Anicio Olibrio*, Naples, 1711, and
Rome, 1722.   (GB-Lbm, Add. 14,121)

This is the 1722 version, which, as can be determined from remnants of
the 1711 version which have not been destroyed, has not been altered
greatly.

MUSICAL EXAMPLE VII (continued)

MUSICAL EXAMPLE VII (continued)

MUSICAL EXAMPLE VII (continued)

MUSICAL EXAMPLE VII (continued)

MUSICAL EXAMPLE VIII

Niccolò Porpora:
"Perchè ad amarmi," from *Flavio Anicio Olibrio.*

The first half seems to be from 1711. Midway through the aria the handwriting changes. This is presumably the 1722 revision, which differs to an unknown extent from the second half of the original.

MUSICAL EXAMPLE VIII (continued)

MUSICAL EXAMPLE VIII (continued)

MUSICAL EXAMPLE VIII (continued)

MUSICAL EXAMPLE VIII (continued)

MUSICAL EXAMPLE IX

Francesco Feo:
"Affetti mi prometti," (I:2) from *Siface, rè di Numidia*, Naples, 1723. (I-Nc, 32.3.27)

MUSICAL EXAMPLE IX (continued)

MUSICAL EXAMPLE IX (continued)

MUSICAL EXAMPLE IX (continued)

MUSICAL EXAMPLE IX (continued)

MUSICAL EXAMPLE IX (continued)

MUSICAL EXAMPLE IX (continued)

tonic, but only of providing a shorter version of the A ritornello. Such a condensation does not become usual for ten or fifteen years in the operas of Feo's contemporaries.

The first composer to take this new style outside of Naples was Leonardo Vinci, who has kept the honor of being the first important proponent of the "Arcadian" opera. In one of his first serious operas, *Astianatte*, (Naples, 1725), we see many new details, which serve as examples of how the da capo aria develops from 1720 to 1730. (Musical Example X) "Temi di vendicarti" has an opening melody phrased in three two-measure groups (2 + 2 + 2), a pattern which Hasse was to emulate and make his own. The preponderance of A_1 and A_2 over B is quite overwhelming. Use of coloratura has increased; the orchestra, despite addition of horns, is subdued and quite subordinate to the voice; and the aria itself, in all its proportions, has reached the size of the "classical" da capo aria. The striking use of the Neapolitan chord in the B stanza draws attention to the geographical location of the origin of this new style (although by this time the chord was known all over Europe). There is no doubt that this is the climax of the scene.

Other arias in *Astianatte* have B sections with new tempos and meters. The idea is certainly not new, but the B sections remain less important than the A stanzas despite this attention. Still other arias show the short A_1 stanza, the lack of the B ritornello, and similar conservative features.

MUSICAL EXAMPLE X

Leonardo Vinci:
"Temi di vendicarti," (II:7) from *Astianatte*, Naples, 1725. (I-Nc, 33.6.2)

MUSICAL EXAMPLE X (continued)

MUSICAL EXAMPLE X (continued)

MUSICAL EXAMPLE X (continued)

MUSICAL EXAMPLE X (continued)

MUSICAL EXAMPLE X (continued)

Vinci was probably only four years older than Hasse. After many successes in comic opera, beginning in 1719, he had been commissioned to write his first opera seria, *Publio Cornelio Scipione*. It was produced at Naples in November, 1722, possibly the same year in which Hasse arrived. In Hasse's first work for the Neapolitans, the serenata *Antonio e Cleopatra*, of 1725, we can see many remnants of the old style: a French "ouverture" with fugal fast section; a duet with imitation between the two voices rather than the homophony that was to become standard practice; lack of coloratura; occasional use of orchestra beyond a simple support for the singer; arias with the short A_1 stanza; lack of B ritornelli; a long B stanza compared to the two A's; use of pauses after internal cadences in B; and the absence of continuo in vocal sections. "Morte, col fiero aspetto" is a typical example, showing many of these points. (Musical Example XI)

This aria has little of the melodic skill that Hasse was soon to develop. It is also quite thick-textured, with five parts often moving at the same time. The violin line seldom doubles the voice. In fact, the equality of the two violin lines, demonstrated as early as mm. 3 and 4, is similar to a Corellian trio-sonata in its textural effect. "Morte," itself quite chromatic, is one of two arias in minor keys, a rather high proportion for a work of only eight arias.[4]

Elsewhere in the serenata, there is another aria, "Pur ch'io posso à te, ben mio," which modulates to the supertonic instead of the dominant, showing this alternative key structure to be a consistent one throughout Hasse's career. B sections are in two instances in a new meter and tempo. B ritornelli are rare, however, and coloratura is not as freely applied as it will become. The lack of continuo during the vocal sections is found in such arias as "Un sol tuo sospiro," and "Come veder potrei." "Là tra i mirti" is exceptional for the invertible counterpoint that is exchanged between viola and first violin. The first duet, "Attendi ad amarmi," is also backward in its use of two sets of words, one for each singer, to be sung at the same time. The "Arcadians" preferred that each singer wait politely for the other to finish, then sing together in verbal (and musical) harmony. The older technique is still found in *Siface*, but Vinci abandons it in *Astianatte*, and it is never found in mature Hasse. The final duet, "Bella etade avventurosa," is an intimation of the typical closing "Coro." It is short, without coloratura, and sung in complete homophony, except for a small imitative section in the B stanza.

By 1726, when Hasse set *Sesostrate* for Naples, he had successfully absorbed Vinci's style. B sections have no pauses, A sections are equal in length and usually each one is longer than the B stanza. "Se di figlia" shows these points clearly, though in total length it is rather

MUSICAL EXAMPLE XI

Johann Adolf Hasse:
"Morte, col fiero aspetto," from *Antonio e Cleopatra*, Naples, 1725.
(A-Wn, Fond Kiesewetter Sa. 68 B. 33.)

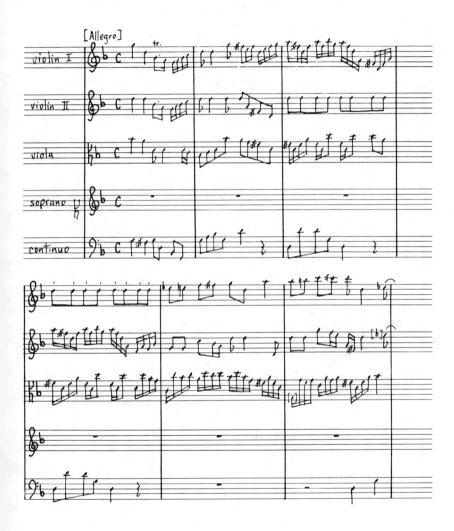

MUSICAL EXAMPLE XI (continued)

MUSICAL EXAMPLE XI (continued)

MUSICAL EXAMPLE XI (continued)

mor- te, cul fiero as- pet-to, or- ror per me non ha, s'io pos- -

so in li- ber- tà, s'io posso in li- ber- tà - - - -

MUSICAL EXAMPLE XI (continued)

MUSICAL EXAMPLE XI (continued)

MUSICAL EXAMPLE XI (continued)

MUSICAL EXAMPLE XI (continued)

MUSICAL EXAMPLE XI (continued)

MUSICAL EXAMPLE XI (continued)

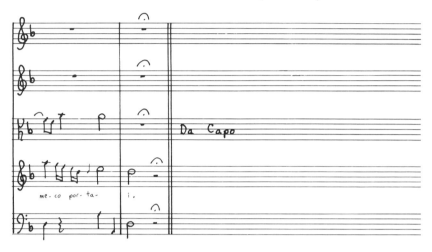

small. (Musical Example XII) The dance-like 6/8 meter is Vinci's favorite one, and the unisono cadential figures abound in his comic and serious works alike. In this aria, Hasse has moved strikingly from the thick-textured harmonies of "Morte, col fiero aspetto." Indeed, most of the aria sounds quite thin, and the B stanza is especially bare in its skeletal harmonies, another testimony to the inspiration of Vinci.

In this piece Hasse approaches a Vincian style of aria writing: one that caters more to the singer and less to the sense of the text. Words are often repeated solely to extend the music, and coloratura is commonly employed on syllables which have no reason for descriptive melismas. Examples of older types of aria decrease in the next five years, in the works of both composers, and by 1730, with the two settings of *Artaserse*, Hasse's for Venice and Vinci's for Rome, the styles are matched, equally mature, with their long A stanzas, short B sections, presence of B ritornelli, coloratura, cadenzas on penultimate syllables, and use of orchestra and continuo throughout the aria.[5]

It is clear that Hasse, in his first years in Naples, absorbed the very latest trends immediately. He matured at the same time Vinci did. It is not likely that he could or would have copied from his great Italian contemporary to the point of becoming obvious. The rivalry pushed Hasse into forming his own musical personality, one that Vinci himself could not have escaped noticing. The five years between 1725 and 1730 must have been quite exciting, with a new form of opera being developed season by season, with intense cross-fertilization among composers. Vinci died in 1730, and, perhaps partly for this reason, opera seria crystallized at this point. Hasse was content for the rest of his long life with a style that scarcely went beyond that of his first *Artaserse*.

MUSICAL EXAMPLE XII

Johann Adolf Hasse:
"Se di figlia acquista," (II:6) from *Sesostrate*, Naples, 1726. (A-Wgm, Q. 1477)

MUSICAL EXAMPLE XII (continued)

MUSICAL EXAMPLE XII (continued)

MUSICAL EXAMPLE XII (continued)

MUSICAL EXAMPLE XII (continued)

MUSICAL EXAMPLE XII (continued)

A comparison of two arias, Vinci and Hasse's settings of "In che t'offende" from their productions of *Catone in Utica* (Vinci's in Rome, 1728, and Hasse's in Turin, 1732) shows how close the styles of these two men became, but also, to some slight extent, a stylistic evolution beyond Vinci on Hesse's part. (Musical Examples XIII and XIV). Despite the total disparity between the meter and tempo of the two (3/4, Lento, e staccato; and C, Più tosto allegro) which changes the affect of the text considerably, the two are obviously based on the same hypothetical model. Both arias have a rather straightforward A_1 stanza, followed by a more complex and lengthier A_2, and a rather brief B stanza, shorter than either of the A stanzas.

Hasse's ritornelli are longer, and in two cases (A_1 ritornello and B ritornello) are used to effect modulations. The A_1 stanzas of both composers modulate from the tonic to the dominant. But Hasse, exceptionally, uses the A_1 ritornello as an exciting, tension-building section, strikingly modulating through B minor to return to the tonic. This ritornello leads without a pause into the next stanza, obviously working against the expectations of the listener. Then, Vinci follows the standard format of using the A_2 stanza to return to the tonic, while Hasse, already in the tonic by the beginning of A_2, remains there throughout the stanza. Hasse's B stanza, beginning on the relative minor, modulates to its (minor) dominant, the most common arrangement. Vinci's B stanza, which remains in the relative minor throughout, uses a less common key structure. In general, the two arias show the range of possibility within the standard five-part da capo format.

MUSICAL EXAMPLE XIII

Leonardo Vinci:
"In che t'offende," (II:6) from *Catone in Utica*, Rome, 1728. (I-Nc, 3.1.9.)

MUSICAL EXAMPLE XIII (continued)

MUSICAL EXAMPLE XIII (continued)

MUSICAL EXAMPLE XIII (continued)

MUSICAL EXAMPLE XIII (continued)

MUSICAL EXAMPLE XIII (continued)

MUSICAL EXAMPLE XIII (continued)

MUSICAL EXAMPLE XIV

Johann Hasse:
"In che t'offende," (II:6), from *Catone in Utica*, Turin, 1732.   (I-Vnm, Cod. It. IV-482)

This aria was also used in Hasse's *Demetrio*, performed in Venice, 1732. This copy is taken from a score of *Demetrio*, and may differ from the original, which is lost.

MUSICAL EXAMPLE XIV (continued)

MUSICAL EXAMPLE XIV (continued)

MUSICAL EXAMPLE XIV (continued)

MUSICAL EXAMPLE XIV (continued)

MUSICAL EXAMPLE XIV (continued)

MUSICAL EXAMPLE XIV (continued)

MUSICAL EXAMPLE XIV (continued)

MUSICAL EXAMPLE XIV (continued)

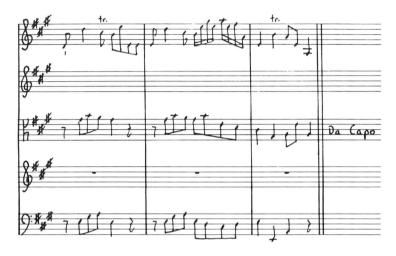

The three-part texture is common to both arias. Hasse uses his standard violin I / viola / continuo, the continuo being a rhythmicised version of a harmonic bass. With the entry of the voice, the violin doubles, to all purposes, the melody line, so the texture remains three-part. Hasse's accompaniment does tend (by the end of the A_1 stanza and through A_2) to become independent, while Vinci's violin has its own part only once, and his A_2 ritornello actually ends with only two parts.

Neither melody line is especially interesting. Both introduce the first four lines without repeat or metric surprise. Vinci's 2 + 2 + 2 + 2 is arranged abb' (sequence) c, and Hasse's, abc (deceptive cadence) c (authentic cadence).

The differences between these two arias are not solely those of artistic temperament. They stem from slightly different conceptions of the importance of the aria within the context of the opera. It would be just as easy to find two arias of which Hasse's was the lighter in effect, and Vinci's the weightier.

Hasse is usually considered to be a follower and a latecomer to the Neapolitan style that was originated by Leo and Feo and brought to fruition by Vinci. This is certainly not the case. Hasse does not copy a style that is already perfected, but instead has an active part in the development of the style. While he is not present at the beginning of the change, he does carry through with the final version, and deserves to be thought of, not as a slavish imitator, forever copying the same models, but as an inventor who in his later years moves only slightly from the style he helps to originate.

CHAPTER VI

CRITICISM OF HASSE'S OPERAS

Hasse became an international figure with *Artaserse*, which was performed not only in Venice, but, within ten years, in eight other cities, including London. Yet it was several years before musical critics began to consider Hasse's music as important. Once they do, it becomes possible to follow his career through observers' perceptions about him. These change as his importance in the musical life of Europe becomes greater. At all times they demonstrate the high esteem in which he was held.

German critics have the most to say about Hasse's music, not only because they acclaimed Hasse as a countryman, despite his Italian style, but because of the general German proclivity toward description and analysis of art. Accordingly, we shall deal mainly with German sources here, and insert those from England, France, and Italy at appropriate places.

Aside from archives and libretti, the first reference to Hasse seems to have been by Johann Georg Keyssler, who, in a letter from Venice in May 1730, calls him the "famous musician" who is to marry Faustina Bordoni.[1]

His own value as a composer begins to be recognized only around 1740, at first mostly by people anxious to show Germany's musical worth in a culture dominated by the Italians and the French. Lorenz Mizler, in his *Neu-eröffnete musikalische Bibliothek* (1737) offers a typical comment:

> Who is it, who has received the approbation of a whole nation, a nation that has always been considered as the most knowledgeable about music? Chapelmaster Hasse, a German, is so famous that the Italians prefer him, a foreigner, to all of their local composers. A certain gentleman . . . has assured me himself that if an opera is to be successful in Italy, it must be composed by Hasse.[2]

Mizler than goes on to name S. L. Weiss as a lutenist, and Handel and Bach as clavier players, who are the best in the world in their respective fields.

Johann Adolph Scheibe's comment in *Critischer Musikus* (1745) is similar. In an anonymous letter to him, conveniently echoing his own views, we find:

> And now, good sir! I will name a man whose fame and fortune have been brought to the highest point not only in Germany, but

> also in Italy. Hasse is well known, and everyone is aware that he has supported the fame of our nation among the Italians in the best possible way. . . . This great man has raised melody to the highest point, and yet never goes to excess. His inventions always correspond with the words, and so far very few have surpassed him in these pieces.

This is followed by a footnote which boasts, "At this time we still have a Hasse and a Graun. Even the most famous Italians have never been able to reach the level of these great men."[3] The quintet of Handel, Bach, Hasse, Graun, and Telemann is to be found in several further places in Scheibe, all with the same reasoning. For example,

> Hasse and Graun, who are also admired by the Italians, show through their inventive, natural, and moving pieces, how beautiful it is to possess and exercise good taste. The creation of good taste in music has thus become a product of the German spirit, and no other nation can vaunt this true advantage.[4]

Scheibe does not know or acknowledge that Hasse's good taste is indistinguishable from Vinci's.

Scheibe does realize that Hasse has started a new style of music. But he eliminates its Italian origins. After mentioning Italians from the first decades of the century, such as Marcello, Gasparini, Bononcini, Conti, Lotti, Porpora, and Vivaldi, who have all "become invisible," ("unsichtbar geworden"), he continues:

> There have already been mentioned two men who have brought fame to our fatherland at this time, in respect to bringing music to its highest point. Hasse and Graun are these excellent men. And one can say truthfully that these are the ones that have begun, as it were, a new period of music. They have shown us the beauty of good taste in such a way, that we can clearly recognize in their works, with what diligence they have followed in the footsteps of those who in so many ways had gone before, and that they truly have reached the ultimate goal that was the object of all endeavors of their predecessors, to follow nature, to imitate it; and the [other] Germans follow their example.[5]

Friedrich Wilhelm Marpurg, in his *Historisch-kritische Beytrage* (1754), takes a more realistic approach. He denies that there is a specifically German style, and links Hasse with Graun as Italianate composers, Handel and Telemann as examples of Germans who follow the French style.[6]

From Hasse's prime years, up to the Seven Years War, there remain only some comments of Mattheson, who as early as 1739 mentioned his "old friend" Hasse, and listed him as one of the three H's (Handel, Heinichen, and Hasse) who had brought the Italian style to Germany.[7]

Christian Gottfried Krause's important aesthetic treatise, *Von der musikalischen Poesie* (1753) makes use of Hasse for selected examples. Like Marpurg, Krause makes no specific application of Hasse's music to his ideas. He uses Hasse as an example of a typical composer writing typical music in good taste. One interesting point in light of the previously cited opinions of German and Italian styles is Krause's original and reasonable belief that Germans mixed the best of French and Italian music, and that Hasse and Graun wrote the best in Italian music (not German):

> In Germany, we have not sworn by the Italian taste in music. Our composers also take beauty from French music, when they find it there . . . Generally . . . good taste consists of that which flatters the ear and moves the heart, and in the Italian opera, the taste has been perfected mostly by Hasse and Graun.[8]

Before considering later comments, we should observe several pages of discussion by both Scheibe and Marpurg, on what they consider to be important aspects of Hasse's style. Scheibe is concerned with Hasse's treatment of the character of Tito Vespasiano, in the opera of the same name, and Marpurg is struck by Hasse's various portrayals of natural effects. Neither makes any attempt at specific analysis.

Scheibe cites Hasse as a general example of the level of taste reached by music in 1745. He chooses to look at the character of Tito since he is the "principal and most beautiful" character of the opera. Tito's first aria (I:5), "Del più sublime soglio," ("Of the highest throne"), supposedly paints his character perfectly. "Majesty shows itself particularly in the opening, and makes known to us, through a very perceptive melody, what the poet wishes to say by 'the only reward is this . . .'" The second stanza shows, by its beauty, Tito's cherishing of his friends.[9] Scheibe's descriptions of several other arias and accompanied recitatives are equally general and unhelpful. Describing "Se all' impero," (III:8), Scheibe can do no better than the following unspecific comment:

> Certainly, the music set to these words is so excellent, that there cannot remain the smallest doubt that great and majestic qualities are expressed through these tones, that understanding and judiciousness reign throughout, and that all of the expressions are reasonable and perceptive. The notes illuminate the words, and express completely the feelings of the heart and all of the therein contained passions.[10]

Indeed, this is a majestic and grand aria, in a moderate tempo, in the heroic key of D, with horns and a march-like dotted rhythm. But it seems to be by dint of imagination alone that one can see this aria fitting Tito and this situation specifically.

Scheibe also singles out Vitellia's aria "Come potesti, o Dio," (II:9), also from *Tito*, which shows her mixture of "love" and "haughtiness." The first three lines show one affect, and the last two, the other. "The exchanges of the affects are among the most notably perceptive."[11] However, Hasse divides the aria, not after the third line, but after the second, playing havoc with the meaning, though Scheibe either does not mind, or does not notice.

While these arias are certainly beautiful, one might well doubt that they all fit the given situation exactly. Either Scheibe is hearing something that modern listeners do not, or his imagination is greater than ours. With no evidence to the contrary, we are forced to assume the latter.

Marpurg's judgment is more musically specific, but more naive according to modern standards. He begins with a rather extravagant praise of Hasse:

> One does not dare, if one is not himself beloved of Apollo, if one is not of the most fiery spirit and possessive of the strongest powers of judgment; if one cannot be equally fortunate in both conception and execution; in short, if one is not himself a Hasse; one does not dare to imitate without hesitation such marvelous phenomena of nature.[12]

He is speaking of *Leucippo*, "Così geloso il cane, / Dell' orticel' custode," (I:9) ("As jealous as the dog that guards the garden"), where the barking of the dog is clearly audible (Musical Example XV). In another part of the aria, "ringhia," ("he growls"), is also closely imitated. But, Marpurg concludes, "One must admire the skill of the master in this aria, and never suspect that things that lie beyond the range of human affects could not also be suited by musical imitation."[13] He seems also to be correcting Scheibe, and cautioning himself, in his next statement:

> We have so much trust in this sort of imitation, and we are so little on our guard in this respect, that we often confuse one meaning with another, or we let our hearing introduce things that otherwise would not at all be suggested. Things that should be understood through a completely different meaning, appear all at once to have changed their nature: we believe that we will find them in the notes, and we truly find them there, as different as they otherwise might truly be.[14]

MUSICAL EXAMPLE XV

Johann Hasse:
"Così geloso il cane," (I:9), excerpts, from *Leucippo*, Dresden, 1747, 1751, 1756(?).   (I-Mc, Part. tr. ms. 155)

This aria is taken from the autograph, presumably the 1756 version, which differs in minor respects from the 1747 aria.

MUSICAL EXAMPLE XV (continued)

Yet, he says, "Uguale e il desio," ("Just as the desire"), from *Leucippo* (II:11), clearly imitates a brook, and "O qual fiamma di gloria" ("Ah, such a blaze of glory"), from *Attilio Regolo* (II:12), "raises a tumult such as a heart, heated through desire for fame and honor, would feel in all its veins."[15] To hear the "rush of the pulse" in this is to recognize "the master's hand."

While this discussion is interesting in respect to the fact that Hasse was appreciated, even cherished, it provides no specific reasons why his music was so popular.

In this epoch, we find very few comments on Hasse by non-Germans. Zanetti's manuscript "Memorie" mentions Hasse as "old and renowned" in an entry of 1743.[16] Much more detailed is the discussion by the President Charles de Brosses in his *Lettres d'Italie*. In his usual witty fashion, he writes from Venice under the date of 29 August 1739:

> The famous Sassone is now the man of the hour. I heard him, at his house, as well as the famous Faustina Bordoni, his wife. She sings with great taste and a charming lightness, but her voice is no longer young. She is without contradiction the most pleasant and the best woman in the world, but she is no longer the best singer.[17]

De Brosses has a long chapter on "Spectacles et Musique," in which Hasse figures prominently, though mostly as the object of anecdotes. While talking of the two styles of French and Italian music, De Brosses inserts, to prove his point that most people cannot like both, an interview with Hasse:

> The famous composer Hasse, detto il Sassone, tried to strangle me in Venice, because of several gentle remonstrances that I wished to make to him, about his indomitable prejudices. "But," I asked him, "have you heard anything of our music? Do you know of our operas by Lully, Campra, Destouches? Have you glanced at the *Hippolyte* of our Rameau?" "Me? No!" he replied. "God save me from ever having to see or hear any music other than Italian."[18]

De Brosses does have a very perceptive historical view of Italian opera and Hasse's place within it; this passage is worth giving in full:

> Latilla is today fashionable in Rome . . . but neither he nor Terradellas, nor any other has the force of those who were composing only a few years ago; and these had surpassed their predecessors, such as Bononcini, Porta, the elder Scarlatti, Sarri (a learned and boring composer), Porpora (natural, but not very original). Vinci, Hasse, usually called il Sassone, and Leo are the ones whose pieces are best-regarded. Vinci is the Lully of Italy, true, simple, natural, expressive, and the best melodic writer in the world, without being obscure; he wrote much although he died

young . . . *Artaserse* is known as his best work; at the same time it is one of the best plays of Metastasio . . . It is the most famous Italian opera. I have never seen it performed, but I know it, having heard almost all of it in concerts, and I have been charmed by it. As excellent as this work of Vinci's is, the scene of Artabano's despair, added by the poet and set to music by il Sassone, surpasses perhaps all the others. The recitative "Eccomi al fine in libertà del mio dolor" is admirable, as well as the following aria, "Pallido il sole . . ." I regard it as one of the most beautiful among the seven or eight hundred arias that I have had copied from various operas. Il Sassone is quite savant; his operas are created with great taste in expression and harmony. Leo has an uncommon talent; he creates good pictures, his harmony is very pure, his melodies have an agreeable and delicate curve, full of refined imagination. They are hard to perform, even though in general Italian music is easier to read and sing than our own, although it does not require as much voice . . .

Pergolesi, Bernasconi, [Giuseppe] Scarlatti, Jommelli, are almost equal to these three of which I have just spoken to you. Among all of these musicians, my favorite is Pergolesi. Ah! the happy talent-- simple and natural. It is not possible to write with more facility, grace, and taste.[19]

Another commentator from this period who appreciated Hasse but preferred Pergolesi was the German transplanted in France, the Baron Grimm. In a letter in *Mercure de France* (2 April 1752), he writes:

I dare also to assure him [a critic] that I know, better than he perhaps, the works, the merit, and the talent of Mr. Hasse, and of Mr. Handel, my contemporaries and my compatriots, and that I am overjoyed that Mr. Hasse should have been the one that the Italians gave the title of Saxon "par excellence," in imitation of which M. de Voltaire has conferred the same title in France to this hero of the century. If I had believed myself able to place this famous artist next to Pergolesi, I would have been too jealous of the glory of my country to avoid doing so. But to overburden great talents with praise that is both excessive and exaggerated without having either sense or truth is to outrage them more than honor them.[20]

Grimm's ally in the "Coin de la Reine," supporting Italian opera, was Jean-Jacques Rousseau. The famous passage from his *Dictionnaire* article on orchestras deserves a place here, for, while it dates from two decades later, it refers to the musical establishment at its height, in the 1750's:

The greatest orchestra in Europe, as far as the number and intelligence of its performers is concerned, is that of Naples; but that which is the best distributed and forms the most nearly perfect ensemble is the orchestra of the opera of the King of Poland at Dresden, directed by the famous Hasse. (This was written in 1754.) (See plate G, figure 1. [Plate XXIX])[21]

After the start of the Seven Years War, Hasse gained status as a respected master, still a good composer, but receiving competition from younger rivals. Francesco Algarotti, to name the most famous advocate of a new kind of music, more dramatic, along with libretti to suit it, is still constrained to admit that there are immortal pieces among the operas of Pergolesi, Vinci, Galuppi, Jommelli, and Hasse.[22] Stefano Arteaga, one of the staunch defenders of the early eighteenth-century style, does not seem to mention Hasse at all, presumably because he is concerned with *Italian* music.

One of the most striking pieces of evidence for Hasse's continued popularity is found in Grosley de Troyes' anonymously published *Nouveaux Mémoires, ou observations sur l'Italie et sur les Italiens, par deux gentilshommes suèdois.* Troyes includes a detailed comment on the first performance of Hasse's Neapolitan *Demofoonte (II)* of 1758:

> The opera of 1758 was the *Demofoonte* of the Abbate Metastasio, set to music for this year by the famous Sassone. These operas are to Italians what motets are to the French: musicians work in emulation of each other, on setting the same words. All of Naples assured [me] that the *Demofoonte* that had already been set to music by so many Virtuosi had never before been so excellently treated. This drama resembles greatly, in its subject and plot, the French *Inès de Castro.* Especially applauded were the duo which closes the second act, and other pieces of this sort; but the tears flowed with the applause of the famous ariette, "Misero pargoletto," which Timante sings to his son whom he holds in his arms. The expression of this entire ariette was that of nature itself; the Frenchmen present at this performance themselves forgot the uncouth appearance of the soprano who filled the role of Timante, and the disparity of his voice with the enormous size of his body, his arms, and his legs, in order to add their tears to those of the Neapolitans.[23]

Grosley neglects to mention that Hasse was not only contending with Leo, Gluck, Jomelli, Graun, Galuppi, Perez, Sarti, and many others who had all set *Demofoonte* in earlier years, but also with his own earlier Dresden version, performed in Naples in 1750.[24]

It was not until 1772 that the first attempt at a biography of Hasse was made. Charles Burney, who visited the composer in Vienna that year, collected the basic facts of his life, and published them in his *Present State of Music.* The account is in all respects quite accurate, but

PLATE XXIX

Distribution of the orchestra of the Dresden Opera

Directed by Mr. Hasse

Key to figures:

1. Harpsichord of the maestro di cappella
2. Harpsichord of the accompanist [of the recitative]
3. Violoncelli
4. Contrabassi
5. First violins
6. Second violins, with backs to the theatre [the stage]
7. Oboes, the same
8. Flutes, the same
a. Violas, the same
b. Bassoons
c. Hunting horns
d. A platform at each side, for the timpani and trumpets

PLATE XXIX

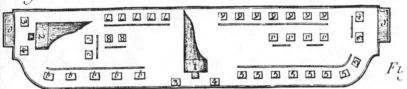

Distribution de l'Orchestre de l'Opera de Dresde,
Fig.1.   Dirigé par le S.ᵣ Hasse.

Renvois des Chiffres.

1. *Clavecin du Maître de Chapelle*
2. *Clavecin d'accompagnement*
3. *Violoncelles*
4. *Contre - basses*
5. *Premiers Violons*
6. *Second Violons, ayans le dos*
   tourné vers le Théatre.
7. *Haubois, de même.*
8. *Flutes, de même.*
a. *Tailles, de meme.*
b. *Bassons.*
c. *Cors de Chasse.*
d. *Une Tribune de Chaque côté pour les*
   Tymballes et Trompettes.

Fig.4.

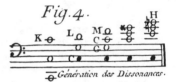

Génération des Dissonances.

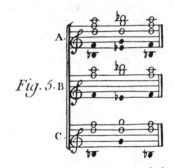

Fig. 5.

Système général

Fig. 7.

Fig. 6.

the information is scattered through several different accounts of visits and is not in chronological order.[25]   Burney also provided some information on Hasse's role in Viennese musical life, stating that he and Metastasio formed the core of a conservative faction facing Gluck and Calzabigi. Burney is responsible for the famous simile comparing Hasse and Gluck to Rafaello and Michelangelo.[26]   General comments by Burney show that Hasse was one of the composers he admired the most: "He may, without injury to his brethren, be allowed to be superior to all other lyric composers, as Metastasio is to all other lyric poets."[27]

The first true biography of Hasse also came during these early years of retirement, this time in the form of one of the rare Italian references to him. Giambattista Mancini, in his *Riflessioni pratiche sul canto figurato*, gives a short description of Hasse's life as a footnote to "Faustina Bordoni, wife of the extremely famous master Johann Hasse, detto il Sassone":

> Johann Hasse moved to Naples in 1722, to study and perfect himself in the art of counterpoint under the direction of the famous Alessandro Scarlatti. It is not necessary for me to extol [him] with my words here in order to extract some profit from it, because although he was young at his first entry [into musical life], in a short time he was known, distinguished, and admired by all of Europe. Because of the marvelous productions of this so distinguished artist, and after having written with repeated approbation different works in the greatest and most diverse theatres of Italy, he entered the service of the Royal and Electoral Court of Saxony, where for many years he wrote much beautiful church music, and operas for that theatre, where to satisfy the exacting taste of those rulers, he was required to produce ever newer and finer compositions.

> It is time, many teachers have decided, that this great man give to the public, by means of the press, if not all, at least part of his so greatly applauded works, which serve as models and instruction for young students.

> He, perhaps too modest, has until now never wished to yield to the petitions of others, and to this date the desires of the musical connoisseurs have remained unsatisfied.   When he entered, as mentioned above, the Electoral service, he did not forego, every few years, travelling to Italy, where he wrote operatic works, always well-received and applauded. His great fame resulted in his being invited to Paris, under the rule of Louis XV, King of France, as well as to Berlin, under Frederick II, King of Prussia, where he had an equal success, and received universal admiration. Also, the Imperial Court at Vienna gave him many distinctions and benefits, and in these last years the Invincible Empress MARIA THERESA, gloriously reigning, is served by this master in the most luminous occasions of the various marriages of the Imperial Family.

The prime of this great man is past, but yet one notices that at all times and in all places he has been appreciated as his merit deserved, and he now lives quietly in Venice, covered with glory, and singled out by all teachers as "the Father of Music."[28]

A more respectful biography could not be imagined.

After 1760, it became less important to German critics that Hasse was a countryman. Johann Adam Hiller conducting various musical societies in Leipzig, reviewed in the *Wöchentliche Nachrichten und Anmerkungen die Musik betreffend* (the house organ of J. G. I. Breitkopf), two of Hasse's operas available in manuscript through Breitkopf: *Romolo ed Ersilia* in 1766 and *Piramo e Tisbe* in 1769. These reviews show a great appreciation for the music, but are more summaries of contents than analyses or criticism.[29] In 1768, Hiller, in his "Entwurf einer musikalischen Bibliothek" places Hasse and Graun above Perez, Galuppi, Ciampi, Traetta, Zoppi, and di Majo for the continuity and suitability of their entire operas, even though as far as individual arias were concerned, he considered them all to be equal.[30] Whether or not this ranking was made for chauvinistic reasons, these reasons are at least disguised and given a rational basis.

Wolfgang Amadeus Mozart let it be known in the dedication of his Opus III (K. 10-15) to Queen Charlotte in 1765 who made up his (or more likely Leopold's) pantheon during his formative years:

Let me live, and one day I will offer to her [the queen] a gift worthy of her and of you [the Genius of Music]; because with your help, I will equal the glory of all the great men of my country, I will become immortal as Handel and Hasse, and my name will be as famous as that of [Johann Christian] Bach.[31]

One of the most important writings on musical style during Hasse's lifetime was set down by Abt Georg Joseph Vogler, in his *Betrachtungen der Mannheimer Tonschule*.[32] In this extensive work, Vogler at one point discusses in detail the aria "Se cerca, se dice" from Galuppi's *L'Olimpiade*, mentioning Hasse's setting of the same text as having more "nobility and elevation." Vogler had been a student of Hasse's in 1774, and, as Mennicke says, Hasse loved him "as a father would love a son."[33] Hasse bade farewell to Vogler with what might well have served as his epitaph: "Che la musica sia chiara, semplice ma sublime"; ("Let music be clear, simple, but sublime.")

At the time of Hasse's death, he was by no means forgotten. An extensive obituary appeared in Carl Friedrich Cramer's *Magazin der Musik*.[34] However, performances of his operas were rare by 1783. Berlin was the only city in which they were performed with any regularity, and this ceased with the death of Frederick the Great in 1786. An *Attilio*

Regolo, performed in Venice in 1792, seems to be Hasse's last staged opera. After this year, except for German translations of *L'Asilo d'amore* (as *Das Wahl des Herakles*) in Dresden (1883), and *Piramo e Tisbe* in Cologne (1939), there were no public performances of Hasse operas until the 1960's.

Though performances ceased almost immediately, historians did not forget Hasse. Cramer's "Abhandlung von der Oper," includes Hasse both in the section on Saxony and that on Venice.[35] Burney's *General History of Music* of course does not omit him.[36] E. L. Gerber's *Lexicon* of 1790 includes a lengthy article on Hasse, including a complete reprinting of Burney's praise from the *Present State* that he calls "concise and true."[37] In 1801, the *Allgemeine Musikalische Zeitung* accorded an important position to Hasse in its serialized history of German music.[38] In 1820, Franz Sales Kandler, a student and assistant of Raphael Georg Kiesewetter, had a memorial to Hasse placed in the church SS. Ermagora e Fortunato (San Marcuola), in Venice.[39] In the same year he published the first full biography of Hasse, *Cenni storico-critici intorno alla vita ed alle opere del cel. Compositore di Musica Gio. Adolfo Hasse detto il Sassone.*[40] Hasse was now alive only in the pages of history books.

Aside from Fürstenau's study of Saxon court music, no scholarly work was done on Hasse until the beginning of the twentieth century. Of the half-dozen or so theses and articles which appeared between 1904 and 1925, only those of Mennicke and Rudolf Gerber are of more than passing interest to the student of Hasse's operas. Since Gerber is the only scholar to have considered these works specifically (aside from Zeller's short thesis on the recitativo accompagnato), it is essential that this chapter include a critique and description of Gerber's inaugural dissertation, *Der Operntypus Johann Adolph Hasses und seine textlichen Grundlagen*, which appeared in 1925, under the aegis of, and dedicated to, Hermann Abert.[41]

Gerber's thesis is a careful study of a large and complex subject. It sets up a sensible framework for a consideration of Hasse's operas, and follows it in a rational, orderly fashion. Perhaps its greatest fault is its attempt to cover all aspects of Hasse's operas: the texts, the construction, the music of the arias, Hasse's development, and his historical importance.

Despite limited access to manuscripts, Gerber succeeded in acquiring a thorough understanding of Hasse's career and his development as an opera composer. Unfortunately, Gerber did not study the early serenatas, and thus missed the only period in which Hasse's music actually changed noticeably. He also assumed that *Tigrane* dated from 1723, thus preceding *Sesostrate*; this negates the changes that do take place between 1725 and 1729. But two of the most complete sections of the thesis deal with techniques of orchestration and harmony used by Hasse to provide emotion in his arias, and the slow expansion of the Dresden orchestra under his direction.[42]   In this exhaustive chapter, Gerber finds wonderful examples of Hasse's orginality of scoring and harmonization, examples which are completely isolated in the mass of his music, and which show no evidence at all of any development in a chronological sense.[43]

His conclusive finding concerning Hasse's instrumentation is, beyond the gradual increase in separate parts and number of performers, that the only instrument which Hasse cultivated in an individual fashion was the bassoon, which gradually received its own staff, and, from that point, its own independent and characteristic line, by the time of the late Viennese operas.

These two discussions are so complete that they make any similar section in the present dissertation unnecessary. They form a considerable part of Gerber's 190-page thesis, and serve as evidence for his sole general judgment of Hasse, which is placed in an emphatic typeface: "Hasse is a rigid, unchanging personality, who succumbs to the influence around him, while his artistic personality proves itself to be, except for a quite unimportant fraction, only prolific."[44]

Despite the evidence amassed by Gerber in the preceding pages, this judgment is harsh and does Hasse a disservice. It is unfair to say that he succumbs to surrounding influences when, in fact, as Gerber himself shows, these influences are sporadic, exceptional, and shortlasting. It is also completely useless as an aid to an appreciation of Hasse's music.

The core of Gerber's thesis deals with the categorization of Hasse's arias into four types. These can be simple defined as: sad, common-time, moderate or fast arias; bravura, 3/8 allegro arias; sweet and pretty "Empfindsamer," triple-time andante or allegretto arias (the most beautiful, Gerber thinks); and slow, common-time, pathetic arias, often in E major.[45]   Gerber has interesting comments to make about all four of these types, including descriptions of the most common effects of each: the ♩ ♩ ♩ rhythm of type 1, with its abb phrases (2+2+2 bars), the five-bar opening phrase in type 2, the consonant intervals of major sixth and perfect fourth, along with feminine cadences in type 3, and the short phrases, often expanded from one measure, in type 4.

This categorization, ultimately, is unsuccessful. There is a great temptation to compile lists of types of arias.[46] After a point, the number of exceptions and hybrid forms overwhelm the easy examples, and the point becomes lost. Hasse's melodies are made up of simple elements, which are then made subject to only the most basic development and organization.   Gerber's efforts to introduce order to this mass of production are justifiable, and indeed often seem to be logical and helpful. But the end result is that Gerber saw more than is actually there, and lost sight of the essential fact, the "clarity and simplicity" for which Hasse was always striving.

Another section of Gerber's thesis takes up the libretti.[47] It is a dense, philosophical and complex consideration of Metastasio's dramatic action, complete with references to Spengler and lesser philosophers. Gerber's conclusion here is that Metastasio's spirit (like Hasse's) was Roman, not German, emphasizing states of being, not developments of character, and existing in space, not time. Thus, it is dead rather than alive, and unconcerned with moving forward in any sense. All the dramatic force of a scene is directed to the aria and the end of the scene. Once reached, the aria drains all of the energy, leaving the recitative of the next scene to begin again to build to the eventual aria. This is a very helpful explanation, though it does not take full cognisance of the ability of Metastasio to build up to a very dramatic climatic scene, such as the last one of *Artaserse*, where, despite the knowledge that the "lieto fine" ("happy ending") is obligatory,[48] there is no idea at all of a dead, static situation existing at the heart of the matter.

The last section of Gerber's thesis is the only one in which his findings are suspect on factual grounds. Most of Chapter D, "Formanalyse der Arien," is devoted to a rather elementary discussion of the organization of Hasse's da capo arias. It includes some derivation of odd-measured phrases from hypothetical four- and eight-bar phrases, which is highly suspect in the first place, and of only minor interest in the second (unless one feels that three-bar phrases are incomplete and unbalanced, and wishes to know how they *should* sound).

Much attention is given to the first appearances of shortened da capo forms in this chapter, and it is Gerber's admittedly tentative conclusion that Hasse was the inventor of this form, with an aria from *Semiramide* of 1747 (actually also found in the 1745 version), and then, in 1755, in the first act of *Il Rè pastore*. But the first example, as he recognizes, is not a truly shortened da capo, but one in which much of A_1 is written out after the B ritornello, in order to accomodate minor changes. It thus has the *form* of a half da capo aria, and uses the mechanical devices, but it is not actually shortened. Recent study has shown, too, that Jommelli's experiments in new forms begin in Stuttgart as early as 1753, thus predating *Il Rè pastore*. This, of course, only strengthens Gerber's argument as to Hasse's rigid, easily influenced personality.

Two streams of thought run continuously through Gerber's work, and detract from his sound conclusions. The first is a background of references to national (Italian and German) characteristics in the drama of Metastasio and the music of Hasse, which distract from attempts to seek real reasons for the differences between the two stylistic backgrounds. The second is an attempt to connect the operas with the shallow, superficial courtly life. But it is clear from the responses of critics of the eighteenth century that Hasse was not often appreciated in the genteel, snide, condescending manner in which Lord Chesterfield appreciated court intrigues, or, even, the President de Brosses appreciated Italian opera. Surely Hasse's music reflects even more the "rational" side of the century, (also acknowleged by Gerber), which assumed a perfectable society, and responsible leadership which would, eventually, show that love and honor, passion and reason, could be reconciled.

As a result, Gerber's dissertation appears as a flawed work. It is a brave attempt to deal with the most important aspect of Hasse's music, his arias. As a ground-breaking work it is enormously important, but much remains to be done in the areas which Gerber opened for study.

A close analysis of one of Hasse's arias is necessary to the understanding of what attracted the eighteenth century to Hasse, what repelled Gerber, and what we ourselves might see of value in his music. There follows a closer look at what might lie behind these various views.

Demetrio was first composed in 1732 for performance in Venice. (See Chapter I, pp. 15, 19 and Chapter IV, pp. 133-139). In 1740 it was revised in almost all respects for Dresden. One of the five arias retained was Demetrio's, from I:10, "Scherza il nocchier talora" (Musical Example XVI). This in itself suggests a certain popularity, as does the existence of some six copies of the aria in manuscript collections in Vienna, Paris, Brussels, Dresden, and Berkeley. The text, which is Metastasian, was also popular, being used in pasticci performed under Hasse's name in Ljubljana (1733, in *Euristeo*), Vienna (1739, with other composers), Pressburg (1741, in a version of *Alessandro nell' Indie* presented by the travelling company of Pietro Mingotti), and Verona (1748, in an *Antigono*).[49]

In the opera, this aria is sung by Alceste, while he is still unaware that he is actually Demetrio, the rightful king of Syria. It comes as a response to a series of insults made to him by Olinto, who, with Alceste, is a claimant for the hand of Cleonice, Queen of Syria and daughter of the usurper Alessandro. Alceste shows his noble blood by restraining his anger and answering Olinto with a series of parables, instead of an attack.

MUSICAL EXAMPLE XVI

Johann Hasse:

"Scherza il nocchier talora," (I:10) from *Demetrio*, Venice, 1732; Dresden, 1740. (I-Vnm, Cod. It. IV-482; F-Pn, Cons. D. 5426-5428.

This is a conflation of the two versions, which have minor differences of phrasing, attack, dynamics, and the like. These have been made uniform throughout the aria.

MUSICAL EXAMPLE XVI (continued)

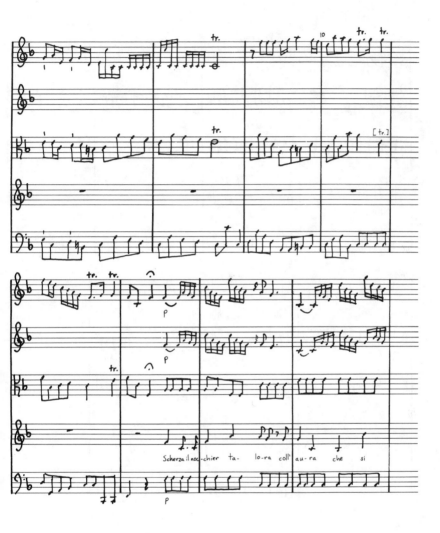

Scherza il noc-chier ta-   lo-ra coll' au-ra   che   si

MUSICAL EXAMPLE XVI (continued)

MUSICAL EXAMPLE XVI (continued)

MUSICAL EXAMPLE XVI (continued)

MUSICAL EXAMPLE XVI (continued)

MUSICAL EXAMPLE XVI (continued)

MUSICAL EXAMPLE XVI (continued)

MUSICAL EXAMPLE XVI (continued)

MUSICAL EXAMPLE XVI (continued)

Scherza il nocchier talora
Coll' aura che si desta;
Ma poi divien tempesta
Che impallidir lo fa.

Non cura il pellegrino
Picciola nuvoletta;
Ma, quando men l'aspetta,
Quella tonando va.

(The seaman mocks the rising breeze,
When first it blows a gentle gale,
But trembles when the wind he sees
With dreadful rage the waves assail.

The pilgrim, with regardless view
Aloft a fleecy cloud espies;
'Till thence unlook'd-for storms ensue
And thunders rattle through the skies.)[50]

The text is exceptional in itself; the usual format of the "comparison" aria contrasts a natural image with the internal state of the singer. The point is that Olinto is in the position of this seaman, mocking a harmless-appearing Alceste who will soon become a tempestuous Demetrio. But Alceste's royal blood shows itself in his restraint in following the first conceit with a second one, even further removed from the actual situation.

Of the four or five general categories of aria (bravura, pastoral, dance-like, passionate, amorous), this is certainly meant by Metastasio to be bravura. The words "tempesta" and "tonando" beg for dramatic coloratura sections, and the meaning of the aria as a whole would certainly be best expressed by a brisk tempo with a rather jagged melodic line. Hasse rarely experiments with music that does not match the obvious sense of the words, and he does not do so here.[51]

Hasse sets this aria in 4/4 time, allegro, F major, with melismas on "tempesta" and "tonando." The violins are given a rather steady sixteenth-note accompaniment figure which suggests movement of wind and waves, and the continuo provides a constant eight-note motion which likewise contributes to the feeling of restlessness. Aside from these general attributes, common to many arias of the same general type and feeling, there is no close portrayal of the text. Hasse is quite careful with the poetry, making sure that all accents are correct and that the structure of the poem, line by line, is kept. But, as Gerber is careful to point out, this does not necessitate a following of the *meaning* of the poetry.[52]

In its broad outlines, "Scherza" is no different from any of Hasse's other arias. Only in its detail does its superior construction become evident, but this only hints at reasons for the popularity of the piece in the eighteenth century.

The aria follows the standard da capo format. It does not have the B ritornello which by this time was becoming obligatory for arias. In the relationship and proportions of its individual parts, it is quite unexceptional:

A ritornello:	11½ mm.	F
A_1 stanza:	18 mm.	F-C
A_1 ritornello:	3½ mm.	C-C (counting ½ m. elision with A_1 stanza)
A_2 stanza:	22 mm.	(begins on $^{o}7$ on C) - F
A_2 ritornello:	8 mm.	F (counting ½ m. elision with A_2 stanza)
B stanza:	11 mm.	d-a

Typically for an early aria, there is no pretense at modulating either to D minor or from A minor, at the beginning or end of the B stanza.

The more exceptional aspects of this piece are found in the melodic and rhythmic cohesiveness, the somewhat unusual harmonic range within the sections, and the uneven, constantly unbalanced structure of phrase and melody.

The A ritornello begins with a 1-1/2 measure violin theme:

Hasse often writes measures twice as long as he needs, and this is clearly the case here.[53] This 1-1/2 measure theme is immediately repeated, on the dominant. The sixteenth-note motion is carried on for another measure, and then 1-1/2 measures more, to the middle of measure 6, where a new staccato rhythm is introduced:

A B♮ at this point shows the first excursion outside of the key. This in itself is not adventuresome, but it is quite rare for Hasse to introduce any chromaticism at all in the A ritornello, no matter how mild.

A dominant pedal in the violins, for 1-1/2 measures, slows down the harmonic rhythm. A ritardando, or perhaps a fermata, may have been intended or added in performance at measure 8. Here, a new rhythm and motive is introduced, one which is of the greatest importance to the organization of the aria:

It is emphasized by its position after the half-cadence, by its downbeat rest, and by its use of the submediant as the opening chord. Besides its use of this secondary triad, a secondary dominant is used, again in measure 9. This 2-1/2 measure phrase ends on a deceptive cadence, and is continued one measure further for a full cadence on F at the end of the ritornello.

The opening ritornello is thus made up of a succession of odd-measured phrases, decreasing and then increasing in length, and then cadencing twice after the introduction of motive 3:

$$1\text{-}1/2 + 1\text{-}1/2 + 1 + 1 + 1/2 + 1 + 1\text{-}1/2 \frown + 2\text{-}1/2 + 1$$

If the measures are divided in half, the arrangement becomes somewhat clearer:

$$3 + 3 + 2 + 2 + 1 + 2 + 3 \frown + 5 + 2$$

The A ritornello is orchestrated in Hasse's standard manner: violin I (doubled by violin II), viola, and continuo.   One would expect the A_1 stanza to continue in his usual arrangement: violin I (with voice), violin II, continuo (doubled by viola).   But we find instead the first violin continues with its motive 1, which is not the theme of the aria, but rather its accompaniment, essentially a "storm motive."   The viola also continues with its constant eighth-note accompaniment.   When the second violin almost immediately enters with its own part (generally in thirds or sixths with the first violin), there are found to be five distinct voices moving, (although in general homophonically), which is quite exceptional for Hasse.

The voice's melodic line explains the derivation of the opening phrases of 1-1/2 measures.[54]   It is possible to hear the opening melody as a contraction from a standard succession of four-bar phrases, with the second repeated:

It is much simpler to hear the phrases as translations into music of the three-foot trochaic lines:

Schērza îl nŏcchiēr tălōră

Cŏll'aūră chē sĭ dēstă;

Mă pōi dĭviēn tĕmpēstă,

Chĕ impāllĭdîr lŏ fā.

This creates a fluid succession of 1-1/2 (or 3) bar phrases, which itself provides a very subtle feeling of flowing restlessness in the aria.

The fourth phrase seems to begin as another 1-1/2 bar structure, but instead it continues into the first section of coloratura, using a new rhythm at first:

and then expanding with the rhythm of motive 1. Motive 4 also reintroduces the B♮, which here serves to begin the modulation to C. Hasse has thus emphasized this structural point with a new rhythm and texture. The word chosen for the modulation, logically, is "tempesta." A pedal on the new dominant, G, closes this section with several interesting points: the voice begins on its lowest note, G, and rises steadily to its highest, d. Measure 22 includes the superimposition of a secondary V^7 over the G, with its striking sound of simultaneous tonic and dominant. The use of the secondary dominant is in itself exceptional.

After the half-cadence on G (equivalent to that in measure 8), motive 4 is reintroduced, on a IV^6 (instead of vi) chord of the new key. It is set to line 4 of the text, used for the first time, and has the sound of a second theme, as it settles firmly in the dominant key. In contrast to the triadic and rhythmically straightforward opening subject, this is stepwise melodically, and somewhat syncopated rhythmically, providing other differentiating factors. A new section of coloratura, on "fa," expands this section which, in the A ritornello, was only 3-1/2 measures long. The first measure of melisma is repeated, expanded by sixteenth-note motion, and followed by a new rhythm:

This new motive is itself repeated, and is followed by the stereotypical cadence of the descending scale. This whole "second subject" has been in the key of C, with not so much as a secondary dominant to disturb the diatonic calm.

The A_1 ritornello seems to be present only to give the singer a chance to breathe, and to strengthen the key of C. Hasse does take the opportunity to bring back motive 2, not heard since the A ritornello.

With the opening of the A_2 stanza, we hear the "deepening" of feeling which Gerber talks of as often being present in the repetition of the A stanza.[55] The opening is immediately modulatory, beginning with a diminished seventh over the C of the preceding cadence. The transposed opening phrase then moves temporarily to G minor, and is continued, in a second 1-1/2 measure phrase, sequentially, with a vii to I in F (thus immediately returning to the tonic). This second phrase is not repeated, as it had been in the A_1 stanza. The third line of the text is immediately introduced, and, as before, leads into the first section of coloratura, on "tempesta."   Here a new idea is introduced, which is treated sequentially, rising from B♭ to F over five measures:

This section of coloratura, like that of A_1, ends with several rather interesting surprises.   Measure 42 (motive 5) corresponds to measure 28, which is from the second thematic area, and Hasse immediately shows how this was derived from motive 2 by doubling its speed and introducing motive 2 itself, for the first time in the vocal line, in measure 43:

Harmonically, this passage is the most development-like of the aria, with the fastest harmonic rhythm (four and six chords per bar), and the greatest amount of chromaticism.   The progression moves:

$$V^6/V - V, V^6/ii - ii, V^6 - I, IV^6 - vii - V - vi - V^6/V - V.$$

Here, in measure 44, the pedal on the dominant equivalent to measure 21-23 is reached.   As before, the secondary dominant seventh over the dominant is included.   But again the "deepening" of affect, which Gerber would try to see as a development, is evident.   Motive 3, with its distinctive downbeat rest, is now taken over by the entire orchestra (measure 46), with the exception of the continuo; formerly, only the voice had the rest, while the entire orchestra played the downbeat.   And, instead of the cadence being delayed by coloratura, the motive cadences in one measure, even more quickly than in the A ritornello.   Then the voice begins line 3 once more (measure 51), and again proceeds to a half-cadence on C, providing in effect 2-1/2 more measures of "development."   Once more, Hasse uses this "development" to unify the aria.   As measure 43 had used motive 2 for the first time in the voice, measure 50 uses the octave sixteenth-note pedal that had not been heard since measures 7-8:[56]

As motive 3 had followed this figure in the A ritornello, so it enters again here, cadencing deceptively at first, as in the A ritornello, and then, in emphasis, cadencing authentically with a Lombard-rhythm figure not otherwise heard in the aria, accompanied by detached chords in the orchestra:

The A_2 ritornello provides a fitting conclusion that does not detract from the voice. The orchestra is again reduced to three parts, the violins play a derivation from the opening theme, and then cadence as in the A ritornello, including the introduction of the "second subject." This does not cadence deceptively, since this technique has just been used in the A_2 stanza, but instead, without hesitation, on the tonic.

B stanzas are often the most imaginative sections of arias. Since they are usually in minor, they can be more chromatic, and there is a standard practice of modulating at least once, with possibly a second modulation several bars before the cadence. In actuality, this stanza is rather anticlimactic. It remains solidly in D minor until measure 66, where, through a $^\flat$VI chord, a modulation to A minor takes place. A minor remains the tonality for the rest of the section. There is not even a short modulation after the voice finishes, to bring the tonality back to F major.

Structurally, the theme follows the example of the A stanzas. There are three 1½ measure phrases, with the fourth being extended into the coloratura section. The rhythm of the first phrase is varied, and the melody is completely new, though it retains the triadic outline of the first subject. The second phrase opens with the rhythm of the first subject, and then continues into motive 3! The short section of coloratura that follows is taken from motive 6, with the grace note removed, which ties it further with motive 2. In measure 71 the actual rhythm of motive 2 appears, while the orchestra plays the emphatic chords of the A_2 stanza cadence. The stanza then ends almost exactly as A_1 had, with motive 5 being derived after motive 2 (instead of the opposite, as in measures 42-43), followed by the standard scalar descent to the tonic. The entire B section strikes the listener as marking time, relaxing with familiar motives in new keys, before returning to the excitement of the A stanzas. It in no way represents an intensification or development of what has gone before.

Despite its outward simplicity, the aria is a carefully-calculated, well-coordinated rhythmic and motivic unity. Its melody is not so carefully wrought. The opening drop of a fourth is reversed to a rise of a sixth (through F) in the next measure, again reversed to a drop of a seventh (to B$\flat$) and again to a rise of an octave in the same measure (14). Once this range has been introduced, the rest of the stanza continues to rise and fall an octave at rather regular intervals, with little or no large-scale intent noticeable.

The A$_2$ stanza is less wave-like and less well organized. Its more diffuse quality is typical for second stanzas in general. The one difference is the addition of a new high note, a grace-note e (eliminated in the 1740 revision: one of the only differences between the two versions).

The B stanza is notable only for a succession of low A's, which must have been inserted to display to advantage the range and quality of the low notes of Antonio Bernacchi, the original singer.

Performance had a great deal to do with the success of an aria. Not indicated in the score are the ornaments and variations added, both in the da capo, and at the cadenzas. The latter are probably only two in number, both in the A$_2$ stanza, and both being probably rather short, performed while the instruments held the notes in measures 51 and 54. It does not seem likely that cadenzas would have been inserted at the ends of the A$_1$ and B stanzas, since they are not prepared in the orchestral parts. There may well have been a cadenza by the concertmaster in measure 60, where a fermata was placed in the 1740 manuscript.

In retrospect, the connoisseur of the eighteenth century would have been attracted by the rhythmic vitality, smooth melodic and harmonic flow, expressive but rare harmonic excursions, and demonstration of the vocal technique of the singer. All of these are present to a highly professional, polished degree in this aria. Hasse was to duplicate these features hundreds of times in dozens of operas over the next forty years. But these attributes are not sufficient for the modern listener. It would take complete sympathy with the ideals and goals of eighteenth-century opera seria to appreciate Hasse's music. Such a sympathy seems to be only a remote possibility. Yet who could have predicted, not many years ago, the present revival of interest in seventeenth-century opera, or, even closer to the point, the renaissance of Handelian opera seria?

The reason for Hasse's immediate and long-lasting fall from popularity was his total devotion to opera seria in its purest form. The music of Metastasian opera seria fits its characters perfectly, but only because both music and character are always general, always universal in their qualities, and are not distinctive in their personalities and situations. When the taste for such universality disappeared, so did the demand for this kind of opera. The last performance of a Hasse opera came only a year after Mozart's setting of *La Clemenza di Tito*. But Mozart had the libretto converted into a much more modern complex of duets, trios, ensembles, and finales before he could write in his thematic catalogue that the work was an "opera seria . . . ridotta a vera opera." By 1791 opera seria was not "true opera." Hasse had not advanced beyond the style of the 1730's, and when public tastes finally moved away from opera seria, his fall was sudden.

It is still easy today to be entranced by the fluid succession of sound found in a typical Hasse aria, and to be amazed by a virtuoso performance of a bravura passage. It is also possible to read a Metastasian drama and be utterly caught up in its poetry, its passions, its conflicts. The lack of verisimilitude found in all opera is present in Hasse's dramas to an only slightly higher degree. Public interest in pre-nineteenth-century opera has gone along with the rise of young performers interested in learning the proper eighteenth-century techniques, and has provided the monetary resources necessary for opulent productions. Let us look forward to the day when Hasse's name again becomes as well-known as those of Handel and Telemann, and it is again possible to understand what the glorious days of Dresden opera were like.

NOTES

CHAPTER I

[1]Biographical sources for Hasse's life include Franz Sales Kandler, *Cenni storico-critici della vita e delle opere di G. A. Hasse* (Venice: Picotti, 1820), G. M. Urbani de Gheltof, *La "nuova Sirena" e il "Caro Sassone,"* (Venice: M. Fontana, 1840), and Moritz Fürstenau, *Zur Geschichte der Musik und des Theaters am Hofe zu Dresden* (Dresden: Rudolf Kuntze, 1861-62). Carl Mennicke includes all of these sources in his 100-page chapter in *Hasse und die Brüder Graun* (Leipzig: Breitkopf und Härtel, 1906). Small additions have been made by Anna Amalia Abert, "Hasse," (*MGG*, v. V, cols. 1771-88), Sven Hostrup Hansell, "Sacred Music at the *Incurabili* in Venice at the Time of J. A. Hasse," (*JAMS*, v. XXIII, 1970, pp. 282-301, 505-521), Karl-Heinz Viertel, "Neue Dokumente zu Leben und Werk Johann Adolf Hasses," (*Analecta Musicologia*, v. 12, 1973, pp. 209-223), and Reinhard Strohm, "Hasse, Scarlatti, Rolle," *Analecta Musicologia*, v. 15, 1975, pp. 220-57. The sixth edition of Grove's Dictionary, forthcoming in 1979, includes most of this information, including the findings of this chapter, which was made available to the author of the "Hasse" article, Sven Hostrup Hansell.

The biography that follows deals only with the outline of Hasse's life in relation to his operas, and follows Mennicke's study for most of the unfootnoted facts; discoveries made since 1906 have been incorporated.

[2]Charles Burney, *The Present State of Music in Germany, the Netherlands, and United Provinces,* (London: T. Becket, J. Robson, G. Robinson, 1775), v. I, p. 350.

[3]Mariä Lichtmess, 2 February, according to Mennicke, p. 356.

[4]Schatz says this was the Laurentius-messe, 11 August. On 10 August, according to Mennicke (the opening of Laurentius-messe?) Hasse sang in Conti's *Don Quichotte*. The libretto of *Antioco* was written by Minato in 1666, greatly rewritten by Zeno and Pariati in 1705, and then revised by Barthold Feind in 1708.

[5]In D-SWl, 4721, No. 59, 68-72. (Reinhard Strohm, *Italienisch Opernarien des Frühen Settecento (1720-1730), Analecta Musicologia*, v. 16 I/II, 1976, v. 11, p. 173.

[6]Due to an error in Florimo (*La Scuola musicale di Napoli e i suoi conservatorii*, Naples: Vincenzo Morano, 1880-82, v. 4, p. 80) Mennicke assumed Hasse's first opera in Naples was *Tigrane*, in 1723, while it was not actually performed until 1729. Bergedorf archives of May 1723 indicate that Hasse was in Italy (they do not say where), but Hansell's discovery of Hasse's marriage document clarifies the situation somewhat. ("Sacred Music," p. 284: *Matrimonio segreto* of 24 June 1730, Archivio della Curia Patriarcale di Venezia.)

[7]Burney, *Present State*, v. I, pp. 347-348: "He studied at first a little while under Porpora, as I had been told before by Barbella; but Hasse denied that it was Porpora who introduced him to old Scarlatti. He says, that the first time Scarlatti saw him, he luckily conceived such an affection for him that he ever after treated him with the

kindness of a father." Hasse carefully studied and revised arias from Scarlatti's *Griselda*, which survive in the Milan Conservatory. (Strohm, "Hasse, Scarlatti, Rolle," pp. 220-257).

[8]Friedrich Wilhelm Marpurg, *Historisch-kritische Beyträge zur Aufnahme der Musik*, (Berlin: Schutzens Wittwe, 1754-62), v. I, 3. Stück, p. 227 ff.

[9]*Ibid*, p. 227. Quantz may be referring here to *Sesostrate*, Hasse's first opus for Naples, performed in May of the *following* year, 1726. Hasse was not formally named, in a libretto, as being connected with the Neapolitan court until 1729 when he was called, in the libretto of *Tigrane*, "maestro sopranumerario della Real Capella di Napoli."

[10]Sven Hostrup Hansell, *Works for Solo Voice of Johann Adolph Hasse (1699-1783)* (Detroit Studies in Music Bibliography, v. 12), (Detroit: Information Coordinators, Inc. 1968), pp. 14-16. Though the manuscript gives the title as *Antonio e Clepatra*, the character is indicated as "Marc' Antonio" throughout the body of the score.

[11]Mennicke lists this as a doubtful opera, as does Abert. The sole copy is in the Osterreiches Nationalbibliothek, and was originally in the possession of Kiesewetter, probably one of the scores purchased for him by Kandler, Hasse's first biographer. No source mentions this work by name, and no libretto exists. But Quantz's first-hand testimony and the information given on the title page both make it extremely likely that this work is Hasse's. The title page reads: *Drama per Musica da/ cantarsi nel Casino di Campagna/ del Regio Consigliere Sig.r D. Carlo/ Carmagnano nell' Estate del 1725./ Poesie di Francesco Ricciardi,/ Musica di Giovanni Hasse detto il Sassone. Maestro di Capella di S.A.S./ il Duca di Wolfenbüttel.*

[12]Ernst Ludwig Gerber seems to have been the first to call Hasse "il caro Sassone," in his *Historisch-biographisches Lexicon der Tonkünstler* (Leipzig: Breitkopf, 1790-92) v. I, col. 593. Hasse himself consistently used "il Sassone" throughout his career. John Mainwaring relates that Italian audiences acclaimed Handel as "il caro Sassone" in 1709, in his *Memoirs of the Life of the Late George Frederick Handel* (London: R. & J. Dodsley, 1760), pp. 51-54.

[13]Ths score, (A-Wgm, Q 1477), stems from the Kiesewetter library, and is in the same hand as *Antonio e Cleopatra.*

[14]Damari and Miride each have an aria following one of their respective master's or mistress's, mimicking it with the same text.

[15]The intermezzo itself is also of a more modern type, being divided into only two parts, while the usual intermezzo that Hasse wrote at Naples was in three parts, the third coming before the last scene of the third act. It would be logical to consider the score as an earlier version of the libretto, but the title page gives the same date as the libretto, and the score includes two arias from *Astarto*, of 1726 (carefully marked, "questa aria non spetta alla stessa opera," in an 18th century hand), suggesting that the score is the less trustworthy of the two sources. The opera was revived with "new arias" on 28 August of the same year, which may explain the discrepancies. (Strohm, *Opernarien*, v. II, p. 173.)

[16]This Ricciardi is probably the same as the Francesco Ricciardo named in a 1727 libretto as "stampatore di Sua Em.i. il Signor Vicere," and in 1730 as administrator of the royal opera.

[17]*La Semele/ o sia/ La Richiesta fatale/ Drama per musica da contarsi/ nell' autunno dell' anno 1726./ Poesia di Francesco Ricciardi/ Musica di Giovanni Adolfo Hass/ detto il Sassone.* (A-Wgm, Q 1476).

[18]Abert says the score is lost, but a manuscript exists. (I-MC, 125/A/2/op. 1.)

[19]"Sacred Music," p. 284.

[20]Col. 1777.

[21]Hansell includes it among feste teatrali. (*Solo Voice*, pp. 13-14.)

[22]Eldest son of Alessandro Scarlatti. This was his only opera.

[23]Hasse is not mentioned on the libretto, and it was Hansell who first connected this libretto with the autograph catalogued as *Lavinia* (the prima donna) in the Sächsische Landesbibliothek: Mus. 2477/F/98 ("Sacred Music," p. 284.) Mennicke listed this work, as *Lavinia*, among works of doubtful authenticity, and Abert has followed this tradition. Another *commedia per musica, Erminia,* also performed in the spring, anonymously, may be by Hasse, for though no score survives, three of the arias, found separately, are identified in various libraries as being by Hasse, including one later used in *Demetrio.* (Strohm, *Opernarien*, v. II, p. 181.)

[23a]Hasse may have met Handel in this year. The latter was in Naples, observing the new style of opera, in this year. He took back to London copies of all of Hasse's early operas. (Reinhard Strohm, "Händels Pasticci," *Analecta Musicologia*, v. 14, 1974, pp. 208-267.)

[24]The careers of these two men paralleled each other very closely. Pietro Trapassi, who had taken the name of his patron, Metastasio, was born in 1698, Hasse in 1699. Metastasio's first work for the theatre was *Gli Orti Esperidi* of 1721, Hasse's *Antioco* also dated from 1721. Metastasio's first opera seria was *Didone abbandonata*, of 1725, Hasse's second (and first mature one) was *Sesostrate*, of 1726. Metastasio received his permanent appointment in Vienna in 1729, Hasse received his permanent appointment in Dresden in 1731. Metastasio's last work was *Ruggiero*, written for Hasse in 1771. It was also Hasse's last opera seria. Metastasio died in 1782, and Hasse followed in 1783.

[25]Though both were composed for the Carnival, Vinci's was clearly the "authorized" version, for it used Metastasio's poem uncut and unchanged. This was a customary honor accorded to the first setting of Metasasio's, and perhaps other dramatists's, works for much of the eighteenth century. Hasse's text was altered by Giovanni Boldini, and included two of thé most famous arias of the century: "Pallido il sole," and "Parto qual pastorello" (Strohm, "Hasse, Scarlatti, Rolli," p. 234).

[26]Cuzzoni was Faustina Bordoni's famous rival on the London stage in Handel's company, during the years 1726-1728.

[27]In the Venetian archival account, Hasse states he had been living in Venice for six or seven months, and had the intention of residing there permanently. (Hansell, "Sacred Music," p. 234.)

[28]Faustina's death certificate in the church of Ss. Ermagora e Fortunato gives her age at her death (4 November 1781) as 81 years (Mennicke, *Hasse*, p. 438). The Venice State Archive *Provveditori alla sanita, 968, Necrologio n.o. 176, 1781*, on the other hand, says she was 88 (Hansell, *Solo Cantatas*, p. 9). Yet the latter age would have her singing her first role at the age of 22, and her last at 58, less likely than the alternative years of activity of 16 to 51. Burney, who is usually trustworthy, calls her seventy-two years old in 1772, (*Present State*, v. 1, p. 315) but also states that Hasse was 10 years younger than his wife (*Ibid.*, p. 278).

[29]The influence of Hasse's early patron König, still court poet in Dresden, is not known.

[30]In the libretto to *Artaserse*, Hasse is still identified as "maestro sopranumerario" to the Neapolitan court.

[31]Faustina sang the part of Dalisa; Angelo Amorevoli, who would join Hasse in Dresden in 1742, had the role of Ottone.

[32]Manuscript notebooks, *Hasse* v. I, in Library of Congress. The latter seems more logical, since the opera, on a Metastasian libretto, includes two arias from *Arminio* and one from *Dalisa*. Cuzzoni was the prima donna in this production. The sole copy of *Ezio* is in GB-Lk, 22 e 17. (Strohm, *Opernarien*, v. II, p. 177.) I have not seen this copy. All other *Ezio* manuscripts are of the second, 1755, version.

[33]Hansell, "Sacred Music," p. 285.

[33a]Hansell, "Hasse," *The New Grove Dictionary*, sixth ed.

[34]Fritz Löffler, *Das Alte Dresden. Geschichte seiner Bauten*, (Dresden: Sachsenverlag Dresden, 1955) p. 354. The Zwinger was not completed until 1732.

[35]*Ibid.*, p. 354.

[36]In 1772 the theatre, in disuse since 1763, was turned into a ballroom. With the renascence of Dresden's musical life in the Wagner era, a new opera house was built (1838-1841). The old Kürfurstliches Theater am Zwinger was destroyed by fire during the 1849 revolution.

[37]Burney, *Present State*, v. II, p. 51.

[38]J. N. Forkel, *Ueber Johann Sebastian Bachs Leben, Kunst und Kunstwerke* (Leipzig: Hoffmeister und Kühnel, 1802). Modern ed., Frankfurt a.M.; H. C. Grahl, 1950), p. 47. In seinem spätern, völlig reifen Alter . . . hielt er . . . viel auf den ehemaligen Kaiserlichen Ober-Capellmeister Fux, auf Händel, auf Caldara, auf Reinh. Kaiser, auf Hasse, beide Graune, Telemann, Zelenka, Benda, u. überhaupt auf alles, was damahls in Dresden and Berlin am vorzüglichsten war. Die ersten vier, nehmlich Fux, Händel, Caldara, und Kaiser, kannte er nicht persönlich, die übrigen aber sämmtlich.

[39]*Ibid.*, pp. 47-48.   In Dresden war die Capelle und die Oper, während Hasse Capellmeister dort war, sehr glänzend und vortrefflich.   Bach hatte schon in frühern Jahren dort viele Bekannte, von welchen allen er sehr geehrt wurde.   Auch Hasse nebst seiner Gattin, der berühmten Faustina, waren unehrere Mahle in Leipzig gewesen, und hatten seine grosse Kunst bewundert.   Er hatte auf diese Weise immer eine ausgezeichnet ehrenvolle Aufnahme in Dresden, und ging oft dahin, um die Oper zu hören.   Sein ältester Sohn musste ihn gewöhnlich begleiten.   Er pflegte dann einige Tage vor die Abreise im Scherz zu sagen: Friedemann, wollen wir nicht die schönen Dresdener Liederchen einmal wieder hören?   So unschuldig dieser Scherz an sich ist, so bin ich doch überzeugt, Dass ihn Bach gegen Keinen andern als gegn diesen sohn geüussert haben würde, der um jene Zeit ebenfalls schon wusste, was in der Kunst gross, und was bloss schön und angenehm ist.

[40]It was repeated in the Carnival season of the next year, after Hasse and Faustina had departed.

[41]It was common practice throughout the century for principal singers to be better paid than composers.   There was no consistent relationship between Taler and ducats; a ducat was worth roughly two to three Taler in value.

[42]The sum remains the best supporting evidence for Mennicke's thesis that Faustina was the Electoral Prince's mistress.   The idea is not a strange one, considering the general reputation of singers and the moral standard of the courts of the era.   Yet it should be pointed out that in 1733, when Faustina and Hasse were formally hired, they each received a yearly salary of 3000 Taler.   A year's salary in advance would have been an honorarium and retaining fee worthy of the Hasses.

[43]Individual arias remain; perhaps as many as twelve of the twenty-eight.

[44]Mennicke makes a strange error, placing this theatre in Rome and putting the intermezzo with *Cajo Fabrizio*, first performed (in Rome's T. Capranica) on 12 January 1732.   (p. 377.)

[45]Women did not sing in theatres in the Papal States at this time.

[46]The score (I-Vnm, Cod. It. IV-482) says 1733; the libretto (by Metastasio) and contemporary chronicles agree on 1732.   The libetto still refers to Hasse as "maestro sopranumerario della real capella di Napoli."   It includes the sinfonia and an aria from *Gerone*, an aria from *Catone in Utica*, and three contrafacta from *Cajo Fabrizio*.

[47]One aria was replaced (in an appendix, showing that the change was made after the libretto was printed) by an aria from *Cajo Fabrizio*.   A second is a contrafactum from *Cajo*; a third, from *Ezio*.   Two more arias, from Metastasio's cantata *Irene*, suggest that this cantata may have been set earlier by Hasse, though it is now lost.   (Hansell, "Hasse," *The New Grove's Dictionary*.

[48]Most sources give 1742 as the date, though this refers to a pasticcio of *Issipile* directed by Leo.   The manuscript (I-MC, 124/G/31, op. 1, 2) has 1732 as the date, which is reinforced by a document from 1742 in the Neapolitan state archives (fasc. 4 e 5, 1741-1744) referring to the 1732 production.   I am thankful to Sven Hansell for communicating this information to me.

[49]The only evidence for such a journey is in Mainwaring's *Memoirs*, (pp. 116-118), where he says that Hasse was the composer at the Hay-market. This is evidently a reference to *Artaserse* and *Siroe*, two works that for the most part used Hasse's music, performed in 1734 and 1736 respectively. Hasse told Burney in 1773 that he had "often been invited, and had often wished to go to England, as he had known many persons of that kingdom, from whom he had received great civilities." (*Present State* v. I, p. 281). See also Millner, "Hasse and London's Opera of the Nobility," (*Music Review*, v. 35, 1974, pp. 240-246).

[49a]Strohm, "Händels pasticci," pp. 253-4. Handel's respect for Hasse was shown by his use of some forty-nine arias from fifteen operas, used in seven pasticci between 1730 and 1734.

[49b]Hansell, "Hasse," *The New Grove's Dictionary*.

[50]The Hasses had three children, Maria (Peppina), Cristina, and Francesco Maria, two of whom are known to have survived their parents. Cristina eventually married Giorgio Torniello, the Italian consul to London. Peppina stayed with her parents and remained unmarried. Almost nothing is known of Francesco.

In the Carnival season *Artaserse* was performed again, presumably with Hasse's revisions. One of the new arias was inserted into the revision of *Cajo Fabrizio*, Hasse's next opera. The role of Artaserse was sung by Cafarello, a soprano, as in Vinci's version, suggesting that this may have been a pasticcio.

[51]The first date is in the Dresden State Archives (Fürstenau, p. 204); the second is in the *Dressdnischen Merkwurdigkeiten* (Mennicke, p. 383).

[52]This cantata, number 66 in Hansell's catalogue, begins with a sinfonia that was later used by Hasse in *Atalanta* of 1737. (Hansell, *Solo voice*, p. 60).

[53]Urbani de Gheltof, p. 40.

[54]Hansell, "Sacred Music," p. 291.

[55]Furthermore, the work was presented in the Teatro San Angelo, one of the secondary theatres of Venice. Hasse never presented an opera himself in this theatre, though other pasticci of his operas were also performed here and in the Teatro San Cassiano. All of the productions which were authorized by Hasse were presented in the Teatro San Giovanni Grisostomo (during Carnival) or in the Teatro San Samuele (during Ascension). There were two possible Hasse pasticci performed in San Giovanni Grisostomo: the 1734 *Artaserse (Ib)*, and the 1743 reworking of *Alessandro nell' Indie (IIc)*, but these are the only exceptions. (Throughout this thesis, different versions of operas will be identified by Roman numerals, referring to completely new settings, and lower case alphabet, referring to revisions. This system is explained in greater detail in Chapter IV.)

[56]Mennicke gives the Dresden performance of 1738 as the first setting (p. 493), but the Pesaro libretto is to be found in the Biblioteca Nazionale Vittorio Emmanuele in Rome. A manuscript exists which may be of this version (I-Nc, Rari 7-4-10). The first two acts match the libretto quite closely. In the third act, substantial differences

appear. Specifically, the final terzetto of the manuscript is found in place of the two final arias of the libretto (and of Metastasio's play). At least one of these arias is found in a loose copy (B-Bc 4121) marked "Pesaro, autunno 1735," which I have not seen. The other discrepancies in the libretto only refer to the recitative. It may be assumed that if any of the Naples manuscript is not by Hasse, it is only the final terzetto, which may belong to the pasticcio performed in Naples on 4 November 1738, with, as the libretto states, "additional music by Palella." Of the nine arias of this manuscript which differ from *Tito Ib* (Dresden, 1738), at least three are taken from earlier Hasse operas.

[57] Three members of the cast, Tesi, Amorevoli, and Margherita Giacomazzi, sang later that year in a pasticcio of this opera presented on 4 November in the Teatro San Bartolomeo of Naples. Carestini was the primo uomo. The music was credited to Hasse, "directed by Giuseppe di Majo," who is also named by the libretto as composer of the prologue. More of the music may have been his, for Hasse had had no ties to the Neapolitan court since 1732.

[58] Fürstenau's date (p. 224). Mennicke says it was 23 January (p. 385).

[59] It was probably not the revised version of *Demetrio* performed in Venice's Teatro San Cassiano for the 1737 Carnival. The libretto shows that almost all the arias were replaced; they have not survived. This *Demetrio* was most likely a pasticcio arranged by Domenico Lalli, who was the maestro di cappella of San Cassiano as well as poet of San Giovanni Grisostomo.

[60] According to singers listed on a manuscript score (D-Mbs, mus. mss. 191).

[61] Anna (1693-1740), a niece of Peter the Great, was empress from 1730. She had intervened in the War of the Polish Succession (1733-1735), along with Charles VI of Austria, on behalf of Saxony, against the Polish claimant Stanislaus I. Frederick Augustus II thus regained the throne held by his father, and in 1735 became King Augustus III of Poland. The war, however, had spread, with Spain and Sardinia joining France against Russia and Austria. Spain recovered its lost Kingdom of the Two Sicilies from Austria in 1734. The shift in Naples from Hapsburg to Bourbon control may have been partially responsible for Hasse's lack of activity in that city, at least temporarily.

[62] Mennicke, p. 385.

[63] According to singers listed on a manuscript score (D-Mbs, mus. mss. 194).

[64] Also in the 1738 Carnival, but in Venice, was another production of *Alessandro nell' Indie*. This was virtually identical to the 1736 production, though it had five new arias, possibly sent by Hasse for the occasion. The arias survive in a manuscript entitled *Arie della nova Aggiunta dell' Opera del Sig. Giov. Hasse Dal Teatro in S. Giov. Grisostomo 1738*, (I-Vnm, Cod. It. IV 478.) Mennicke states (p. 385) that Faustina went to Venice to sing in the revival, and did not sing in *Irene*. Nevertheless, her name is not on the *Alessandro nell' Indie* libretto, and is on that of *Irene*.

[65] Hansell, "Sacred Music," p. 291.

[66]They had performed it in Dresden. Both had been hired in 1724 and thus were the longest-tenured members of the company. (Fürstenau, p. 160.) Also in 1739, the intermezzo *Rimario e Grilantea* was performed, in an unknown location. It is not known if this was actually by Hasse.

[67]Simultaneously, a pasticcio of *Demetrio* under the title *Cleonice* was presented in Venice under Hasse's name. Like the 1737 version of *Demetrio*, this consisted mainly of substitute arias which are no longer extant. Though Hansell assumes the two 1740 productions were the same ("Sacred Music," p. 292), there seems to be no connection between them.

[68]This was the first time since 1730 that a work by a composer other than Hasse had been presented in the Electoral Court Theatre.

[69]An anonymous bass singer had participated in *Atalanta* (1737). It was quite exceptional for opera seria to include a bass role, but Hasse consistently used one for the role of the confidant or general from 1742 unil 1756. Joseph Schuster's son, of the same name, born in 1748, became Church composer in Dresden in 1772, along with Naumann.

[70]Fürstenau, p. 237.

[71]As listed in I-Vc, Ospedaletto XIX 324.

[72]Pietro Trapassi, *detto* Metastasio, *Tutte le opere di Pietro Metastasio*, Bruno Brunelli, ed., (Milan: Arnoldo Mondadori, 1943-54) v. III, pp. 230-231, (and notes 2 and 3, pp. 1209-1210). Francesco Algarotti's *Saggio sopra l'opera* was published in 1755. As a friend of Frederick the Great, he was occasionally involved in revisions of libretti set by C. H. Graun. In Dresden from 1742 to 1747, he was closely allied with the court of Frederick Augustus II, though he does not seem to have been further connected with Hasse's libretti.

[73]Benedetto Croce, *I Teatri di Napoli*, (Naples: Tip. di Francesco Giannini, 1891) p. 410, says that this was given in Naples in July of 1742. Abert repeats the date (*MGG* col. 1776). But Hasse could not have been present, for the Electoral court was in residence in Dresden that summer, and Hasse would not have been allowed to leave. Manuscript #834 in the music library of the University of California at Berkeley includes the sinfonia, with the information that it was performed with "the serenata" (unnamed) at the Neapolitan Court in 1744. This is a more logical date.

[74]There is some doubt about the actual first performance of *Antigono*. Mennicke gives *L'Asilo d'amore* as 7 Oct. 1743, and *Antigono* as 20 Jan. 1744. Schatz listed both as 7 Oct. 1743. Sonneck, Loewenberg, and Abert all have 10 Oct. 1743 for *Antigono*. There do not seem to be any libretti extant for *L'Asilo d'amore*; the Carnival libretto for *Antigono* was printed in 1743, which may have caused the confusion. Mennicke's answer still seems to be the best.

[75]Brunelli, ed., *Metastasio: Tutte le opere.* V. I, p. 1024.

[76]Hansell, "Sacred Music," p. 294.

[77]Hansell ("Sacred Music," p. 294) says it was first performed on 4 November 1744 in Naples, but this seems to be based on faulty evidence. Quite a few Hasse operas were performed there between 1738 and 1747; all seem to be pasticcios, with additions by Palella or Leo.

[78]He probably did not help produce two puppet operas given in this year. *Lo Starnuto d'Ercole* and *Eurimedonte e Timocleone* were both given at the private theatre of the Abate Angelo Labia; the first on Trinity Sunday, the second on 29 June, according to information in a handwritten addition to a copy of Antonio Groppo's *Cataloghi di tutti i drammi per musica recitati nei teatri di Venezia* (Venice, 1746) in the Biblioteca Marciana of Venice. Additional information is given by Schatz (manuscript notebooks). The librettists were Giacopo Martelli and Girolamo Zanetti respectively. *Eurymedonte* may have been an all-Hasse pasticcio: of the twenty-one arias and choruses, only three cannot be identified as being taken from a previous Hasse opera, and these could easily have been contrafacta. *Lo Starnuto d'Ercole* names Andrea Adolfati as being the composer along with Hasse, and the arias are much less identifiable.

[79]For further information, see Chapter IV, pp. 116-133.

[80]There is no doubt that Hasse was involved in the revision of *Demetrio* produced at San Giovanni Grisostomo during the Carnival season of 1747. Four of the new arias are from earlier Hasse operas (*Antigono, Didone, Ipermestra,* and *La Sorella amante*). Two more of the new arias are found in the Sächsische Landesbibliothek (Ms. mus. 1/F/28, 12). These originated in the Munich collection of Princess Maria Antonia Walpurgis, and must have been given to her by Hasse on either of his stays in Munich at this time.

[81]Sources on Maria Antonia include Alan Yorke-Long, *Music at Court, Four Eighteenth Century Studies.* (London: Weidenfeld and Nicolson, 1954), pp. 72-93, and H. Drewes, *Maria Antonia Walpurgis als Komponistin,* Ph.D. Diss. Köln, 1934.

[82]Writing to Brühl, in reference to a copy of *Il Trionfo della fedeltà,* a festa teatrale which Metastasio had just finished editing, she complained, "Metastasio has cruelly mutilated it. He has not left alone a single one of my arias, which makes me want to cry; even worse, he has changed them in such a way that even if one wished, one could not put my melodies on them." ("Metastasio l'a cruellement mutilé, il n'en a pas laisser un seul de mes airs dont je voudrais pleure et ce qu'il y a de pis, c'est qu'il a changé de façon, que quand on le voudrait, on ne pouvait y metre mes airs.") (Mennick. p. 397) Brühl had written to her that Hasse had not yet begun to set the text to music; possibly she had given him the melody line to harmonize; the music, though eventually published under her name, was certainly Hasse's to a great degree.

[83]*Tutte le opere,* v. III, pp. 337-340, 342-348. Burney (*Present State,* v. I, p. 160) says that Hasse wrote the aria "Se tutti i mali miei" for Mingotti, hoping that the adagio tempo and pizzicato accompaniment would show off Mingotti's voice at its worst, but that she made it a success. "Se tutti i mali miei" is, however, one of Faustina's arias, "un poco sostenuto, ma poco," and not pizzicato. Mingotti, in fact, does not have an aria slower than allegretto in the opera.

[84]Hansell surmises this ("Sacred Music," p. 300). Mennicke assumes that since Frederick Christian and Maria Antonia did not go to Warsaw, Hasse must have stayed in Dresden with them. The argument is unconvincing in the face of the evidence to the contrary.

[85]F-Pn, Cons. D. 5468 and 5469 (isolated arias). A version half-way between the Dresden and Venice productions is also in Paris: Cons. D. 5426-5428. Since the title page gives Dresden as the place of performance, this may be a version performed later during the 1748 Carnival. One of the substitute arias, "Per lei mi nacque amore," is from *La Spartana generosa*, and when Hasse completely rewrote *Demofoonte* in 1758 he thought enough of the text to keep it, though he set it to new music.

[86]Schatz notebooks. Mennicke (p. 404) and later sources say 7 October.

[87]Brunelli's introduction to the libretto (*Tutte le Opere*, v. I, p. 972) makes it clear that the drama was first set to music in 1750. Abert, however, seems to think that it was composed in 1740: "Already written in 1740 for Vienna, but because of the death of Emperor Charles VI not performed." ("Schon 1740 f. Wien geschrieben, aber wegen des Todes Kaiser Karls VI nicht aufgef.") (*MGG*, col. 1776)

[88]*Tutte le Opere*, v. III, p. 427 ff., (20 October 1749). Certainly the letter would not have been necessary had the opera been set nine years earlier.

[89]A great many scores of Hasse operas, surviving with book plates from the library of the *Menus plaisirs*, testify to the interest of the French court in Italian opera seria. Hasse also composed four harpsichord sonatas, titled on the manuscript, "fatte per la Real Delfina di Francia," and a cantata on a French text.

[90]This may well have been partly in retaliation for Frederick's hiring away of J. J. Quantz, first flute in the Saxon cappella, in 1742. Quantz's price for leaving was 2000 Taler a year, further pay for compositions, independence from the Berlin cappella, and exclusive use of the King's private chamber orchestra.

[91]This organ was built at the incredible cost of 20,000 Taler, not counting any of the decorative carpentry. Although the case was destroyed in World War II, the pipes were saved and it is being rebuilt.

[92]Teresa Albuzzi-Todeschini, a soprano, was, according to Fürstenau, (p. 272), the mistress of Brühl. She had been hired on 1 January 1750 to replace Anna Maria Negri. At that time she and Mingotti were the highest-paid singers in the company (besides Faustina), with salaries of 2000 Taler each.

[93]A contemporary report of Hasse's dislike for Mingotti that was not known to Fürstenau or Mennicke is found in a letter from Pisendel to Telemann, printed in Viertel, "Neue Dokumente," pp. 217-218.

[94]This may have been planned then or later for a 7 October performance, for the autograph includes a licenza in honor of Frederick Augustus.

[95]It is this version that Gerber used as the basis of his *Das Erbe Deutsche Musik*, (vols. 26-27) edition (Leipzig: Breitkopf und Härtel, 1957). The arias from 1745 are

included in the appendix. Since the changes were made for the sake of variety and for new singers, and not primarily because the composer was dissatisfied with the first version, it is the first version which probably should be used as the basis of such an edition. Later alterations would be better placed in the appendix.

[96]The bass Schuster was replaced by Führich, at least in the libretto.

[97]He may have gone to Italy during the summer. On 30 November Metastasio wrote to Farinelli that he had seen Hasse "several months ago" on his way through Vienna. (*Tutte le opere*, v. III, pp. 871-872).

[98]With one exception: Coltellini's *Piramo e Tisbe*, Hasse's penultimate stage work, written in 1768.

[99]This was the first Hasse opera produced in that city. Hasse later told Burney that he had frequently attended the court in Warsaw (*Present State*, v. I, p. 349). Mennicke states that the performance (and six repetitions) took place in Dresden (p. 118), though Fürstenau (p. 280) and the libretto (according to Sartori's manuscript catalogue of opera libretti--the only copy is in the Krakow Jagiellonska Museum Narodowe) agree that it was in Warsaw.

[100]Of twenty-four arias, seven were substitutes in 1730, all of which were replaced in 1755, six by the original Metastasian texts and one by a new substitute. Five more arias were given substitute texts in 1755, making a total of twelve of the twenty-four on new texts. Strohm says ths version is "strongly differentiated musically" from the 1730 opera. (*Opernarien*, v. II, p. 177.)

[101]Fürstenau, pp. 283-4. The cast included Belli, Albuzzi, Monticelli, Pilaja, Amorevoli, and Rochetti (again active in the Cappella.)

[102]This opera was probably a fourth version of *Leucippo*. The autograph score of *Leucippo* does not fit any surviving libretto. It includes pre-war copyists' hands and has a cast of five sopranos and a bass that fits this period perfectly: Pilaja, Albuzzi, Belli, Putini, Monticelli, and Führich or Schuster. Performance of an old opera on the 7 October holiday had not occurred since *Asteria* in 1737, and the opera included an aria from another Dresden opera, *Attilio Regolo*, which was also not customary, so there does remain some doubt that this version of *Leucippo* was to have been performed at this time. Unsettled conditions prior to the war may have caused the breaks from tradition.

[103]The war, fought in Europe, North America, and India, saw France, Russia, and Austria allied against England and Prussia. Its causes were the 1748 loss of Silesia to Prussia, Russia's desire to expand into European politics, and colonial rivalry between France and England. In 1763, the status quo was restored in Central Europe, while England gained colonial supremacy over France.

[104]It had originally been presented 31 March 1741, in Dresden.

[105]Algarotti had revised the poetry of this scene for Hasse, and presumably had a copy of the music. (See p. 38).

[106]I-Bc, Ms. FF 244.

[107]It may well have been made, however, for Hasse eventually saved about twenty of his manuscripts dating from before 1757.

[108]*Nouveaux memoires ou observations sur l'Italie,* (London: Jean Nourse, 1764), v. II, p. 54.

[108a]*La Clemenza di Tito* included one substitute aria and at least eleven contrafacta, from *L'Olimpiade, Il Rè pastore,* and *Ezio II,* leaving at most only ten newly-composed arias. See Chapter IV, pp. 173-92. *Artaserse II* also included some prior-composed music, especially the sinfonia, borrowed from *Ezio II.*

[109]From there, they passed to his daughter Peppina on his death. In her old age, she sold the manuscripts to the Royal Conservatory in Milan, as stated in the *Allgemeine Musicalische Zeitung* of 1817 (v. 19, p. 506). Three, however, remained in Venice, where they became part of the collection of the Conservatorio Benedetto Marcello. There is no reason to believe that any Hasse operas were lost forever through the bombardment of Dresden; the only missing ones date from before 1731, and were probably lost long before 1760.

[110]On 7 October *Semiramide* was repeated in Warsaw. Hasse could not have been present.

[111]That *Il Trionfo di Clelia* was not written for Warsaw is evident from the autograph title page: *Il Trionfo di Clelia/ posto in Musica/ da/ Giovanni Adolfo Hasse/ detto il Sassone./ in Vienna/ 1762.*

[112]It was evidently finished in great haste. (See Chapter IV, pp. 152-169).

[113]Mennicke says he may have visited Dresden during the Carnival season of 1762, when Frederick Christian and Maria Antonia re-entered the city.

[114]The Warsaw librettos did not include the casts, so we do not know who accompanied the court to that city.

[115]Elisabeth Teyber (born 1746, known also as Teiber, Teuber, or Tayber) was a pupil of Hasse and Vittoria Tesi. She made her debut in this opera, at age 17. She was the elder sister of Theresa Teyber, the first Blonde in Mozart's *Entführung aus dem Serail,* and sang extensively in Vienna herself.

[116]Fürstenau, p. 370. This cast would fit any of the first three versions of the opera (a, b, or c) without transposition. I do not know Fürstenau's source for the information that the intended opera was indeed *Leucippo.* The 1748 libretto is misprinted MDCCXLXIII (for XLVIII) which Fürstenau may have mis-read as LXIII.

[117]A. G. Meissner, in his *Brüchstuche zur Biographie J. G. Naumanns* (Prague: 1803-04; Vienna: 1814, p. 124 footnote), says that the Hasses were owed 30,000 Taler, of which they were paid 12,000. This is the equivalent of five years' pay at 6000 Taler a year; there seems to be no other evidence for it. Logically, Hasse may have claimed he was owed 42,000 Taler (seven years' pay) of which he was paid 12,000 for the two years he officiated at Warsaw, leaving 30,000 unpaid. (Mennicke, p. 425.)

[118]This had been operating under the auspices of Biaggio Campagnari beginning in October 1746.

[119](F-Pn, Vm.[4] 35.) A copy, made in Dresden, of the 1756 version, is the only Hasse opera manuscript in the Turin Biblioteca Nazionale (Foà 52). This copy may well have been sent on ahead by Hasse so the cast could start learning the recitatives.

[120]Burney, for example, tells us that "Metastasio and Hasse, may be said, to be at the head of one of the principal sects, and Calsabigi and Gluck of another. The first, regarding all innovations as quackery, adhere to the ancient form of the musical drama, in which the poet and musician claim equal attention from an audience; the bard in the recitatives and narrative parts; and the composer in the airs, duos, and chorusses. The second party depend more on theatrical effects. . ." (*Present State*), v. I, p. 237.

[121]Mennicke, p. 428.

[122]*Present State*, v. I, p. 280.

[123]Mennicke, p. 432. But the autograph has no sign of any changes.

[124]This has been published in a modern edition as Volume I of the *Concentus Musicus* series, by the German Historical Institute in Rome. (Klaus Hortschansky, ed., Cologne: Volk, 1973).

[125]The autograph, however, has no copied sections, and thus must be a fair copy.

[126]Letter to Ortes, 5 October. (Mennicke, p. 433).

[127]Letter to Ortes, 30 October. (Mennicke, p. 434).

[128]Letter of L. Mozart, 19 October 1771. Wilhelm Bauer and Otto Deutsch, eds., *Mozart, Briefe und Aufzeichnungen* (Kassel: Bärenreiter, 1962) v. I, p. 444. "Kurz, mir ist leid. Die Serenata des Wolfgang hat die opera von Hasse so niedergeschlagen, dass ich es nicht beschreiben kann."

[129]*Briefe*, 2 November 1771, v. I, p. 449. "Heute ist die *Opera* des Hasse; weil aber der Papa nicht ausgeht, kann ich nicht hinein. Zum Glück weiss ich schier alle Arien auswendig, und also kann ich sie zu Hause in meinen Gedanken hören und sehen."

[130]The *Incurabili*, in which he had invested much of his savings, was near bankruptcy at this time (Hansell, "Sacred Music," p. 515).

[131]*Magazin der Musik*, (Hamburg: 2nd year, 1784), pp. 30-31. 10) Aus Italien, vom 3ten Januar) Zu Venedig ist der berühmte chursächsische Obercapellmeister, Herr Hasse, in einem hohen alter mit Tode abgegangen.5)

5) Es versteht sich von selbst, dass man bey der Nachricht, von dem Tode eines der verehrungswürdigsten Componisten, der in seiner Kunst mit die erste Zierde des Jahrhunderts gewesen ist, und in der Gattung der theatralischen Sing(s)musik keinen unter der ganzen Nation der Deutschen, als Händel, Graun, Gluck und Benda für seines Gleichen erkennt, nicht gern das Publicum mit der nackten, traurigen Botschaft: *auch Er ist gewesen!* abspeist. Unterdess weis ich nicht, wie es zugeht, dass ausser den bekannten Umständen, "dass er aus Bergedorf gebürtig, dass er einst mit Händel in London revalisirt, hernach viele Jahre nebst seiner Gattinn Faustina, der Vater und

der Stolz der glänzendisten Bühne Europas, der Dresdenschen war, nach ihrer Aufhebung sein Privatlleben in Wien fortsetze, (wo *Piramo und Thisbe* sein leztes, durch edlen Werteifer mit Gluck vielleicht auch vortreflichstes Werk ward) und zulezt in Venedig es beschlossen hat," dass, sage ich, ausser diesen Umständen, und seinen Werken, von denen ich vielleicht einmal eine vollständigere Recension im Magazin gebe, nie eben ein biographischer Detail von ihm bekannt geworden ist. Wer daher von seiner Lebensgeschichte besser als ich unterrichtet ist, und mir einen genauern Aufsatz, oder auch nur Data dazu zu selbst beliebiger Anwendung mittheilen wollte, der dürfte wohl so sicher auf das Wohlgefallen der Kunstfreunde rechnen, als auf die Dankbarkeit, wodurch er mich sich verbinden würde.

The "London journey" probably stems from Mattheson's translation of Mainwaring (*op. cit.*), published in Hamburg in 1761. *Piramo* was not Hasse's last opera, but it was certainly his most modern, the one which bears closest comparison to Gluck. (See Chapter II, p. 53).

CHAPTER II

[1]The term was not standard during Hasse's lifetime, the usual expression being the more general "dramma per musica." The term "opera seria" was, however, used and understood by the middle of the century.

[2]The generalizations made in the first part of this chapter refer to opere serie, and not to the other large secular works known as serenate, feste teatrali, or azioni teatrali. These are discussed separately in the last part of this chapter.

[3]Exceptions to this "lieto fine" are famous. Metastasio wrote only three dramas without it: *Didone abbandonata* (1723), his first seria libretto, *Catone in Utica* (1728), his third, (later rewritten with a happy ending), and *Attilio Regolo* (1740), which is neither tragic nor amorous, but rather heroic in its ending.

[4]These shorter arias, usually being only one stanza in length, are known by this name only in the latter half of the century. The name derives from *cavata*, an arioso section within a passage of recitativo obbligato; this term is defined as such in Walther's *Lexicon* of 1732.

[5]For the sake of clarity, simple final choruses, intended to be sung by the cast, will be referred to as cori. More complex pieces, meant for separate choirs of voices, shall be called choruses.

[6]This may reflect the structure of French classical tragedy.

[7]These are *Sesostrate, Didone abbandonata,* and *Catone in Utica*. The latter two, being tragedies, could not end with the usual joyful coro.

[8]Mennicke has two extensive chapters on Hasse's ouvertures and sinfonie: (*Hasse*, pp. 90-112, 142-199). Feste teatrali also use the Italian sinfonia, except for *Alcide al bivio* and *Piramo e Tisbe*, which have ouvertures.

[9]This has been known as such since at least 1925, when Gerber described it in *Der Operntypus Johann Adolf Hasses und seine textlichen Grundlagen* (Leipzig: Kistner und Siegel, 1925), p. 36. Downes has given the best modern English description in

his dissertation, *The Operas of Johann Christian Bach as a Reflection of the Dominant Trends in Opera Seria 1750-1780*, Ph.D. dissertation, Harvard University, 1958).

[10]An exceptional instance of an A_1 ritornello which modulates through several keys before reaching the tonic can be found in Chapter V, Musical Example IX.

[11]This term, and its separation into various types, has been invented and defined by Downes, *op. cit.*

[12]Manuscripts differ, and some autographs show that full da capo arias were made into half da capos at a later date, perhaps even after the work was performed. (See Chapter IV, pp. 154-155, for an example.)

[13]Of the two trios mentioned above, one is also through-composed. Note also the four-movement sinfonia used for this opera.

[14]Charles de Brosses praises the scene beginning, "Eccomi al fine," (II:15) added to *Artaserse*, in his *Lettres d'Italie* (Dijon: 1927), pp. 284-285, dated 1739. Johann Adolf Scheibe singles out for special attention the recitatives of Act III, scenes 4, 6 and 7 of *Tito Vespasiano*, in his *Critischer Musicus* (Leipzig: Breitkopf, 1745), pp. 781-2. (See Chapter VI, pp. 253-54, 277-78.) Neither critic specifically distinguishes these passages from recitativo semplice, however.

[15]Hansell (*Solo Voice*, pp.. 42-43, 59) includes these in his catalogue of Hasse's seventy-six cantatas, though he recognizes that they are hybrid pieces: *Antonio* as Cantata 23, "*Da quel salso elemento*," and "*Sei tu, Lidippe*," as Cantata 66.

[16]Aside from these two, (described below), only one cantata has more than three arias: Cantata 2, "*Ah Nice, ah gia rosseggia*," with four arias and a duet, dating from 1775. Only seven have instrumental preludes: Numbers 2, 3, 8, 24, 29, 39 and 67. Of these, only the last has a full three-part sinfonia.

[17]No other cantata has more than two voices.

[18]*Les Intermèdes Comiques Italiens au XVIIIe Siècle, en France et en Italie* (Paris: Editions du centre national de la Recherche Scientifique, 1972). Ortrun Landmann has also done much work in this area, in her *Quellenstudien zum Intermezzo Comico per Musica und zu seiner Geschichte in Dresden* (Ph.D. dissertation, University of Rostock, 1972).

[19]Brunelli, *op cit.*, v. II.

[20]Though Hansell says, "Its similarities to the chamber cantata are . . . easier to recognize than its resemblance to the other known genres of music composed by Hasse." (*Solo Voice*, p. 16.).

[21]The Milan copy (Part. tr. ms. 181), transcribed in Dresden, divides the larger chorus into two small groups: "solo coro" and "l'altro coro," implying the same division.

[22]Brunelli, *op. cit.*, v. II, p. 292.

[23]This idea has been put forward by Raymond Monelle ("Gluck and the 'Festa Teatrale,'" *Music and Letters*, v. 54, 1973, pp. 308-325.

CHAPTER III

[1]Notably *Gerone, II Rè pastore*, and *Demofoonte II.*

[2]Actually, only two operas that are found in autograph were not written for cities with resident cappelle: *Cajo Fabrizio a* (Rome, Teatro Capranica, 1732) and *L'Olimpiade b* (Turin, Teatro Reggio, 1765).

[3]This is the case when entire sections of recitative are copied over for revised operas.

[4]There is no aria between scenes 1 and 2, and the recitative is composed without a break.

[5]This autograph is probably a fair copy in any case. See above, p. 58.

[6]Vincenzo Manfredini, *Regole armoniche* (Venice: Guglielmo Zerletti, 1775), p. 134 (quoted in Mennicke, *Hasse*, p. 442). Hasse never wrote more than two new operas a year with the exception of the years 1729 to 1732, when he consistently wrote three or four a year, and 1737, which included the small *Atalanta.*

[7]This recitative passage may either have been originally written on a new fascicle and then discarded, or not written at all, with the idea that, as a small passage (only six lines long) it could later be composed and inserted between the arias.

CHAPTER IV

[1]Burney, *Present State*, pp. 310-311. Hasse (or Burney) exaggerated slightly. Hasse did set all of Metastasio's twenty-six opere serie except for *Temistocle*, but even with the most liberal definition of "setting," there do not seem to be more than ten that were set more than once, though another seven were performed at later times (in Dresden or Warsaw), apparently unchanged. Of the ten multiply-set operas, five were set twice; three, three times; and two, four times.

[2]Mennicke, for instance, includes *Olimpia in Ebuda* (London, 1740, a pasticcio), and *Lo Starnuto d'Ercole* and *Eurimedonte e Timocleone*, (Venice, 1746), two puppet operas, perhaps wholly on Hasse's music, but not authorized by him, as far as can be determined) among his works. (*Hasse*, p. 494.) Abert includes a *Cleonice* (Vienna, 1734) and an *Issipile* (Naples, 1742), which are both probably unauthorized productions. (*MGG*, col. 1776.) Hansell mentions a whole series of Neapolitan productions between 1744 and 1747, which were probably not connected to Hasse either. ("Sacred Music," pp. 294-295.)

[3]There are exceptions. Many scores from Berlin productions directed by Graun have survived. (These are usually altered only by transposition of the vocal parts.) Some of the music from London pasticci ascribed to Hasse was printed. A very few substitute arias are found in collections of loose arias.

Much music ascribed to Hasse can be located neither in authentic works nor in pasticci. Aside from at least sixty loose arias, there are two operas, *Didone abbandonata* (I-Mc, Noseda F-67), and *Tito Vespasiano* (I-Nc, Rari 7.4.10), which seem to be either pasticci or hitherto unidentified revisions. Otherwise, all of the hundreds of scores and thousands of loose arias attributed to Hasse seem to be his.

[4]Operas repeated in Dresden were, as far as can be determined, not revised. The two exceptions, *Leucippo c* (1751) and *Arminio IIb* (1753), seem to have been reworked for specific singers. Operas repeated in Warsaw likewise were probably not altered.

[5]Libretto by Salvi.

[6]Libretto by Pasquini.

[7]Based on Metastasio's *Alessandro nell'Indie*, revised by Boccardi.

[8]Perhaps the same as *Leucippo a* or *c*.

[9]Hasse may not have supervised this opera himself.

[10]With the probable exception of operas produced in Warsaw.

[11]The only exception to this is *Cleofide I* (Dresden, 1731), designed as a vehicle for Faustina, and so completely prima-donna oriented that Hasse could not produce the opera elsewhere, but instead had to revert to the original *Alessandro* of Metastasio.

[12]This correlates with the common placement of substitute texts, both in original and in revised versions. (See below and in Chapter III.) It also correlates with the evidence (in Chapter III) that Hasse composed his operas chronologically from beginning to end.

[12a]Another form of revision, borrowing arias from the works of other composers, is not considered in this thesis. It should be remembered that such practice was standard in the eighteenth century, and might reasonably be expected to occur in the works of Hasse.

[13]It is also possible that the substituted texts from old operas may have had new music, and that arias which used the same text may also have had new music. Yet the surviving arias from *Demofoonte Ib* (Bibliothèque Nationale Cons. D. 5468, 5469, in loose-aria form, out of order, and with no recitatives; identified "Venice, 1749," and missing four of the 26 arias listed in the libretto) show that this is not the case. (The music to *Leucippo b* and *Demetrio c* does not exist, at least in a form identified as such, though two of the new arias for the latter are to be found in the Sächsische Landesbibliothek, Mus. 1/F/28,12.) (See p. 295 n. 80.)

[14]"Arias newly added to the opera of Signor Hasse, of the Theatre of San Giov. Grisostomo, 1738." (I-Vnm, Cod. It. IV 478 (=10002)) (See p. 293 n. 64.)

[15]The text is a non-Metastasian substitute, which lessens the chance that someone else set the music.

[15a]Nor were his arias even new. All three are contrafacta taken from *Cajo Fabrizio a*. (Appiani did not sing in *Cajo Fabrizio a*, nor were the three arias sung by any one singer.)

[16]Alfred Loewenburg, *The Annals of Opera*, 1597-1940 (Geneva: Societas Bibliographica, 1955), v. 1, col. 207.

[17]Loewenburg lists a Dresden, 1761 performance, but this is impossible, since the court was in exile at this time. *Ibid.*

[18]F-Pn, Cons. D. 5435-5437.

[19]A secondary copy, British Museum ms. Add. 32027, gives Denner as the singer of Climene's part; this must be an error. Theresa Albuzzi, who sang in the Venetian production, made her Dresden debut in the following fall, and may have actually had her premiere with *Leucippo*: British Museum ms. Add. 32026 lists her as singing in *Ciro riconosciuto*, also performed during the Carnival season of 1751. (The libretto names Mingotti as singing her role.) She was hired on 1 January 1750. (See Chapter I, p. 26.)

[20]Most of the exceptions to this rule occur when the primo uomo also happens to be a father, as in *Attilio Regolo*.

[21]All 1745 scores seem to agree with each other. A Paris manuscript (F-Pn, Cons. D. 5454), which is Venetian in origin, was indeed copied from the autograph as it originally existed, for in most cases, arias and whole scenes match the autograph exactly, down to the placement of measures on the page.

[22]The numbering of the following scenes, 12 and 13, is not changed. This scene is only six lines long, but scene 12 is also on a new fascicle. This suggests that Hasse originally wished to set this aria, and thus when he composed the recitative he used a new fascicle, to provide space for the aria. Otherwise, he would have merely continued immediately into scene 12. At a later time, plans for the aria were dropped, and the libretto was printed without it. But at the last moment, Hasse found that he had the time to write it, and space to include it. This would not make sense if the entire scene had been added later, for the recitative would not have been found in the libretto either, and the following scenes would have had to have their numbering changed.

[23]There is no doubt that the scores are of the Dresden version, and not the Warsaw, even though they match the Warsaw libretto more closely. The Dresden-copied manuscripts all match the autograph, and give the date 1747 on them. The state of the autograph also belies the possibility that it is the result of two revisions, one for Dresden and a further one for Warsaw. The missing arias were indeed never set.

[24]The fifth is from *Gerone, tiranno di Siracusa*, of 1728. Though Caterina and Filippo Giorgi sang in both *Catone* and *Demetrio b* of 1740, neither sang the one aria from *Catone*.

[25]This part was sung in 1732 by Antonio Maria Bernacchi, one of the most famous castrati of the early eighteenth century. He was then forty-seven years old and at the end of his career. In 1740, Annibali sang the role.

[26]Faustina's other arias in 1740 go as high as f', g', and even a', but in general the 1732 arias are higher.

[27] The one minor-key aria in 1732 was given to Barsene.

[28] Thirteen of the 1731 arias were on substitute texts; of these, five can be identified as coming from earlier operas: *Gerone, La Sorella amante, Tigrane,* and *Ezio I.* At least two other substitute texts are parodies of arias from *Attalo* and *Gerone.*

[29] The Viennese cast is not known.

[30] The Viennese role is in soprano clef until Act III, scene 5, when it becomes tenor clef. Since tenor parts often were written in soprano clef, it must be presumed that Plistene had been a tenor all along, despite the rarity of the use of a tenor for the role of secondo uomo.

[31] The Dresden cappella had to hire a non-member, Lodovico Cornelius, to sing this second tenor part.

[32] This practice is also visible in first versions of operas, where the copyist has only been entering the words to the recitative. See Chapter III, pp. 77-83.

[33] Since it is hard to imagine that Viennese court singers were any less skilled than those of Dresden, it is possible that either Viennese taste allowed for simpler arias, or that Viennese singers were accustomed to adding more ornamentation themselves.

[34] I am deeply indebted to Eric Weimer, of the University of Chicago, for calling my attention to the great number of contrafacta in this opera.

[35] The final coro is also a paraphrase of the borrowed music's original text; the stereotypical content of cori removes any possible interest in this process.

[36] Strohm. *Opernarien,* v. 1, p. 260. "Man möchte fast sagen: Nicht der Inhalt oder gar der Affekt dieser beiden Texte stimmt überein und ermöglicht somit die Parodie, sondern geradezu das Desinteresse am Inhalt und die Abwesenheit von Affekt."

[37] D-Dl, Mus. 2477/F/22; US-BE, uncat. ms. 714; D-Mbs, mus. mss. 6312.

CHAPTER V

[1] If a distinction must be made, "protoclassic," with its prefix implying "first among the forms that can be identified with . . ." has none of the pejorative or non-musical characteristics of the others.

[2] Both examples below show revisions made in the manuscript (GB-Lbm, Add. 14,121), possibly in Porpora's hand.

[3] This orchestration is probably incomplete, for five staves were reserved at all points. A remnant of the 1711 version (cancelled following the new aria) shows that the orchestration was never intended to be elaborate. Yet it seems certain that there should be, for example, a repetition of the eighth-note string accompaniment on the repetition of the coloratura on "speranza" in A_2.

[4]According to Reinhard Strohm ("Hasse, Scarlatti, Rolli"), many of these aspects are still found in the cantatas or "arie da camera" of the time; especially typical are the longer B stanzas and extensive voice-crossing of the violins.

[5]Dropping the continuo was a practice limited to Naples. Strohm, "Hasse, Scarlatti, Rolli," p. 224.

CHAPTER VI

[1]"Berühmten Musico," *Fortsetzung neuester Reisen durch Deutschland,* (Hannover: 1740), p. 709.

[2](Leipzig: im Verlag des Verfassers und bey Brauns Erben, v. III, 1737), p. 9.

Wer ist der, so sich den Beyfall einer gantzen Nation, die man allezeit vor die beste Kennerin der Musik gehalten, erworben? Herr Capellmeister Hasse, ein Deutscher hat es so weit gebracht, dass ihn die Italiäner, als einen Ausländer, allen ihren einheimischen Componisten vorziehen. Ein gewisser Cavalier . . . hat mich selbsten versichert, dass, wenn eine Oper Beyfall in Italien finden sollte, müsste sie von Herrn Hassen componiret seyn.

[3](Leipzig: Breitkopf, 1745), p. 65.

Nunmehro, mein Herr! will ich ihnen einen Mann nennen, der seinen Ruhm und sein Glück nicht nur in Deutschland, sondern so gar in Italien, aufs höchste gebracht hat. Der Herr *Hasse* ist bekannt; und wer weis nicht, dass er den Ruhm seiner Nation unter den Italienern selbst auf das beste erhalten . . . Dieser grosse Mann hat die Melodie auf das höchste getrieben, und er wird selten darinnen ausschweifen. Seine Erfindungen stimmen mit dem Worten überein, und bisher sind ihm sehr wenige in diesem Stucke nachgekommen.

Zur Zeit haben wir nur noch einen Hassen und einen Graun. Auch die berühmtesten Italiener haben diese grossen Männer noch nie erreichen können.

[4]*Ibid.,* pp. 148-9.

Hasse und Graun, die auch von den Italienern bewundert werden, beweisen durch ihre erfindungsreichen, natürlichen und rührenden Werke, wie schön es ist, den guten Geschmack zu besitzen und auszuüben. Die Herstellung des guten Geschmacks in der Musik, ist also ein Werk des deutschen Witzes gewesen; und keine andere Nation wird sich dieses wahren Vorzuges rühmen können.

[5]*Ibid.,* pp. 766-767, from an "Abhandlung vom itzigen Geschmack in der Musik."

Es ist bereits zweener Männer Erwähnung geschoben, welche zu unsern Zeiten den Ruhm unsers Vaterlandes, in Ansehung der Musik aufs höchste gebracht haben. Hasse und Graun sind diese vertrefflichen Männer. Und man kann mit Recht sagen, dass sie diejenigen sind, mit welchen sich gleichsam ein neuer Periodus in der Musik anfängt. Sie haben uns die Schönheit des guten Geschmackes auf eine solche Art gewiesen, dass wir durch ihre Werke ganz deutlich erkennen, mit welchem Fleisse sie in die Fusstapfen derjenigen getreten sind, die ihnen auf so vielfältige Art vorgegangen waren, und dass sie wirklich den Endzweck erreichen haben, der die Absicht aller Bemühungen ihrer Vorgänger gewesen sind, der Natur zu folgen, ahmen ihnen nach, und die Deutschen folgen ihrem Beyspiele.

[6]v. I, p. 22.

(Die Deutschen haben keinen ihnen eigenen Geschmack in der Musik. Aber unser Händel und Telemann hommen wenigstens den Franzosen, und Hasse und Graun den Italiänern bey.)

This seems to refer primarily to orchestral music. Both Handel and Telemann cultivated the French "ouverture" extensively. The same point is made again on pages 37-38. Marpurg also mentions a greater taste in Germany for Italian music, and credits this to the melancholy character shared by the two nations, which sing and dance less than the French!

Telemann and Hasse are again linked together by Marpurg, slightly later, in his *Kritische Briefe über die Tonkunst* (Berlin: Birnstiel, 1760, XI Brief, 1 September 1759). He closes a lament on the death of Graun with the plea, "Stop, cursed Fates, and leave us a Telemann and Hasse for a while." ("Haltet ein, verwünschte Göttinnen, und lasset uns noch lange einen Telemann und Hassen!")

[7]*Vollkommene Kapellmeister*, (Hamburg: Herold, 1739), p. 128. ("Mein Freund nicht von gestern," p. 36.)

[8](Berlin: J. F. Voss, 1753), pp. 395-6.

Wir haben in Deutschland nicht auf den italiänischen Geschmack in der Musik geschworen. Unsere Componisten nehmen das Schöne auch aus den französischen Musik, wenn sie es da finde . . . Ueberhaupt . . . bestehet der gute Geschmack darinn, dass man dem Ohre schmeichelt und das Herz rühret; und in den italiänischen Opern ist der Geschmack hauptsächlich, von Herr Hassen und Herr Graunen vollkommen gemacht worden.

[9]*Op. cit.*, pp. 779-780.

Die Majestät zeiget sich sonderlich im Anfange, und giebt uns durch eine sehr scharfsinnige Tonfolge zu erkennen, was der Poet unter den Worten 'L'unico frutto e questo' sagen will.

[10]*Ibid.*, p. 782.

Gewiss, die Musik zu diesen Worten ist so vortrefflich, dass auch nicht der geringste Zweifel übrig bleiben kann, ob auch grosse und majestätische Eigenschaften durch die Töne auszudrücken sind. Dass überall Verstand und Einsicht darinnen herrschen, und dass alle Ausdrücke regelmässig und scharfsinning sind. Die Töne erklaren die Worte, und drücken die Empfindungen des Herzens und alle darinnen enthaltene Leidenschaften vollkommen aus.

[11]*Ibid.*, p. 784. "Die Abwechselungen der Affecten sind auf das scharfsinnigste bemerket."

[12]Op. cit., p. 533.

Man wage es im übrige nicht, wenn man nicht ein Liebling des Apollo selber ist; wenn man nicht den feurigsten Geist und die stärkste Beurtheilungskraft besitzet; wenn man nicht in der Wahl und der Ausführung gleich glücklich seyn kann; kurz, wenn man nicht ein Hasse selber ist; man wage es nicht, so sonderbare Dinge in der Natur ohne Unterschied nachzuahmen.

[13]*Ibid.*, p. 534.

Man wird die Geschicklichkeit des Meisters in dieser Arie bewundern, und niemals zweifeln, dass sich nicht auch Dinge ausser dem Gebiethe der menschlichen Affecten zur Nachahmung in der Musik sehr wohl schicken."

[14]*Ibid.*

Wir haben so viel Vertrauen zu dieser Art der Nachahmung, und wir sind so wenig darbey auf unsrer Hut, das wir öfters einen Sinn durch den andern täuschen lassen; oder wir lassen dem Gehör Dinge vorstellen, die sich sonst für dasselbe gar nicht schickten. Dinge die durch einen ganz andern Sinn sollten begriffen werden, scheinen auf einmal ihre Natur geändert zu haben: wir glauben sie in den Tönen zu finden, und wir finden sie wirklich darinnen, so weit sie sonst davon unterschieden sind.

[15]*Ibid.* "tobt ein solcher Aufruhr, den ein Herz, durch Begierde nach Ruhme und Ehre erhitzt, in allen Adern zu fühlen nur im Stande ist."

[16]Archivio Veneto, Anno XV, Nuova Serie, Tomo XXIX, Parte I, p. 116 ("Vecchio e rinomato").

[17]Dijon, 1927, vol. 1, p. 158.

Le fameux Saxon est aujourd'hui l'homme fêté. Je l'ai ouï chez lui aussi bien que la célèbrè Faustina, sa femme, qui chante d'un grand goût et d'une légèreté charmante; mais ce n'est plus une voix neuve. C'est sans contredit la plus complaisante et la meilleure femme du monde; mais ce n'est pas la meilleure chanteuse.

[18]*Ibid.*, II: 254.

Le fameux compositeur *Hasse, detto il Sassone,* pensa s'en étrangler avec moi à Venise, à propos de quelques douces représentations que je voulais lui faire, sur son indomptable préjugé. Mais, lui disais-je, avez-vous entendu quelque chose de notre musique? Savez-vous ce que c'est que nos opéras de Lulli, de Campra, de Destouches? Avez-vous jeté les yeux sur l'*Hippolyte* de notre Rameau? Moi! non, reprit-il, Dieu me garde de voir jamais ni d'entendre d'autre musique que l'italienne. . .

The passage ends, quite humorously, with Hasse becoming so angry that, "he had already become chromatic, and if Faustina, his wife, had not intervened, he would have harpooned me with a sixteenth-note, and struck me down with a sharp." (il tenait déjà du chromatique; et si la Faustine, sa femme, ne s'était mise entre nous deux, il m'allait harper avec une double croche et m'accabler de diezis.")

[19] *Ibid.*, 284-85.

. . . Latilla est aujourd'hui à la mode à Rome . . . mais ni lui, ni Terradellas et autres, ne sont de la force de ceux qui travaillaient le plus il y a peu d'années; et ceux-ci avaient surpassé leurs prédécesseurs, tels que Buononcini, Porta, l'aîné Scarlatti, Sarri, compositeur savant et triste, Porpora, naturel, mais peu inventif. Vinci, Adolphe Hasse, communément nommé le Saxon, et Leo, sont ceux dont les pièces ont le plus de réputation. Vinci est le Lulli de l'Italie, vrai, simple, naturel, expressif et le plus beau chant du monde, sans être recherché; il a beaucoup travaillé quoique mort jeune . . . *Artaxerce* passe pour son plus bel ouvrage; c'est en même temps l'une des meilleures pièces du Métastase . . . C'est le plus fameux opéra italien. Je ne l'ai pas vu jouer, mais je le connais pour l'avoir ouï presque tout entier en concerts, et j'en été charmé. Tout excellent qu'est cet ouvrage de Vinci, la scène du désespoir d'Artaban, ajoutée par le poete et mise en musique par le Sassone, surpasse peut-être encore toutes les autres. Le récitatif *Eccomi al fine in libertà del mio dolor* est admirable, ainsi que l'air qui suit: *Pallido il sole* . . . Je le regarde comme ce que j'ai de plus beau parmi sept ou huit cents airs que j'ai fait copier de diverses pièces. Le Saxon est très savant; ses opéras sont travaillés d'un grand goût d'expression et d'harmonie. Leo a un génie peu commun; il rend bien les images; son harmonie est très pure; ses chants sont d'une tournure agréable et delicate, pleins d'une invention recherchée. Ils ne sont pas trop faciles à déchiffrer, quoiq'en général la musique italienne soit plus aisée a lire et à chanter que la nôtre, outre qu'elle n'exige pas tant de voix. . .

Pergolèse, Bernasconi, Scarlatti, Jomelli, sont presque égaux aux trois dont je viens de parler. Parmi tous ces musiciens, mon auteur d'affection est Pergolèse. Ah! le joli génie, simple et naturel. On ne peut pas écrire avec plus de facilité, de grâces et de goût.

(There is no evidence that Metastasio was the author of the added scene, "Eccomi al fine." See p. 289 n. 25.)

[20]Mennicke, *Hasse*, p. 413.

J'ose aussi l'assurer que je connais peut'être autant que lui les ouvrages, le mérite et le talent de M. Hasse et de M. Haendel, mes contemporains et mes compatriotes, et que je suis tout aussi glorieux que M. Hasse peut l'être lui-meme du titre de Saxon par excellence que les Italiens lui ont donné et qu'à leur imitation M. de Voltaire a conféré en France, au héros du siècle. Si j'avois cru pouvoir placer cet artiste célèbre à côté de Pergolèse, j'aurais été trop jaloux de la gloire de ma patrie pour y manquer. Mais accabler les grands talents de louanges excessives et outrées sans y attacher ni de sens ni de vérité, c'est les outrager plutôt que les honorer.

[21]*Dictionnaire de Musique*, (Paris: Duchesne, 1768), p. 359.

Le premier *Orchestre* de l'Europe pour le nombre & l'intelligence des Symphonistes est celui de Naples; mais celui qui est le mieux distribué & forme l'ensemble le plus parfait est l'Orchestre de l'Opera du Roi de Pologne à Dresde, dirigé par l'illustre Hasse. (Ceci s'écrivoit en 1754.) (Voyez Pl. G. fig 1.)

[22]*Saggio sopra l'opera in musica*, (Berlin: 1755), p. 39.

[23](London, Jean Nourse, 1764), vol. III, pp. 95-6.

L'Opéra de 1758 étoit le Démophoon de l'Abbé Métastase, mis en musique pour cette année, par le célèbre Sassone: car les Opéras sont en Italie ce que sont en France les Motets, les Musiciens travillant à l'envi sur les mêmes paroles. Tout Naples assuroit que le Démophoon déjà mis en musique par plusieurs *Virtuoses*, n'avoit point encore été traité aussi supérieurement. On fait que ce Drame ressemble beaucoup, pour le sujet & pour l'intrigue, a l'Inès de Castro Françoise. On applaudit généralement au Duo qui terminoit le second Acte, & à d'autres morceaux de ce genre; mais les larmes se mêlèrent aux applaudissemens dans l'Ariette connue, *Misero Pargoletto*, que Timante adresse à son fils qu'il tient dans ses bras: l'expression de toute cette Ariette étoit celle de la Nature: les François présens à ce spectacle, oublièrent eux-mêmes l'air gauche du *Soprano* qui remplissoit le rôle de Timante, & la dissonance de sa voix avec l'énormité de sa taille, de ses bras, de ses jambes, pour mêler leurs larmes à celles des Napolitains.

[24]There is a review of this production in d'Orbessan's *"Voyage d'Italie,"* (*Melanges historiques critiques*, Paris: 1768, v. I, part 2, pp. 493ff.), which, according to Mennicke (*Hasse*, p. 410), includes some adverse criticism.

[25]*Op. cit.*, v. I, pp. 229-237, 273-278, 310-317, 343-350.

[26]*Ibid.*, v. I, pp. 349-350.

[27]*Ibid.*, v. I, p. 236. John Mainwaring was actually the first Englishman to mention Hasse, in his *Memoirs of the Life of the Late George Frederic Handel*, (London: R. & J. Dodsley, 1760) pp. 116-118. Mainwaring sums up Hasse's style quite succinctly: "He is remarkable for his fine elevated air, with hardly so much as the show of harmony to support it."

[28](Milano: Giuseppe Galeazzi, 3rd ed. 1777) (1st ed. 1775), pp. 29-30.

Giovanni *Hasse* si trasferî in Napoli nel 1722, per proseguire, e perfezionarsi nell'arte del contrappunto sotto la direzione del celebre Alessandro *Scarlatti*. Non occorre, che io qui esalti co' miei detti qual profitto ne ritraesse, poichè quantunque giovane di prima uscita, in breve tempo si fece conoscere, distinguere ed ammirare da tutta l'Europa. Colle maravigliose sue produzioni questo sî distinto Artista, dopo aver scritto con reiterate approvazione varie opere nei primi, e diversi Teatri d'Italia, abbracciò il servigio della Reale ed Elettorale Corte de Sassonia, dove per molti anni ha fatto molte bellissime Musiche de Chiesa, ed Opere per quel Teatro, dove per soddisfare al fino gusto di que' Sovrani, vi volevano sempre nuove e più finite composizione.

E assai tempo, che disiderano molti Professori, che questo grand'uomo dia al Pubblico per mezzo delle stampe, so non in tutto, almeno in parte, i suoi tanto applauditi lavori, acciò servano di modello e d'istruzione alla gioventù studiosa.

Egli però eccessivamento modesto, finora non ha mai voluto cedere alle altrui istanze, e finora restano delusi i desideri de' coltivatori della Musica. Quantunque abbracciasse, come si disse, il servigio Elettorale, non mancò in diversi anni di trasferirsi in Italia, ove scrisse Opere Teatrali, sempre bene accolto ed applaudito. La sua gran fama lo fece chiamare a Parigi sotto il governo di Luigi XV Rè di Francia, non meno che a Berlino dal Regnante Federico II Rè di Prussia, ove ebbe l'eguale successo, è ne riscosse l'universale ammirazione. Anche dall' Impero Corte ebbe molte distinzione e beneficinze; ed in quest' ultimi tempi l'Invitta Imperatrice MARIA THERESA gloriosamente Regnante si è servita di questo Maestro nelle occasione più luminose de' vari matrimone dell' Imperiale Famiglia.

Ristretta è l'epoca di questo grand' uomo, ma pure vi si scorge che in ogni tempo ed in ogno   parte fu apprezzato come lo meritava, ed ora vive placidamente in Venezia, pieno di gloria, e per eccellenza chiamato da Professori tutti *Il Padre della Musica.*

[29]V. 1, pp. 103-107; 3rd year, 4th quarter, pp. 135-139.   Hiller also produced several Hasse operas and oratorios between 1768 and 1784.

[30]*Wöchentliche Nachrichten,* 3rd year, 1st quarter, pp. 57-59.

[31]*Chronoligisch-thematisches Verzeichnis sämtlicher Tonwerke Wolfgang Amadé Mozart.* Dr. Ludwig Ritter von Kochel, (Wiesbaden: B & H, 7th ed., 1965), p. 13.

Mais que je vive, et un jour je lui offrirai un don digne d'elle et de toi: car avec ton sécours, j'égalerai la gloire de tous les grands hommes de ma patrie, je deviendrai immortel comme Händel, et Hasse, et mon nom sera aussi célèbre que celui de Bach.

[32](Mannheim, 1778-80).

[33]Mennicke, *Hasse,* p. 435.

[34]Hamburg, 2nd year, 1784), pp. 30-31. See Chapter I for the text (pp. 34-35).

[35]*Magazin der Musik,* 20 April 1785, 2:1, pp. 670-672.

[36](London: T. Becket, J. Robson, and G. Robinson, 1776-1789), v. IV, pp. 341, 446, 457, etc.

[37]*Op. cit.,* v. I, cols. 590-601. ("kurz und richtig.")

[38]V. III, pp. 275 ff.

[39]The memorial, with an incorrect date of Hasse's death (1784), still exists in the floor of the nave.

[40](Venice: Picotti, 1820).

[41](Berliner Beitrage zur Musikwissenschaft, ed. Hermann Abert, v. 2, 1925. Leipzig: Kistner und Siegel 1925). This thesis has just been reprinted by Olms (Hildesheim and New York: 1973).

[42]Chapter C: "Satztechnische Beschaffenheit der Aria," pp. 97-141.

[43]Gerber reaches the rather confusing conclusion that Hasse does indeed develop, but not chronologically. Perhaps a better expression would be that Hasse's experiments in this direction go far from his norm, but do not influence this norm.

[44]*Ibid.*, p. 143: "Hasse ist ein starrer unbeweglicher Typus, der den Einflüssen um sich her unterliegt, während sich seine Künstlerische Persönlichkeit bis zu einem ganz geringen Grade nur als produktive erweist."

[45]*Ibid.*, pp. 45-88.

[46]A typical 18th century one is by Carlo Goldoni: "Il primo Soprano, la prima Donna, e il Tenore, che sono i tre principali Attori del Dramma, devono cantare cinque Arie per ciascheduno, una patetica, una di bravura, una parlante, una di mezzo carettere, ed una brillante."

From his *Comedie*... Tomo XI (Venice: 1761), preface.

[47]*Op. cit.*, pp. 1-26.

[48]In fact it was not; for by 1730, two of Metastasio's seven opere serie had had tragic endings.

[49]Two different versions, both under Hasse's name, are found in Milan: Noseda 0 41-41 and Noseda 0 42-2. The copies of this aria in Brussels and Vienna, which I have not seen, may match either of these different versions. It is not at all certain that the versions in any of the four pasticci are actually by Hasse.

[50]Translation by John Hoole. *Dramas & Other Poems of the Abbe Pietro Metastasio* (London: H. Baldwin and Son, printers, 1800), v. I, p. 338.

[51]Another possibility, which he might have used, but also did not, would have been setting the first two lines to slow, melodic music, and the second two in a more excited manner.

[52]*Op. cit.*, pp. 88-97.

[53]The B stanza also begins on the first beat of the measure, but the A_1 and the A_2 stanzas, which use the same theme, begin on the third beat.   The other significant downbeat, first found on measure nine, beat one (♩ ♪ ♪ ♪), is found again on beat one in the A_1 stanza, but on beat three the next three times it appears. In fact, the copyist of the 1740 version purposely placed his bar-lines inconsistently (some bars being of four beats, and others of two) so that this downbeat would always fall on beat one.

[54]It is certain that the vocal line was sketched before the opening ritornello was, and that the latter follows the former chronologically in composition.

[55]*Op. cit.*, p. 162 ff.

[56]This actually shows only Hasse's skill in combining all of the motives of the aria, later, while writing the A ritornello, but it is impossible to hear the aria in this fashion.

WORK	LIBRETTIST	FIRST PERFORMANCE		GENRE
Antioco	Minato/Zeno/Feind	11 August 1721	Wolfenbüttel	opera seria
Antonio e Cleopatra	Ricciardi	summer, 1725	Naples	serenata
Sesostrate	Carasale	13 May 1726	Naples	opera seria
Miride e Damari	Carasale?	13 May 1726	Naples	intermezzo
Semele	Ricciardi	autumn, 1726	Naples	serenata
Astarto	Zeno/Pariati	December, 1726	Naples	opera seria
Larinda e Vanesio a	Salvi	December, 1726	Naples	intermezzo
Enea in Caonia	Stampiglia	1727	Naples	serenata
Gerone	Aureli	19 November 1727	Naples	opera seria
Porsugnacco e Grilletta	Molière/?	19 November 1727	Naples	intermezzo
Attalo	Silvani	spring, 1728	Naples	opera seria
Pantaleone e Carlotto	?	spring, 1728	Naples	intermezzo
La Contadina a	Belmuro	fall, 1728	Naples	intermezzo
Ulderica	?	29 January 1729	Naples	opera seria
La Fantesca	Saddumene	29 January 1729	Naples	intermezzo
La Sorella amante	?	spring, 1729	Naples	commedia

WORK	LIBRETTIST	FIRST PERFORMANCE		GENRE
Tigrane	Silvani	4 November 1729	Naples	opera seria
La Serva scaltra	?	4 November 1729	Naples	intermezzo
Artaserse Ia	Metastasio/Boldini	February, 1730	Venice	opera seria
Dalisa	Minato/Lalli ?	April, 1730	Parma	opera seria
Arminio I	Salvi	28 August 1730	Milan	opera seria
Ezio I	Metastasio	fall?, 1730 (or Carnival, 1730)	Naples	opera seria
Il Tutore a	?	fall?, 1730 (or Carnival, 1730)	Naples	intermezzo
Cleofide I (= Alessandro)	Metastasio/Boccardi	13 September 1731	Dresden	opera seria
Catone in Utica	Metastasio	26 December 1731	Turin	opera seria
Caio Fabrizio a	Zeno/ ?	12 January 1732	Rome	opera seria
Demetrio a	Metastasio	January, 1732	Venice	opera seria
Euristeo	Lalli	Ascension, 1732	Venice	opera seria
Issipile	Metastasio	fall?, 1732	Naples	opera seria
Siroe a	Metastasio	2 May 1733	Bologna	opera seria
Artaserse Ib	Metastasio	Carnival, 1734	Venice	opera seria
Caio Fabrizio b	Zeno/ ?	8 July 1734	Dresden	opera seria
L'Artigiano gentiluomo b	Salvi/ ?	8 July 1734	Dresden	intermezzo

WORK	LIBRETTIST	FIRST PERFORMANCE		GENRE
"Sei tu, Lidippe"	?	3 August 1734	Dresden	cantata pastorale
Tito Vespasiano Ia	Metastasio	24 September 1735	Pesaro	opera seria
Alessandro IIa	Metastasio	Carnival, 1736	Venice	opera seria
Senocrita	Pallavicino	27 February 1737	Dresden	opera seria
Atalanta	Pallavicino	26 July 1737	Dresden	opera seria
Don Tabarano b (= La Contadina)	Belmuro	26 July 1737	Dresden	intermezzo
Asteria	Pallavicino	3 August 1737	Dresden	opera seria
Alessandro IIb	Metastasio	Carnival, 1738	Venice	opera seria
Tito Vespasiano Ib	Metastasio	17 January 1738	Dresden	opera seria
Irene	Pallavicino	8 February 1738	Dresden	opera seria
Alfonso	Pallavicino	11 May 1738	Dresden	opera seria
Il Tutore b	?	11 May 1738	Dresden	intermezzo
Viriate	Metastasio?/Lalli	Carnival, 1739	Venice	opera seria
Demetrio b	Metastasio	8 February 1740	Dresden	opera seria
Artaserse Ic	Metastasio	9 September 1740	Dresden	opera seria
Numa	Pallavicino	7 October 1741	Hubertusburg	opera seria
Pimpinella e Marcantonio	Pallavicino	7 October 1741	Hubertusburg	intermezzo
Lucio Papirio	Pallavicino	18 January 1742	Dresden	opera seria

WORK	LIBRETTIST	FIRST PERFORMANCE		GENRE
Didone abbandonata	Metastasio/Algarotti	7 October 1742	Hubertusburg	opera seria
Alessandro IIc	Metastasio	Carnival, 1743	Venice	opera seria
L'Asilo d'amore	Metastasio	7 October 1743	Hubertusburg	festa teatrale
Ipermestra	Metastasio	8 January 1744	Vienna	opera seria
Antigono	Metastasio	20 January 1744 (or 10 October 1743)	Dresden	opera seria
Semiramide a	Metastasio	26 December 1744	Venice	opera seria
Arminio IIa	Pasquini	7 October 1745	Hubertusburg	opera seria
Demetrio c	Metastasio	Carnival, 1747	Venice	opera seria
Semiramide b	Metastasio	11 January 1747	Dresden	opera seria
La Spartana generosa	Pasquini	14 June 1747	Dresden	opera seria
Leucippo a	Pasquini	7 October 1747	Hubertusburg	opera seria
Demofoonte Ia	Metastasio	9 February 1748	Dresden	opera seria
Demofoonte Ib	Metastasio	Carnival, 1749	Venice	opera seria
Leucippo b	Pasquini	Ascension, 1749	Venice	opera seria
Il Natal di Giove	Metastasio	3 August 1749 (or 7 October 1749)	Hubertusburg	azione teatrale
Attilio Regolo	Metastasio	12 January 1750	Dresden	opera seria
Leucippo c	Pasquini	7 January 1751	Dresden	opera seria

WORK	LIBRETTIST	FIRST PERFORMANCE		GENRE
Ciro riconosciuto	Metastasio	20 January 1751	Dresden	opera seria
Ipermestra b	Metastasio	7 October 1751	Hubertusburg	opera seria
Adriano in Siria	Metastasio	17 January 1752	Dresden	opera seria
Arminio IIb	Pasquini/Migliavacca?	8 January 1753	Dresden	opera seria
Solimano	Migliavacca	5 February 1753	Dresden	opera seria
L'Eroe cinese	Metastasio	7 October 1753	Hubertusburg	opera seria
Artemisia	Migliavacca	6 February 1754	Dresden	opera seria
Ezio II	Metastasio	20 January 1755	Dresden	opera seria
Il Rè pastore	Metastasio	7 October 1755	Hubertusburg	opera seria
L'Olimpiade a	Metastasio	16 February 1756	Dresden	opera seria
Leucippo d	Pasquini	7 October 1756 (?)	Hubertusburg(?)	opera seria
Nitteti	Metastasio	Carnival, 1758	Venice	opera seria
Demofoonte II	Metastasio	4 November 1758	Naples	opera seria
La Clemenza di Tito II	Metastasio	20 January 1759	Naples	opera seria
Achille in Sciro	Metastasio	4 November 1759	Naples	opera seria
Artaserse II	Metastasio	20 January 1760	Naples	opera seria
Alcide al bivio	Metastasio	8 October 1760	Vienna	festa teatrale

WORK	LIBRETTIST	FIRST PERFORMANCE		GENRE
Zenobia	Metastasio	7 October 1761	Warsaw	opera seria
Il Trionfo di Clelia	Metastasio	27 April 1762	Vienna	opera seria
Siroe b	Metastasio	Carnival, 1763	Warsaw	opera seria
Leucippo e ?	Pasquini	7 October 1763 (planned)	Dresden	opera seria
Egeria	Metastasio	24 April 1764	Vienna	festa teatrale
L'Olimpiade b	Metastasio	26 December 1764	Turin	opera seria
Romolo ed Ersilia	Metastasio	6 August 1765	Innsbruck	opera seria
Partenope	Metastasio	9 September 1767	Vienna	festa teatrale
Piramo e Tisbe a	Coltellini	November 1768	Vienna	intermezzo tragico
Piramo e Tisbe b	Coltellini	September 1770	Vienna	intermezzo tragico
Ruggiero	Metastasio	16 October 1771	Milan	opera seria

APPENDIX B: Alphabetical list of all operas attributed to Hasse

All known operas performed under the name of Hasse are listed here: alphabetically and in chronological order. The great majority of these are to be found in the manuscript libretto catalogues of Sartori and Schatz, and in the published *Annals* of Loewenberg. Especially doubtful attributions have sources named. Pasticci are identified as such only when either other composers are named specifically, or when the libretto itself states that the music is by Hasse "e autori diversi." Where the music is identified in the libretto as being by Hasse with specific arias by one other composer, the second composer is identified.

First performances of Hasse operas are preceded by an asterisk (*); later performances which can be closely identified with Hasse are preceded by (H). Specific versions are identified only in these two cases. It should be remembered that all works with neither an asterisk nor an (H) are probably pasticci, whether or not they are identified as such.

Titles are standardized, with alternative titles provided. Hyphenated dates refer to a Carnival season beginning in December and continuing into the new year.

Achille in Sciro
    *Naples, 1759
    Berlin, 1766 (Mennicke)

Adriano in Siria
    *Dresden, 1752
    Naples, 1755
    Cassel, 1777

Alcide al bivio
    *Vienna, 1760
    (H)Vienna, 1761
    Florence, 1766
    Copenhagen, 1774
    Leipzig, 1777
    Vienna, 1781 (concert performance)
    Dresden, 1883 (as *Die Wahl des Herakles)*
    Ceský Krumlov, ? (Záloha)

Alessandro in Persia
    London, 1741 (pasticcio)

Alessandro nell'Indie
> *Dresden, 1731 (as *Cleofide)* (version I)
> Milan, 1732 (as *Cleofide;* Strohm: doubtful, probably by Predieri)
> Munich, 1735 (as *Cleofide)*
> *Venice, 1736 (version IIa)
> Naples, 1736 (with de Majo)
> Ferrara, 1737 (with Vivaldi)
> *Venice, 1738 (version IIb)
> Graz, 1738 (Müller: Mingotti)
> Verona, 1740
> Pressburg, 1741
> *Venice, 1743 (version IIc)
> Vienna, 1746
> Verona, 1754
> Berlin, 1754 (Mennick: 1753)
> Lucca, 1759
> Berlin, 1777 (as *Cleofide*)

Alfonso
> *Dresden, 1738

Andromeda
> Vienna, 1750 (pasticcio)

Annibale in Capua
> London, 1746 (pasticcio)

Antigono
> *Hubertusburg, 1743
> (H)Dresden, 1744
> Hamburg, 1744 (perhaps by Scalabrini)
> Naples, 1744 (with Palella)
> Brunswick, 1746 (with Schürmann)
> Florence, 1747 (listed on aria in F:Pn)
> Milan, 1747
> Verona, 1748 (with Galuppi)
> Parma, 1753 (as *Alessandro rè d'Epiro*)
> London, 1776 (pasticcio: Hansell)

Antioco
> *Brunswick, 1721

Antonino Commodo
>Brunswick, 1747 (pasticcio)

Antonio e Cleopatra
>*Naples, 1725

Armida Placata
>Vienna, 1750 (pasticcio)

Arminio
>*Milan, 1730 (libretto by Salvi) (version I)
>Milan, 1733 (listed on aria in GB-Lk)
>*Dresden, 1745 (Pasquini libretto. Autograph catalogued as *Egeste e Tusnelda* in I-Mc, after main characters, Segeste and Tusnelda, presumably to differentiate from Salvi's libretto.) (version IIa)
>Berlin, 1746-7
>Vienna, 1747 (ballets by Holzbauer)
>Brunswick, 1747 (some music by Schürmann)
>*Dresden, 1753 (version IIb)
>(H)Warsaw, 1761
>Berlin, 1773

Artaserse
>*Venice, 1730 (version Ia)
>Genoa, 1730 (Loewenberg: probably)
>Bologna, 1730 (diversi autori)
>Lucca, 1730
>Turin, 1730 (Strohm: pasticcio possibly with Giay)
>Milan, 1731 (Strohm: with Vinci)
>Verona, 1733
>*Venice 1734 (no author: probably Hasse) (version Ib)
>London, 1734 (pasticcio)
>Madrid, 1738 (Loewenberg: probably Hasse)
>Bergamo, 1738
>Graz, 1738
>Modena, 1739 (Schatz: probably Hass)
>Ljubljana, 1740
>*Dresden, 1740 (version Ic)
>Pressburg, 1741
>Bologna, 1745 (with Antonio Paganello)
>Ferrara, 1745 (with Vinci)
>Brunswick, 1751 (Loewenberg: probably Hasse)

Lübeck, 1752
London, 1754 (Loewenberg: "altered")
*Naples, 1760 (version II)
(H)Warsaw, 1760
(H?)Naples, 1762
Ferrara, 1764-5
Lodi, 1765
London, 1766

Artemisia
*Dresden, 1754
(H)Dresden, 1755
Berlin, 1777-8
Berlin, 1785-6

L'Artigiano gentiluomo (See *Larinda e Vanesio*)

L'Asilo d'amore
Naples, 1742 (Mennicke) (doubtful)
*Hubertusburg, 1743
Naples, 1744 (listed on US-BE score)
Leipzig, 1777

Astarto
*Naples, 1726 (with *Larinda e Vanesio*)
Milan, 1733 (listed on aria in GB-Lam)

Asteria
*Dresden, 1737 (August)
(H) Hubertusburg, 1737 (October)

Atalanta
*Dresden, 1737 (with *Don Tabarano*)

Attalo, rè di Bitinia
*Naples, 1728 (with *Pantaleone*)
Brussels, 1730 (Mennicke: possibly Hasse)
Ferrara, 1739

Attilio Regolo
*Dresden, 1750
Vienna, 1750
Rome, 1750 (probably not a performance)

Berlin, 1775
Rome, 1891

Bacocco e Serpilla: See *Serpilla e Bacocco*

II Baron Cespuglio
    Madrid, 1747 (almost certainly a pasticcio)
    Florence, 1751 (as *La Donna accorta.* Schatz: pasticcio)

La Baronessa d'Arbella: see *Larinda e Vanesio*

Berenice
    London, 1756 (Schatz: pasticcio)

II Bevitore
    Dresden, 1747
    Potsdam, 1749 (no author listed)
    Dresden, 1767

II Bottegaro gentiluomo: See *Larinda e Vanesio*

Cajo Fabrizio
    *Rome, 1732 (with *La Contadina*) (version a)
    Naples, 1733 (with *La Contadina*)
    London, 1733 (recitatives by Handel. 21 of 26 arias are by Hasse)
    Urbino, 1734
    *Dresden, 1734 (with *L'Artigiano gentiluomo*) (version b)
    Jaromeriz, 1734 (as *Pirro*)
    Venice, 1735
    Salzburg, 1737
    Leghorn, 1740 (pasticcio)
    Lucca, 1740
    Bologna, 1743 (Loewenberg: probably Hasse)
    Graz, 1743 (Loewenberg: probably Hasse)
    Frankfurt a.M., 1755
    Berlin, 1766
    Berlin, 1785

II Calandrano
    Frankfurt a.M., 1755 (Schatz: pasticcio)

II Capitan Galoppi e Malina serva finta d'duna vedova: **See *La Fantesca***

II Capitan Galoppo e Merlina serva finta d'una vedova: See *La Fantesca*

Il Capitan Galloppo: See *La Fantesca*

Catone in Utica
    *Turin, 1731-2
    Naples, 1746

Cesare in Egitto
    Holleschau, 1736 (pasticcio, possibly Giacomelli)

Circe
    Hamburg, 1734 (mainly Keiser)

Ciro riconosciuto
    *Dresden, 1751
    Prague, 1751
    Stuttgart, 1752
    (H)Warsaw, 1762

La Clemenza di Tito
    *Pesaro, 1735 (as *Tito Vespasiano*) (version Ia)
    *Dresden, 1738 (version Ib)
    Naples, 1738 (with Palella)
    Verona, 1738
    Madrid, 1739
    (H)Dresden, 1740
    Moscow, 1742
    Berlin, 1743 (Loewenberg: 1744)
    Ferrara, 1743 (pasticcio)
    Brunswick, 1743
    St. Petersburg, 1743
    Brunswick, 1744
    Hamburg, 1745 (prologue by Scalabrini)
    Dresden, 1746
    St. Petersburg, 1747
    Hamburg, 1748
    Copenhagen, 1748
    *Naples, 1759 (version II)
    Palermo, 1764
    London, 1765 (mainly Cocchi)
    Cremona, 1769-70
    Verona, 1773

Cleofide: See *Alessandro nell'Indie*

Cleonice: See *Demetrio*

La Contadina
    *Naples, 1728 (with P. Scarlatti's *Clitarco)*
    Venice, 1731 (no composer; possibly Hasse; with Porpora's
      Annibale)
    Trieste, 1731 (same libretto as above)
    Parma, 1734
    Naples, 1733 (with *Cajo Fabrizio*)
    (H)Dresden, 1737 (as *Don Tabarano,* with *Atalanta*)
    Bologna, 1738 (as *Don Tabarano*)
    Graz, 1738
    Milan, 1738 (no composer named; possible Hasse)
    Bergamo, 1738 (matches above)
    "Teatro de Lucque," 1740 (Mamczarz)
    Sinigaglia, 1741 (as *Don Tabarano,* Mamczarz)
    Florence, 1742 (Mamczarz)
    Venice, 1744 (Mamczarz)
    Bologna, 1744 (as *Il Tabarano*)
    Hamburg, 1745 (as *Il Tabarano*)
    Venice, 1746 (as *Il Tabarano,* with *Orlando Furioso*)
    Dresden, 1747 (as *Don Tabarano*)
    Berlin, 1748 (as *Don Tabarano*)
    Copenhagen, 1748, (as *Il Tabarano,* with *Temistocle*)
    Potsdam, 1748 (as *Don Tabarano:* Mamczarz)
    Brunswick, 1749 (as *Il Tabarano*)
    Berlin, 1750
    Prague, 1750 (as *Don Tabarano)*
    Wolfenbüttel, 1750 (as *Don Tabarano*)
    Frankfurt a.M., 1753 (as *Don Tabarano e la bella Contadina*)
    Treviso, 1755
    Copenhagen, 1756
    Dresden, 1763 (as *Don Tabarano*)

La Contessina
    Venice, 1743 (pasticcio)

La Costanza vincitrice: See *Dalisa*

Dafne e Leucippo: See *Leucippo*

Dalisa
>*Parma, 1730
>(H) Venice, 1730
>Cesena, 1741 (as *La Costanza vincitrice*)
>Florence, 1742

Demetrio
>*Venice, 1732 (version a)
>Genoa, 1732
>Bruna-Swoboda, 1733
>Verona, 1733
>Vienna, 1733 (Mennicke)
>Vienna, 1734 (as *Cleonice*: Schatz)
>Parma, 1736 (1737?)
>Ferrara, 1737 (Strohm: with Vivaldi)
>Rimini, 1737 (libretto says "Rimino")
>Venice, 1737
>Madrid, 1738
>Modena-Reggio, 1739 (pasticcio)
>Venice, 1740 (as *Cleonice*)
>*Dresden, 1740 (with Pergolesi's *La Serva padrona*) (version b)
>Cremona, 1740
>Lucca, 1741
>Hamburg, 1744 (Loewenberg: mostly Scalabrini)
>Gorizia, 1744-5
>Ferrara. 1746
>*Venice, 1747 (version c)
>Turin, 1748
>Milan, 1748 (pasticcio, Hansell: perhaps Hasse)
>Milan, 1749 (no composer named; doubtful)
>Cremona, 1749-50
>Frankfurt a.M., 1755 (Schatz: probably Hasse)
>Arezzo, 1762
>Cassel, 1767
>Mantua, 1770

Demofoonte
>*Dresden, 1748 (version Ia)
>*Venice, 1749 (version Ib)
>Mannheim, 1750
>Naples, 1750
>Vicenza, 1753-4
>London, 1755 (pasticcio)

*Naples, 1758 (version II)
(H)Warsaw, 1759
Catania, 1760
Valletta, 1765

Didone abbandonata
    *Hubertusburg, 1742
    (H)Dresden, 1743
    Naples, 1744
    London, 1748 (Schatz: mostly Hasse)
    Versailles, 1753
    Berlin, 1752-3
    Berlin, 1766 (Mennicke)
    Berlin, 1769
    Berlin, 1780 (planned and cancelled)

La Donna accorta: See *Il Baron Cespuglio*

Don Tabarano: See *La Contadina*

Egeria
    *Vienna, 1764
    Florence, 1764
    (H?) Naples, 1764

Enea in Caonia
    *Naples, 1727

Ercole al Termodonte
    Brunswick, 1749 (Schatz: mostly Hasse)

Die Erkannte Semiramis: See *Semiramide riconosciuto*

Erminia
    *? Naples, 1729 (Strohm: probably Hasse)

L'Eroe cinese
    *Hubertusburg, 1753
    (H)Warsaw, 1754 (Mennicke: Dresden)
    Hamburg, 1754
    Potsdam, 1773

Eumene
> London, 1765 (pasticcio)

Euridice
> Vienna, 1750 (pasticcio)

Euristeo
> *Venice, 1732
> Warsaw, 1733 (Manferrari)
> Ljubljana, 1733
> Padua, 1747 (Strohm: probably Caldara)

Eurymedonte e Timocleone
> Venice, 1746 (pasticcio)

Ezio
> *Naples, 1730 (with *Il Tutore)* (version I)
> *Dresden, 1755 (version II)
> London, 1755 (pasticcio)
> (H)Dresden, 1756
> Naples, 1772 (listed on B-Bc aria)
> Cassel, 1785 (Hansell)

La Fantesca
> *Naples, 1729 (with *Ulderica*)
> Rome, 1737 (as *Il Capitan Galoppi e Malina serva finta d'una vedova*)
> Leghorn, 1739 (as *Il Capitan Galoppo e Merlina serva finta d'una vedova*)
> Venice, 1741, (as *Il Capitan Galoppo;* Sonneck: Hasse)
> Dresden, 1747 (Mennicke)
> Venice, 1751 (as *Il Capital Galoppo*)
> Ravenna, 1752 (as *Il Capitan Galoppo*; Mamczarz)
> Lisbon and/or Salvaterra, 1753 (as *Capitan Galoppo*)
> Lisbon, 1758 (as *Capitan Galoppo*; Mamczarz)
> Dresden, 1767 (Mennicke)

Die Farbe macht die Königin
> Hamburg, 1737 (pasticcio)

La Finta tedesca: See *Pantaleone e Carlotta*

Galatea ed Acide
>Potsdam, 1748 (no author listed; Sonneck: mostly Hasse)

Gerone, tiranno di Siracusa
>*Naples, 1727 (with *Porsugnacco e Grilletta)*
>Corfu, 1733 (no composer listed; Schatz: Hasse)

Gianguir
>London, 1742 (pasticcio)

Il Giocatore
>Dresden, 1746 (Schatz)
>Potsdam, 1748 (Schatz)
>Frankfurt a.M., 1755 (Schatz)
>Frankfurt a.M., 1759 (Schatz)
>Mainz, 1757 (Schatz)
>Berlin, 1777 (Minnicke)

Die Hochzeit der Statira
>Hamburg, 1737 (pasticcio)

L'Ingratitudine punita
>London, 1748 (pasticcio)

L'Innocenza difesa
>Vienna, 1733 (Strohm; probably an alternative title for *Siroe*)

Ipermestra
>*Vienna, 1744 (ballets by Holzbauer, final coro by Predieri)
>   (version a)
>Naples, 1746 (with Palella)
>*Hubertusburg, 1751 (version b)
>(H)Dresden, 1752
>London, 1754 (with Lampugnani)

Irene
>*Dresden, 1738

Issipile
>*Naples, 1732
>Naples, 1742 (with Leo)
>Naples, 1763-4 (pasticcio)

Ixion
　　Brunswick, 1746 (with Bernasconi)

Larinda e Vanesio
　　*Naples, 1726 (with *Astarto)*
　　(H)Dresden, 1734 (with *Cajo Fabrizio,* as *L'Artigiano gentiluomo*)
　　St. Petersburg, 1734 (as *L'Artigiano gentiluomo*: Mamczarz)
　　Venice, 1739 (as *Il Bottegaro gentiluomo,* with Chiarini's *Achille in sciro*)
　　Potsdam, 1755 (as *La Baronessa d'Arbella*: Mamczarz; extremely doubtful)

Lavinia: See *La Sorella amante*

Leucippo
　　*Hubertusburg, 1747 (version a)
　　Brunswick, 1747
　　(H)Dresden, 1748
　　Salzthal, 1748 (as *Dafne e Leucippo*)
　　Vienna, 1748
　　*Venice, 1749 (version b)
　　*Dresden, 1751 (version c)
　　Prague, 1752
　　Frankfurt a.M., 1754
　　*Hubertusburg, 1756 (probably planned, but not performed) (version d)
　　Mannheim, 1757
　　Pressburg, 1759
　　Dresden, 1761 (Loewenberg. Doubtful)
　　*Hubertusburg, 1763 (Mennicke: rehearsed but not performed) (version e)
　　London, 1764 (or 1755; pasticcio: Hansell)
　　Berlin, 1765
　　Brunswick, 1765

Lucio Papirio
　　*Dresden, 1742
　　Brunswick, 1744 (Loewenberg: recitatives by Schürmann)
　　Naples, 1746
　　Berlin, 1766
　　Berlin, 1784

The Maid of the Mill
>London, 1765 (two arias attributed to Hasse)
>London, 1781 (see above)
>London, 1791 (see above)
>London, 1808 (see above)

Miride e Damari
>*Naples, 1726 (with *Sesostrate*)

Il Natal di Giove
>*Hubertusburg, 1749
>? ; 1756 (B-Bc libretto)

Nerone
>London, 1753, (pasticcio)

Nicomede
>? , 1728 (Strohm: ms lost in war, probably *Attalo*)

Nitteti
>*Venice, 1758
>Florence, 1758
>(H) Warsaw, 1759
>Lodi, 1765

Numa
>*Hubertusburg, 1741 (with *Pimpinella*)
>(H)Dresden, 1743 (with *Pimpinella*)

L'Olimpiade
>*Dresden, 1756 (version a)
>(H) Warsaw, 1761
>*Turin, 1764-5 (version b)

Olimpia in Ebuda
>London, 1740 (pasticcio)

Orfeo
>London, 1735 (pasticcio)
>London, 1736 (pasticcio)

Oronte, rè di Sciti
>   Graz, 1742 (mostly Scalabrini)
>   Hamburg, 1745 (mostly Scalabrini)

Pandolfo; See *Il Tutore*

Pantaleone e Carlotta
>   *Naples, 1728 (with *Attalo*)
>   St. Petersburg, 1734 (Mamczarz)
>   Naples, 1734 (with Conti's *Cajo Marzio Coriolano*)
>   Hamburg, 1746 (as *La Finta tedesca*; Müller)
>   Pescia, 1748 (as *La Finta tedesca*)
>   Potsdam 1749 (as *La Finta tedesca*)
>   Copenhagen, 1756 (as *La Finta tedesca)*

Partenope
>   *Vienna, 1767
>   (H?)Naples, 1767
>   (H?)Palermo, 1767
>   Berlin, 1767
>   Potsdam, 1775

Penelope
>   London, 1754 (pasticcio)

La Petite Maison
>   Paris, 1757 (pasticcio; one aria attributed to Hasse)

Pharamundus
>   Wolfenbüttel, 1748 (pasticcio)

Pimpinella e Marcantonio
>   *Hubertusburg, 1741 (with *Numa)*
>   (H)Dresden, 1743 (with *Numa*)
>   Versailles, 1753 (with *Didone abbandonata*)

Piramo e Tisbe
>   *Vienna, 1768 (version a)
>   *Vienna, 1770 (version b)
>   Potsdam, 1771
>   Hamburg, 1774
>   Dresden, 1775 (Schatz: 1776)

London, 1776 (libretto says Rauzzini; printed excerpts include
  Hasse)
Mainz, 1777
Frankfurt a.M., 1777
Copenhagen, 1778
Berlin, 1782
Cologne, 1939 (in German translation)

Pirro: See *Cajo Fabrizio*

Porsugnacco e Grilletta
    *Naples, 1727 (with *Gerone*)
    London, 1737 (Mamczarz: perhaps Hasse)
    Dresden, 1747 (Mennicke)

Il Rè pastore
    *Hubertusburg, 1755
    (H)Dresden, 1756
    London, 1757
    (H?)Vienna, 1760 (private performance)
    (H)Warsaw, 1762
    Potsdam, 1770

Rimario e Grillantea
    *Dresden, 1739
    Dresden, 1883

Romolo ed Ersilia
    *Innsbruck, 1765
    (H?) Naples, 1765-6
    Leipzig, 1766 (concert performance)
    Leipzig, 1768
    Hamburg, 1775
    Venice, 1795
    Ceský Krumlov, ? (Záloha)

Rosmira
    Ljubljana, 1740 (pasticcio)

Ruggiero, ovvero l'eroica gratitudine
    *Milan, 1771
    (H)Naples, 1772

Sabrina
>London, 1737 (pasticcio)

Segeste e Tusnelda: See *Arminio*

Semele, o sia la richiesta fatale
>*Naples, 1726

Semiramide riconosciuta
>*Venice, 1744-5 (version a)
>S. Giovanni in Pesiceto, 1745 (Loewenberg)
>Graz, 1746
>Prague, 1746
>Leipzig, 1746
>*Dresden, 1747 (version b)
>Brescia, 1748
>London, 1748
>Brunswick, 1748 (as *Die Erkannte Semiramis,* recitatives and some
>   arias by Schürmann)
>Prague, 1760
>(H)Warsaw, 1760

Senocrita
>*Dresden, 1737

Serpilla e Bacocco
>Trieste, 1731 (Mennicke) (Probably by Porta)
>Venice, 1739 (Lazarevich: pasticcio of Orlandini's intermezzo,
>   with one aria by Hasse)

La Serva padrona ossia la serva favorita
>Turin, 1730 (Hansell: pasticcio)

La Serva scaltra ovvero la moglie a forza
>*Naples, 1729 (with *Tigrane)*
>Venice, 1737 (with Albinoni's *Ardelinda)*
>Potsdam, 1752 (possibly Hasse)

Sesostrate
>*Naples, 1726 (with *Miride e Damari)*

Siroe, rè di Persia
>*Bologna, 1733 (version a)

Vienna, 1733 (under title *L'Innocenza difesa* (?): Strohm)
Bologna, 1735
London, 1736 (mostly Hasse)
Florence, 1736
Padua, 1737
Graz, 1738
Madrid, 1739
Parma, 1742 (no composer listed; Loewenberg: Hasse)
Rimini, 1743
Naples, 1747
Lucca, 1748
*Warsaw, 1763 (version b)
(H) Dresden, 1763
(H?)Vienna, 1763
London, 1764
Siena, 1765
Brunswick, 1767 (pasticcio)

Il Sogno di Scipione
Warsaw, 1758 (Schatz. Doubtful: Mennicke)

Solimano
*Dresden, 1753
(H)Dresden 1754
London, 1758 (pasticcio; Hansell)
Pesaro, 1772 (Loewenberg: doubtful)

La Sorella amante
*Naples, 1729 (no composer listed on libretto; autograph score in
D-Dl, under *Lavinia*)
Valletta, 1736

La Spartana generosa, ovvero Archidamia
*Dresden, 1747
(H)Dresden, 1748

Lo Specchio della verità
Vienna, 1733 (pasticcio: Grove)

Lo Starnuto d'Ercole
Venice, 1746 (certainly a pasticcio)

The Stratagem
> London, 1761 (pasticcio: Grove)

A Summer's Tale
> London, 1765 (two arias attributed to Hasse)

Il Tabarano: See *La Contadina*

Tarconte, principe de' Volsci
> Vienna, 1734 (pasticcio: Grove)

Tigrane
> *Naples, 1729, (with *La Serva scaltra)*
> Naples, 1745 (with Palella)

Tito Vespasiano ovvero la clemenza de Tito: See *La Clemenza de Tito*

Tomiri
> Brunswick, 1749 (pasticcio)

Tom Jones
> London, 1769 (one aria attributed to Hasse)

Il Trionfo della fedeltà
> Berlin, 1753 (pasticcio) (Originally written by Maria Antonia Walpurgis with help of Hasse. Hasse not given credit; thus not to be considered a pasticcio. Performance in question a true pasticcio)

Il Trionfo di Clelia
> *Vienna, 1762
> (H)Warsaw, 1762
> (H?) Naples, 1763
> Prague, 1766
> Ceský Krumlov, ? (Záloha)

The Tutor: See *Il Tutore*

Il Tutore
> *Naples, 1730 (with *Ezio)*
> (H) Dresden, 1738 (with *Alfonso)*
> Rome, 1739 (as *Pandolfo*; Mamczarz)
> Venice, 1739 (as *Pandolfo*, with Chiarini's *Achille in Sciro*)

Pardo, 1740
Hamburg, 1744 (as *Il Tutore e la pupilla*)
Venice, 1745 (as *Pandolfo,* Mamczarz)
Venice, 1746 (as *Pandolfo,* Mamczarz)
Bologna, 1746
Vienna, 1747 (as *Il Tutore e la pupilla)*
Florence, 1747
London, 1759 (as *The Tutor*)
London, 1762 (as *Il Tutore e la pupilla*)
Vienna, 1771 (as *Il Tutore e la pupilla*)
Paris, 1797 (as *Pandolfo*: Mamczarz)

Il Tutore e la pupilla: See *Il Tutore*

Ulderica
         *Naples, 1729 (with *La Fantesca*)

La Vedova ingegnosa
         Dresden, 1747 (probably a pasticcio)

Viriate
         *Venice, 1739
         Copenhagen, 1750

Die Wahl des Herakles: See *Alcide al bivio*

Zenobia
         Warsaw, 1761
         (H?)Vienna, 1763

APPENDIX C: Chronological list of all operas attributed to Hasse

This is intended to be a cross-reference to Appendix B. Pasticci and suspect performances are not usually identified. Operas supervised by Hasse are indicated by asterisks for first performances, (H) for revivals. See Appendix B for sources and further information.

1721

Antioco, Brunswick

1725

Antonio e Cleopatra, Naples

1726

Astarto, Naples
Larinda e Vanesio, Naples (with *Astarto*)
Miride e Damari, Naples (with *Sesostrate*)
Semele, o sia la richiesta fatale, Naples
Sesostrate, Naples

1727

Enea in Caonia, Naples
Gerone, tiranno di Siracusa, Naples
Porsuganacco e Grilletta, Naples (with *Gerone*)

1728

Attalo, rè di Bitinia, Naples
La Contadina, Naples
Pantaleone e Carlotta Naples (with *Attalo*)

1729

*? *Erminia*, Naples
La Fantesca, Naples (with *Ulderica*)
La Serva scaltra, Naples (with *Tigrane*)
La Sorella amante, Naples
Tigrane, Naples
Ulderica, Naples

1730

Arminio, Milan (version I)
Artaserse, Bologna
Artaserse, Genoa
Artaserse, Lucca
Artaserse, Turin
Artaserse, Venice (version Ia)
Attalo, Brussels
Dalisa, Parma
(H)*Dalisa*, Venice
Ezio, Naples (version I)

La Serva padrona, ossia la serva favorita, Turin
Il Tutore, Naples (with *Ezio*)

1731

*Alessandro nell'Indie, Dresden (as *Cleofide*; version I)
*Catone in Utica, Turin
La contadina, Trieste
La Contadina, Venice
Serpilla e Bacocco, Trieste

1732

Alessandro nell'Indie, Milan
Arminio, Vienna
*Cajo Fabrizio, Rome (version a)
Demetrio, Genoa
*Demetrio, Venice (version a)
*Euristeo, Venice
*Issipile, Naples

1733

Arminio, Milan
Artaserse, Verona
Astarto, Milan
Cajo Fabrizio, London
Cajo Fabrizio, Naples
La Contadina, Naples (with *Cajo*)
Demetrio, Bruna-Swoboda
Demetrio, Verona
Demetrio, Vienna
Euristeo, Ljubljana
Euristeo, Warsaw
Gerone, Corfu
*Siroe, Bologna (version a)
Siroe, Vienna
Lo Specchio della verità, Vienna

1734

Artaserse, London
*Artaserse, Venice (version Ib)
*Cajo Fabrizio, Dresden (version b)
Cajo Fabrizio, Jaromeriz
Cajo Fabrizio, Urbino
Circe, Hamburg
La Contadina, Parma
Demetrio, Vienna
(H)*Larinda e Vanesio*, Dresden (with *Cajo*)
Larinda e Vanesio, St. Peterburg

Pantaleone, Naples
Pantaleone, St. Petersburg
Tarconte, principe de Volsci, Vienna

1735

Alessandro nell' Indie, Munich
Cajo Fabrizio, Venice
**La Clemenza di Tito*, Pesaro (as *Tito Vespasiano;* version Ia)
Orfeo, London

1736

Alessandro nell'Indie, Naples
**Alessandro nell'Indie*, Venice (version IIa)
Cesare in Egitto, Holleschau
Demetrio, Parma
Orfeo, London
Siroe, Florence
Siroe, London
La Sorella amante, Valletta

1737

Alessandro nell'Indie, Ferrara
*Asteria, Dresden (August)
Atalanta, Dresden
(H)*Atalanta*, Hubertusburg (October)
Cajo Fabrizio, Salzburg
(H)*La Contadina*, Dresden (with *Atalanta*)
Demetrio, Ferrara
Demetrio, Rimini
Demetrio, Venice
La Fantesca, Rome
Die Farbe macht die Königin, Hamburg
Die Hochzeit der Statira, Hamburg
Porsugnacco, London
Sabrina, London
*Senocrita, Dresden
La Serva scaltra, Venice
Siroe, Padua

1738

Alessandro nell'Indie, Graz
**Alessandro nell'Indie*, Venice (version IIb)
*Alfonso, Dresden
Artaserse, Bergamo
Artaserse, Graz
Artaserse, Madrid
**La Clemenza di Tito*, Dresden (as *Tito Vespasiano*, version Ib)

La Clemenza de Tito, Naples
La Clemenza de Tito, Verona
La Contadina, Bergamo
La Contadina, Bologna
La Contadina, Graz
La Contadina, Milan
Demetrio, Madrid
*_Irene_, Dresden
Siroe, Graz
(H)*Il Tutore*, Dresden (with *Alfonso*)

1739

Artaserse, Modena
Attalo, Ferrara
La Clemenza di Tito, Madrid
Demetrio, Modena-Reggio
Demetrio, Naples
La Fantesca, Leghorn
Larinda e Vanesio, Venice
*?*Rimario e Grillantea*, Dresden
Siroe, Madrid
Il Tutore, Rome
Il Tutore, Venice
*_Viriate_, Venice

1740

Alessandro nell'Indie, Verona
Arminio, Vienna
*_Artaserse_, Dresden (version Ic)
Artaserse, Ljubljana
Cajo Fabrizio, Leghorn
Cajo Fabrizio, Lucca
(H)*La Clemenza de Tito*, Dresden
La Contadina, Teatro de Lucque
*_Demetrio_, Dresden (version b)
Demetrio, Venice
Demetrio, Cremona
Olimpia in Ebuda, London
Rosmira, Ljubljana
Il Tutore, Pardo

1741

Alessandro in Persia, London
Alessandro nell'Indie, Pressburg
Artaserse, Pressburg
La Contadina, Sinigaglia

Dalisa, Cesena
Demetrio, Lucca
La Fantesca, Venice
*Numa, Hubertusburg
**Pimpinella e Marcantonio*, Hubertusburg (with *Numa*)

1742

*? *Asilo d'amore*, Naples
La Clemenza de Tito, Moscow
La Contadina, Florence
Dalisa, Florence
**Didone abbandonata*, Hubertusburg
Gianguir, London
Issipile, Naples
*Lucio Papirio, Desden
Oronte, rè di Sciti, Graz
Siroe, Parma

1743

**Alessandro nell'Indie*, Venice (version IIc)
Antigono, Hubertusburg
**L'Asilo d'amore*, Hubertusburg (perhaps only a second
   performance)
Cajo Fabrizio, Bologna
Cajo Fabrizio, Graz
La Clemenza di Tito, Berlin
La Clemenza di Tito, Brunswick
La Clemenza di Tito, Ferrara
La Clemenza di Tito, St. Petersburg
La Contessina, Venice
(H)*Didone abbandonata*, Dresden
(H)*Numa*, Dresden
(H)*Pimpinella e Marcantonio*, Dresden (with *Numa*)
Siroe, Rimini

1744

(H),*Antigono*, Dresden
Antigono, Hamburg
Antigono, Naples
L'Asilo d'amore, Naples
La Clemenza di Tito, Berlin
La Clemenza di Tito, Brunswick
La Contadina, Bologna
La Contadina, Venice
Demetrio, Gorizia
Demetrio, Hamburg

Didone abbandonata, Naples
Ipermestra, Vienna (version a)
Lucio Papirio, Brunswick
Semiramide, Venice (version a)
Il Tutore, Hamburg

1745

Arminio, Dresden (version IIa)
Artaserse Bologna
Artaserse, Ferrara
La Clemenza di Tito, Hamburg
La Contadina, Hamburg
Oronte, rè di Sciti, Hamburg
Semiramide, S. Giovanni in Pesiceto
Tigrane, Naples
Il Tutore, Venice

1746

Alessandro nell'Indie, Vienna
Annibale in Capua, London
Antigono, Brunswick
Arminio, Berlin
Catone in Utica, Naples
La Clemenza di Tito, Dresden
La Contadina, Venice
Demetrio, Ferrara
Eurymedonte e Timocleone, Venice
Il Giocatore, Dresden
Ipermestra, Naples
Ixion, Brunswick
Lucio Papirio, Naples
Pantaleone, Hamburg
Semiramide, Graz
Semiramide, Leipzig
Semiramide, Prague
Lo Starnuto d'Ercole, Venice
Il Tutore, Bologna
Il Tutore, Venice

1747

Antigono, Florence
Antigono, Milan
Antonino Commodo, Brunswick
Arminio, Brunswick
Arminio, Vienna
Il Baron Cespuglio, Madrid

Il Bevitore, Dresden
La Clemenza di Tito, St. Petersburg
La Contadina, Dresden
*Demetrio, Venice (version c)
Euristeo, Padua
La Fantesca, Dresden
Leucippo, Brunswick
*Leucippo, Hubertusburg (version a)
Porsugnacco e Grilletta, Dresden
*Semiramide, Dresden (version b)
Siroe, Naples
*La Spartana generosa, Dresden
Il Tutore, Vienna
Il Tutore, Florence
La Vedova ingegnosa, Dresden

1748

Antigono, Verona
La Clemenza di Tito, Copenhagen
La Clemenza di Tito, Hamburg
La Contadina, Berlin
La Contadina, Copenhagen
La Contadina, Potsdam
Demetrio, Milan
Demetrio, Turin
*Demofoonte, Dresden (version Ia)
Didone abbandonata, London
La Fantesca, Dresden
Galatea ed Acide, Potsdam
Il Giocatore, Potsdam
L'Ingratitudine punita, London
(H)*Leucippo*, Dresden
Leucippo, Salzthal
Leucippo, Vienna
Pantaleone, Pescia
Pharamundus, Wolfenbüttel
Semiramide, Brescia
Semiramide, Brunswick
Semiramide, London
Siroe, Lucca
(H)*La Spartana generosa*, Dresden

1749

Il Bevitore, Potsdam
La Contadina, Brunswick

Demetrio, Cremona
Demetrio, Milan
*Demofoonte, Venice (version Ib)
Ercole al Termodonte, Brunswick
*Leucippo, Venice (version b)
*Il Natal di Giove, Hubertusburg
Pantaleone, Potsdam
Tomiri, Brunswick

1750

Andromeda, Vienna
Armida placata, Vienna
*Attilio Regolo, Dresden
Attilio Regolo, Vienna
Attilio Regolo, Rome
La Contadina, Berlin
La Contadina, Prague
La Contadina, Wolfenbüttel
Demofoonte, Mannheim
Demofoonte, Naples
Euridice, Vienna
Viriate, Copenhagen

1751

Artaserse, Brunswick
Il Baron Cespuglio, Florence
*Ciro riconosciuto, Dresden
Ciro riconosciuto, Prague
La Fantesca, Venice
*Ipermestra, Hubertusburg (version b)
*Leucippo, Dresden (version c)

1752

*Adriano in Siria, Dresden
Artaserse, Lübeck
Ciro riconosciuto, Stuttgart
Didone abbandonato, Berlin
La Fantesca, Ravenna
(H)*Ipermestra*, Dresden
Leucippo, Prague
La Serva scaltra, Potsdam

1753

Antigono Parma
*Arminio, Dresden (version IIb)
La Contadina, Frankfurt a.M.
Demofoonte, Vicenza

Didone abbandonata, Versailles
*L'Eroe cinese, Hubertusburg
La Fantesca, Lisbon/Salvaterra
Nerone, London
Pimpinella e Marcantonio, Versailles
*Solimano, Dresden
Il Trionfo della fedeltà, Berlin

1754

Alessandro nell'Indie, Verona
Alessandro nell'Indie, Berlin
Artaserse, London
*Artemisia, Dresden
L'Eroe cinese, Hamburg
(H)*L'Eroe cinese,* Warsaw
Ipermestra, London
Leucippo, Frankfurt a.M.
Penelope, London
(H)*Solimano,* Dresden

1755

Adriano in Siria, Naples
(H)*Artemisia,* Dresden
Cajo fabrizio, Frankfurt a.M.
Il Calandrano, Frankfurt a.M.
La Contadina, Treviso
Demetrio, Frankfurt a. M.
*Ezio, Dresden (version II)
Ezio, London
Demofoonte, London
Il Giocatore, Frankfurt a.M.
Larinda e Vanesio, Potsdam
*Il Rè pastore, Hubertusburg

1756

La Contadina, Copenhagen
(H)*Ezio,* Dresden
*Leucippo, Hubertusburg (version d?)
Il Natal di Giove, ?
*L'Olimpiade, Dresden (version a)
Pantaleone, Copenhagen
(H)*Il Rè pastore,* Dresden

1757

Il Giocatore, Mainz
Leucippo, Mannheim

La Petite Maison, Paris
Il Rè pastore, London

1758

*Demofoonte, Naples (version II)
La Fantesca, Lisbon
Nitteti, Florence
*Nitteti, Venice
Il Sogno di Scipione, Warsaw
Solimano, London

1759

*Achille in Sciro, Naples
Alessandro nell'Indie, Lucca
*La Clemenza di Tito, Naples (version II)
(H)*Demofoonte,* Warsaw
Il Giocatore, Frankfurt a.M.
Leucippo, Pressburg
(H)*Nitteti,* Warsaw
Il Tutore, London

1760

*Alcide al bivio, Vienna
*Artaserse, Naples (version II)
(H)*Artaserse,* Warsw
Demofoonte, Catania
(H?)*Il Rè pastore,* Vienna
Semiramide, Prague
(H)*Semiramide,* Warsaw

1761

(H)*Alcide al bivio,* Vienna
(H) *Arminio,* Warsaw
Leucippo, Dresden
(H)*L'Olimpiade,* Warsaw
The Stratagem, London
Zenobia, Warsaw

1762

(H?)*Artaserse,* Naples
(H)*Ciro riconosciuto,* Warsaw
Demetrio, Arezzo
(H) *Il Rè pastore,* Warsaw
*Il Trinofo di Clelia, Vienna
(H) *Il Trionfo di Clelia,* Warsaw
Il Tutore, London

1763

La Contadina, Dresden
Issipile, Naples

(H?)*Leucippo,* Hubertusburg (version e?)
(H)*Siroe,* Dresden
(H?)*Siroe,* Vienna
**Siroe,* Warsaw
(H?)*IlTrionfo di Clelia,* Naples
(H?)*Zenobia,* Vienna

1764

Artaserse, Ferrara
La Clemenza di Tito, Palermo
Egeria, Florence
(H?) *Egeria,* Naples
**Egeria,* Vienna
Leucippo, London
**L'Olimpiade,* Turin (version b)
Siroe, London

1765

Artaserse, Lodi
Berenice, London
La Clemenza de Tito, London
Demofoonte, Valletta
Eumene, London
Leucippo, Berlin
Leucippo, Brunswick
The Maid of the Mill, London
Nitteti, Lodi
**Romolo ed Ersilia,* Innsbruck
(H?) *Romolo ed Ersilia,* Naples
Siroe, Siena
A Summer's Tale, London

1766

Achille in Sciro, Berlin
Alcide al bivio, Florence
Artaserse, London
Cajo Fabrizio, Berlin
Didone abbandonata, Berlin
Lucio Papirio, Berlin
Romolo ed Ersilia, Leipzig
Il Trionfo di Clelia, Prague

1767

Il Bevitore, Dresden
Demetrio, Cassel
La Fantesca, Dresden
Partenope, Berlin

(H?) *Partenope*, Naples
Partenope, Palermo
*Partenope, Vienna
Siroe, Brunswick

1768

*Piramo e Tisbe, Vienna (version a)
Romolo ed Ersilia, Leipzig

1769

La Clemenza di Tito, Cremona
Didone abbandonata, Berlin
Tom Jones, London

1770

Demetrio, Mantua
*Piramo e Tisbe, Vienna (version b)
Il Rè pastore, Potsdam

1771

Piramo e Tisbe, Potsdam
*Ruggiero, Milan
Il Tutore, Vienna

1772

Ezio, Naples
(H)*Ruggiero*, Naples
Solimano, Pesaro

1773

Arminio, Berlin
La Clemenza di Tito, Verona
L'Eroe cinese, Potsdam

1774

Alcide al bivio, Copenhagen
Piramo e Tisbe, Hamburg

1775

Attilio Regolo, Berlin
Partenope, Potsdam
Piramo e Tisbe, Dresden
Romolo ed Ersilia, Hamburg

1776

Antigono, London
Piramo e Tisbe, Dresden
Piramo e Tisbe, London

1777

Adriano in Siria, Cassel
Alcide al bivio, Leipzig
Alessandro nell'Indie, Berlin

Artemisia, Berlin
L'Asilo d'amore, Leipzig
Il Giocatore, Berlin
Piramo e Tisbe, Frankfurt a.M.
Piramo e Tisbe, Mainz

1778
　　Piramo e Tisbe, Copenhagen

1780
　　Didone abbandonata, Berlin

1781
　　Alcide al bivio, Vienna
　　The Maid of the Mill, London

1782
　　Piramo e Tisbe, Berlin

1784
　　Lucio Papirio, Berlin

1785
　　Artemisia, Berlin
　　Cajo Fabrizio, Berlin
　　Ezio, Cassel

1791
　　The Maid of the Mill, London

1795
　　Romolo ed Ersilia, Venice

1797
　　Il Tutore, Paris

unknown, 18th century:
　　Alcide al bivio, Ceský Krumlov Castle
　　Romolo ed Ersilia, Ceský Krumlov Castle
　　Il Trionfo di Clelia, Ceský Krumlov Castle
　　Il Tutore, London

1808
　　The Maid of the Mill, London

1883
　　Alcide al bivio, Dresden

1883
　　Rimario e Grilantea, Dresden

1891
　　Attilio Regolo, Rome

1939
　　Piramo e Tisbe, Cologne

APPENDIX D: List by city of all operas attributed to Hasse

This is intended to be a second cross-reference to Appendix B. Pasticci and suspect performances are not usually indicated. Operas supervised by Hasse are indicated by asteriks for first performances, and (H) for revivals. See Appendix B for sources and further information.

Arezzo:	1762:	*Demetrio*
Bergamo:	1738:	*Artaserse*
	1738:	*La Contadina*
Berlin/Potsdam:	1743:	*La Clemenza di Tito*
	1744:	*La Clemenza di Tito*
	1746:	*Arminio*
	1748:	*La Contadina*
	1748:	*La Contadina* (P)
	1748:	*Galatea ed Acide* (P)
	1748:	*Il Giocatore* (P)
	1749:	*Il Bevitore* (P)
	1749:	*Pantaleone* (P)
	1750:	*La Contadina*
	1752:	*Didone abbandonata*
	1752:	*La Serva scaltra* (P)
	1753:	*Il Trionfo della fedeltà*
	1754:	*Alessandro nell'Indie*
	1755:	*Larinda e Vanesio* (P)
	1765:	*Leucippo*
	1766:	*Achille in Sciro*
	1766:	*Cajo Fabrizio*
	1766:	*Didone abbandonata*
	1766:	*Lucio Papirio*
	1767:	*Partenope*
	1769:	*Didone abbandonata*
	1770:	*Il Rè pastore* (P)
	1771:	*Piramo e Tisbe* (P)
	1773:	*Arminio*
	1773:	*L'Eroe cinese* (P)
	1775:	*Attilio Regolo*
	1775:	*Partenope* (P)
	1777:	*Alessandro nell'Indie*
	1777:	*Artemisia*
	1777:	*Il Giocatore*

	1780:	*Didone abbandonata*
	1782:	*Piramo e Tisbe*
	1784:	*Lucio Papirio*
	1785:	*Artemisia*
	1785:	*Cajo Fabrizio*
Bologna:	1730:	*Artaserse*
	*1733:	*Siroe*
	1738:	*La Contadina*
	1743:	*Cajo Fabrizio*
	1744:	*La Contadina*
	1745:	*Artaserse*
	1746:	*Il Tutore*
Brescia:	1748:	*Semiramide*
Bruna-Swoiboda:	1733:	*Demetrio*
Brunswick/ Wolfenbüttel:	*1721:	*Antioco*
	1743:	*La Clemenza di Tito*
	1744:	*La Clemenza di Tito*
	1744:	*Lucio papirio*
	1746:	*Antigono*
	1746:	*Ixion*
	1747:	*Antonino Commodo*
	1747:	*Arminio*
	1747:	*Leucippo*
	1748:	*Pharamundus* (W)
	1748:	*Semiramide*
	1749:	*La Contadina*
	1749:	*Ercole al Termodonte*
	1749:	*Tomiri*
	1750:	*La Contadina* (W)
	1751:	*Artaserse*
	1765:	*Leucippo*
	1767:	*Siroe*
Brussels:	1730:	*Attalo*
Cassel:	1767:	**Demetrio**
	1777:	**Adriano in Siria**
	1785:	**Ezio**

Catania:	1760:	*Demofoonte*
Cesena:	1741:	*Dalisa*
Ceský Krumlov Castle:	? :	*Alcide al bivio*
	? :	*Romolo ed Ersilia*
	? :	*Il Trionfo di Clelia*
Cologne:	1939:	*Piramo e Tisbe*
Copenhagen:	1748:	*La Clemenza di Tito*
	1748:	*La Contadina*
	1750:	*Viriate*
	1756:	*La Contadina*
	1756:	*Pantaleone*
	1774:	*Alcide al bivio*
	1778:	*Piramo e Tisbe*
Corfu:	1733:	*Gerone*
Cremona:	1740:	*Demetrio*
	1749:	*Demetrio*
	1769:	*La Clemenza di Tito*
Dresden/ Hubertusburg:	*1731:	*Alessandro nell'Indie* (as *Cleofide*, version I)
	*1734:	*Cajo Fabrizio* (version b)
	(H) 1734:	*Larinda e Vanesio*
	*1737:	*Asteria* (August performance)
	(H) 1737:	*Asteria* (October performance) (Hb)
	*1737:	*Atalanta*
	(H) 1737:	*La Contadina*
	*1737:	*Senocrita*
	*1738:	*Alfonso*
	*1738:	*La Clemenza di Tito* (as *Tito Vespasiano*, version Ib)
	*1738:	*Irene*
	(H) 1738:	*Il Tutore*
	*? 1739:	*Rimario e Grillantea*
	*1740:	*Artaserse* (version Ic)
	(H) 1740:	*La Clemenza di Tito*

*1740:	*Demetrio* (version b)
*1741:	*Numa* (Hb)
*1741:	*Pimpinella e Marcantonio* (Hb)
*1742:	*Didone abbandonata* (Hb)
*1742:	*Lucio Papirio*
*1743:	*Antigono* (Hb)
*1743:	*L'Asilo d'amore* (Hb)
(H) 1743:	*Didone abbandonata*
(H) 1743:	*Numa*
(H) 1743:	*Pimpinella e Marcantonio*
(H) 1744:	*Antigono*
*1745:	*Arminio* (version IIa)
1746:	*La Clemenza di Tito*
1746:	*Il Giocatore*
1747:	*Il Bevitore*
1747:	*La Contadina*
1747:	*La Fantesca*
*1747:	*Leucippo* (Hb)
1747:	*Porsugnacco e Grilletta*
*1747:	*Semiramide* (version b)
*1747:	*La Spartana generosa*
1747:	*La Vedova ingegnosa*
*1748:	*Demofoonte* (version Ia)
1748:	*La Fantesca*
(H) 1748:	*Leucippo*
(H) 1748:	*La Spartana generosa*
*1749:	*Il Natal di giove* (Hb)
*1750:	*Attilio Regolo*
*1751:	*Ciro riconosciuto*
*1751:	*Ipermestra* (version b) (Hb)
*1751:	*Leucippo* (version c)
*1752:	*Adriano in Siria*
(H) 1752:	*Ipermestra*
*1753:	*Arminio* (version IIb)
*1753:	*L'Eroe cinese* (Hb)
*1753:	*Solimano*
*1754:	*Artemisia*
(H) 1754:	*Solimano*
(H) 1755:	*Artemisia*
*1755:	*Ezio* (version II)
*1755:	*Il Rè pastore* (Hb)
(H) 1756:	*Ezio*
*1756:	*Leucippo* (version d?) (Hb)

	*1756:	*L'Olimpiade* (version a)
	(H) 1756:	*Il Rè pastore*
	1761:	*Leucippo*
	1763:	*La Contadina*
	*1763:	*Leucippo* (version e?) (Hb)
	(H) 1763:	*Siroe*
	1767:	*Il Bevitore*
	1767:	*La Fantesca*
	1775:	*Piramo e Tisbe*
	1776:	*Piramo e Tisbe*
	1883:	*Alcide al bivio*
	1883:	*Rimario e Grillantea*
Ferrara:	1737:	*Alessandro nell'Indie*
	1737:	*Demetrio*
	1739:	*Attalo*
	1743:	*La Clemenza di Tito*
	1745:	*Artaserse*
	1746:	*Demetrio*
	1764:	*Artaserse*
Florence	1736:	*Siroe*
	1742:	*La Contadina*
	1742:	*Dalisa*
	1747:	*Antigono*
	1747:	*Il Tutore*
	1751:	*Il Baron Cespuglio*
	1758:	*Nitteti*
	1764:	*Egeria*
	1766:	*Alcide al bivio*
Frankfurt a.M.:	1753:	*La Contadina*
	1754:	*Leucippo*
	1755:	*Cajo Fabrizio*
	1755:	*Il Calandrano*
	1755:	*Demetrio*
	1755:	*Il Giocatore*
	1759:	*Il Giocatore*
	1777:	*Piramo e Tisbe*
Genoa	1730:	*Artaserse*
	1732:	*Demetrio*
Gorizia	1744:	*Demetrio*

Graz	1738:	*Alessandro nell'Indie*
	1738:	*Artaserse*
	1738:	*La Contadina*
	1738:	*Siroe*
	1742:	*Oronte, rè di Sciti*
	1743:	*Cajo Fabrizio*
	1746:	*Semiramide*
Hamburg:	1734:	*Circe*
	1734:	*Die Farbe macht die Königin*
	1737:	*Die Hochzeit der Statira*
	1744:	*Antigono*
	1744:	*Demetrio*
	1744:	*Il Tutore*
	1745:	*La Clemenza di Tito*
	1745:	*La Contadina*
	1745:	*Oronte, rè di Sciti*
	1746:	*Pantaleone*
	1748:	*La Clemenza di Tito*
	1754:	*L'Eroe cinese*
	1774:	*Piramo e Tisbe*
	1775:	*Romolo ed Ersilia*
Holleschau	1736:	*Cesare in Egitto*
Innsbruck	*1765:	*Romolo ed Ersilia*
Jaromeriz	1734:	*Cajo Fabrizio*
Leghorn	1739:	*La Fantesca*
	1740:	*Cajo Fabrizio*
Leipzig	1746:	*Semiramide*
	1766:	*Romolo ed Ersilia*
	1768:	*Romolo ed Ersilia*
	1777:	*Alcide al bivio*
	1777:	*L'Asilo d'amore*
Lisbon and/ or Salvaterra	1753:	*La Fantesca*
	1758:	*La Fantesca*

Ljubljana	1733:	*Euristeo*
	1740:	*Artaserse*
	1740:	*Rosmira*
Lodi:	1765:	*Artaserse*
	1765:	*Nitteti*
London	1733:	*Cajo Fabrizio*
	1734:	*Artaserse*
	1735:	*Orfeo*
	1736:	*Orfeo*
	1736:	*Siroe*
	1737:	*Porsugnacco e Grilletta*
	1737:	*Sabrina*
	1740:	*Olimpia in Ebuda*
	1741:	*Alessandro in Persia*
	1742:	*Gianguir*
	1746:	*Annibale in Capua*
	1748:	*Didone abbandonata*
	1748:	*L'Ingratitudine punita*
	1748:	*Semiramide*
	1753:	*Nerone*
	1754:	*Artaserse*
	1754:	*Ipermestra*
	1754:	*Penelope*
	1755:	*Demofoonte*
	1755:	*Ezio*
	1757:	*Il Rè pastore*
	1758:	*Solimano*
	1759:	*Il Tutore*
	1761:	*The Stratagem*
	1762:	*Il Tutore*
	1764:	*Leucippo*
	1764:	*Siroe*
	1765:	*Berenice*
	1765:	*La Clemenza di Tito*
	1765:	*Eumene*
	1765:	*The Maid of the Mill*
	1765:	*A Summer's Tale*
	1766:	*Artaserse*
	1769:	*Tom Jones*
	1776:	*Antigono*
	1776:	*Piramo e Tisbe*

	1781:	*The Maid of the Mill*
	1791:	*The Maid of the Mill*
	1808:	*The Maid of the Mill*
	? :	*Il Tutore*
Lübeck:	1752:	*Artaserse*
Lucca:	1730:	*Artaserse*
	1740:	*Cajo Fabrizio*
	1741:	*Demetrio*
	1748:	*Siroe*
	1759:	*Alessandro nell'Indie*
Madrid:	1738:	*Artaserse*
	1738:	*Demetrio*
	1739:	*La Clemenza di Tito*
	1739:	*Siroe*
	1747:	*Il Baron Cespuglio*
Mainz:	1757:	*Il Giocatore*
	1777:	*Piramo e Tisbe*
Mannheim:	1750:	*Demofoonte*
	1757:	*Leucippo*
Mantua:	1770:	*Demetrio*
Milan:	*1730:	*Arminio*
	1732:	*Alessandro nell'Indie*
	1733:	*Arminio*
	1733:	*Astarto*
	1738:	*La Contadina*
	1747:	*Antigono*
	1748:	*Demetrio*
	1749:	*Demetrio*
	*1771:	*Ruggiero*
Modena/Reggio:	1739:	*Artaserse*
	1739:	*Demetrio* (R)
Moscow:	1742:	*La Clemenza di Tito*
Munich:	1735:	*Alessandro nell'Indie*

Naples

*1725:	*Antonio e Cleopatra*
*1726:	*Astarto*
*1726:	*Larinda e Vanesio*
*1726:	*Miride e Damari*
*1726:	*Semele, o sia la richiesta fatale*
*1726:	*Sesostrate*
*1727:	*Enea in Caonia*
*1727:	*Gerone, tiranno di Siracusa*
*1727:	*Porsugnacco e Grilletta*
*1728:	*Attalo, rè di Bitinia*
*1728:	*La Contadina*
*1728:	*Pantaleone e Carlotta*
*?1729:	*Erminia*
*1729:	*La Fantesca*
*1729:	*La Serva scaltra*
*1729:	*La Sorella amante*
*1729:	*Tigrane*
*1729:	*Ulderica*
*1730:	*Ezio*
*1730:	*Il Tutore*
*1732:	*Issipile*
1733:	*Cajo Fabrizio*
1733:	*La Contadina*
1734:	*Pantaleone*
1736:	*Alessandro nell'Indie*
1738:	*La Clemenza di Tito*
1739:	*Demetrio*
*?1742:	*L'Asilo d'amore*
1742:	*Issipile*
1744:	*Antigono*
1744:	*L'Asilo d'amore*
1744:	*Didone abbandonata*
1745:	*Tigrane*
1746:	*Catone in Utica*
1746:	*Ipermestra*
1746:	*Lucio Papirio*
1747:	*Siroe*
1750:	*Demofoonte*
1755:	*Adriano in Siria*
*1758:	*Demofoonte* (version II)
*1759:	*Achille in Sciro*
*1759:	*La Clemenza di Tito* (version II)
*1760:	*Artaserse* (version II)

	(H?) 1762:	*Artaserse*
	1763:	*Issipile*
	(H?) 1763:	*Il Trionfo di Clelia*
	(H?) 1764:	*Egeria*
	(H?) 1765:	*Romolo ed Ersilia*
	(H?) 1767:	*Partenope*
	1772:	*Ezio*
	(H) 1772:	*Ruggiero*
Padua:	1737:	*Siroe*
	1747:	*Euristeo*
Palermo:	1764:	*La Clemenza di Tito*
	1767:	*Partenope*
Pardo:	1740:	*Il Tutore*
Paris:	1757:	*La Petite Maison*
	1797:	*Il Tutore*
Parma:	1730:	*Dalisa*
	1734:	*La Contadina*
	1736:	*Demetrio*
	1742:	*Siroe*
	1753:	*Antigono*
Pesaro:	*1735:	*La Clemenza di Tito* (as *Tito Vespasiano*, version Ia)
	1772:	*Solimano*
Pescia:	1748:	*Pantaleone*
Prague:	1746:	*Semiramide*
	1750:	*La Contadina*
	1751:	*Ciro riconosciuto*
	1752:	*Leucippo*
	1760:	*Semiramide*
	1766:	*Il Trionfo di Clelia*
Pressburg:	1741:	*Alessandro nell'Indie*
	1741:	*Artaserse*
	1759:	*Leucippo*
Ravenna:	1752:	*La Fantesca*

| Rimini: | 1737: | *Demetrio* |
| | 1743: | *Siroe* |

Rome:	*1732:	*Cajo Fabrizio*
	1737:	*La Fantesca*
	1739:	*Il Tutore*
	1750:	*Attilio Regolo*
	1891:	*Attilio Regolo*

St. Petersburg:	1734:	*Larinda e Vanesio*
	1734:	*Pantaleone*
	1743:	*La Clemenza di Tito*
	1747:	*La Clemenza di Tito*

| Salzburg: | 1737: | *Cajo Fabrizio* |

| Salzthal: | 1748: | *Leucippo* |

| San Giovanni in Pesiceto: | 1745: | *Semiramide* |

| Siena: | 1765: | *Siroe* |

| Sinigaglia: | 1741: | *La Contadina* |

| Stuttgart: | 1752: | *Ciro riconosciuto* |

| Teatro de Lucque: | 1740: | *La Contadina* |

| Treviso: | 1755: | *La Contadina* |

| Trieste: | 1731: | *La Contadina* |
| | 1731: | *Serpilla e Bacocco* |

Turin:	1730:	*La Serva padrona, ossia la serva favorita*
	1730:	*Artaserse*
	*1731:	*Catone in Utica*
	1748:	*Demetrio*
	*1764:	*L'Olimpiade* (version b)

| Urbino: | 1734: | *Cajo Fabrizio* |

| Valletta: | 1736: | La Sorella amante |
| | 1765: | Demofoonte |

Venice:	*1730:	Artaserse (version Ia)
	(H) 1730:	Dalisa
	1731:	La Contadina
	*1732:	Demetrio (version a)
	*1732:	Euristeo
	*1734:	Artaserse (version Ib)
	1735:	Cajo Fabrizio
	*1736:	Alessandro nell'Indie (version IIa)
	1737:	Demetrio
	1737:	La Serva scaltra
	*1738:	Alessandro nell'Indie
	1739:	Larinda e Vanesio
	1739:	Il Tutore
	*1739:	Viriate
	1740:	Demetrio
	1741:	La Fantesca
	*1743:	Alessandro nell'Indio (version IIc)
	1743:	La Contessina
	1744:	La Contadina
	*1744:	Semiramide (version a)
	1745:	Il Tutore
	1746:	La Contadina
	1746:	Eurymedonte e Timocleone
	1746:	Lo Starnuto d'Ercole
	1746:	Il Tutore
	*1747:	Demetrio (version c)
	*1749:	Demofoonte (version Ib)
	*1749:	Leucippo (version b)
	1751:	La Fantesca
	*1758:	Nitteti
	1795:	Romolo ed Ersilia

Verona:	1733:	Artaserse
	1733:	Demetrio
	1738:	La Clemenza di Tito
	1740:	Alessandro nell'Indie
	1748:	Antigono
	1754:	Alessandro nell'Indie
	1773:	La Clemenza di Tito

Versailles:	1753:	*Didone abbandonata*
	1753:	*Pimpinella e Marcantonio*
Vicenza:	1753:	*Demofoonte*
Vienna:	1733:	*Arminio*
	1733:	*Demetrio*
	1733:	*Siroe*
	1733:	*Lo Specchio della verità*
	1734:	*Demetrio*
	1734:	*Tarconte, principe de' Volsci*
	1740:	*Arminio*
	*1744:	*Ipermestra* (version a)
	1746:	*Alessandro nell'Indie*
	1747:	*Arminio*
	1747:	*Il Tutore*
	1748:	*Leucippo*
	1750:	*Andromeda*
	1750:	*Armida placata*
	1750:	*Attilio Regolo*
	1750:	*Euridice*
	*1760:	*Alcide al bivio*
	(H?) 1760:	*Il Rè pastore*
	(H) 1761:	*Alcide al bivio*
	*1761:	*Zenobia*
	*1762:	*Il Trionfo di Clelia*
	(H?) 1763:	*Siroe*
	(H?) 1763:	*Zenobia*
	*1764:	*Egeria*
	*1767:	*Partenope*
	*1768:	*Piramo e Tisbe* (version a)
	*1770:	*Piramo e Tisbe* (version b)
	1771:	*Il Tutore*
	1781:	*Alcide al bivio*
Warsaw:	1733:	*Euristeo*
	(H) 1754:	*L'Eroe cinese*
	1758:	*Il Sogno di Scipione*
	(H) 1759:	*Demofoonte*
	(H) 1759:	*Nitteti*
	(H) 1760:	*Artaserse*
	(H) 1760:	*Semiramide*
	(H) 1761:	*Arminio*

(H) 1761:	*L'Olimpiade*
*1761:	*Zenobia*
(H) 1762:	*Ciro riconosciuto*
(H) 1762:	*Il Rè pastore*
(H) 1762:	*Il Trionfo di Clelia*
*1763:	*Siroe*

Unknown:	1756:	*Il Natal di Giove*

BIBLIOGRAPHY

(A) Books and Secondary Sources

Abert, Anna Amalie, "Hasse," *MGG*, v. 5, cols. 1771-88.

Algarotti, Francesco, *Saggio sopra l'opera in musica*, Livorno: Coltellini, 1763.

Allgemeine Musikalische Zeitung, Leipzig: Breitkopf und Härtel, Vols. II, III, XIX, 1800, 1801, 1816.

"Biographie von Adolf und Faustina Hasse," *Neujahrs geschenk an die zürchesche Jugend von der allgemeinen Musik-Gesellschaft*, v. XLI, 1853, pp. 3-5.

Bollert, Werner, "Hasse," *Enciclopedia dello Spettacolo*, v. 6, col. 193 ff.

Breitkopf, J. G. I., *The Breitkopf thematic catalogue*, Barry S. Brook, ed., New York: Dover, 1966.

Burney, Charles, *A General History of Music*, London: T. Becket, J. Robson, and G. Robinson, 1776-1789, 4 vols.

_____, *The Present State of Music in Germany, the Netherlands, and United Provinces*, London: T. Becket, J. Robson, G. Robinson, 1773-5, 2 vols.

Burt, Nathaniel, "Opera in Arcadia," *Musical Quarterly*, v. XLI, 1955, pp. 145-70.

Cramer, Carl Friedrich, *Magazin der musik*, Hamburg: in der Musicalischen Niederlage, 1783-1785.

Croce, Benedetto, *I Teatri di Napoli*, Naples: Tip. di Francesco Giannini, 1891. 4th ed, revised; Bari: Giuseppe Laterza e figli, 1947.

De Brosses, Charles, *Lettres d'Italie*, Dijon: 1927, 2 vols.

De Filippis, Felice, and Arnese, R., *Cronache del Teatro di san Carlo, 1737-1960*, Naples: Edizioni Politica Popolare, 1961-63, 2 vols.

De Gheltof, G. M. Urbani, *La "nuova Sirena" e il "Caro Sassone,"* Venice: M. Fontana, 1840.

Downes, E. O. D., "The Neapolitan Tradition in Opera," *Report of the Eighth Congress of the International Musicological Society, New York, 1961*, Kassel: Barenreiter, 1961, pp. 277-84.

_____, *The Operas of Johann Christian Bach as a Reflection of the Dominant Trends in Opera Seria, 1750-1780*, Ph. D. Dissertation, Harvard University, 1958.

_____, "*Secco* Recitative in Early Classical Opera Seria (1720-80)," *Journal of the American Musicological Society*, v. XIV, 1961, pp. 50-69.

Drewes, H., *Maria Antonia Walpurgis als Komponistin*, Ph.D. Dissertation, Köln, 1934.

Drummond, P., "The Concertos of J. A. Hasse," *Proceedings of the Royal Music Association*, v. 99 1973, pp. 91 ff.

Eitner, Robert, *Biographisch-bibliographisches Quellen Lexicon der Musiker*, Graz: Akademische Druck- and Verlagsanstalt, 1959, 11 vols.

Engel, Hans, "Hasses *Ruggiero* und Mozarts Festspiel *Ascanio*," Mozart-Jahrbach, 1960-61.

Florimo, Francesco, *La Scuola musicale di Napoli e i suoi conservatorii*, Naples: Vincenzo Morano, 1880-82, 4 vols.

Forkel, J. N., *Ueber Johann Sebastian Bachs Leben, Kunst und Kunstwerk*, Leipzig: Hoffmeister und Kühnel, 1802, Reprinted: Frankfurt a.M.: H. C. Grahl, 1950.

Freeman, Robert, *Opera without Drama*, Ph. D. Dissertation, Princeton University, 1967.

Fürstenau, Moritz, *Zur Geschichte der Musik und des Theaters am Hofe zu Dresden*, Dresden:　Rudolf Kuntze, 1861-62, 2 vols.

Gaspari, Gaetano, *Catologo della biblioteca del Liceo Musicale di Bologna*, Bologna: Libreria romagnoli dell'acqua, 1890-1905. Reprinted:　Bologna:　Arnoldo Forni, 1961, 4 vols.

Gerber, Ernst Ludwig, *Historisch-biographisches Lexicon der Tonkünstler*, Leipzig: Breitkopf, 1790-92, 2 vols.

Gerber, Rudolf, ed. Hasse's *Arminio*, preface and notes, *Das Erbe deutsche Musik*, vols. 26-27, Leipzig:　Breitkopf und Härtel, 1957.

_____, *Der Operntypus Johann Adolf Hasses und seine textlichen Grundlagen*, Leipzig: Kistner und Siegel, 1925.

Goldoni, Carlo, *Commedie*, Venice: 1761-1778, 17 vols.

Groppo, Antonio, *Cataloghi di tutti i drammi per musica recitati nei teatri di Venezia*, Venice:　A. Groppo, 1746.

Grosley de Troyes, Pierre Jean, *Nouveaux Memoires ou observations sur l'Italie*, London: Jean Nourse, 1764, 3 vols.

Hammitzsch, Martin, *Der moderne theaterbau, der höfische theaterbau, der anfang der modernen theaterbaukunst, ihre entwicklung und betätigung zur zeit der renaissance, des barock, und des rokoko*, Berlin:　E. Wasmuth, 1906.

Hansell, Sven, and Hansell, Kathleen, Review of Hasse's *Ruggiero*, ed. by Klaus Hortschansky, *JAMS*, v. 29, 1976, pp. 308-19.

Hansell, Sven Hostrup, "Sacred Music at the *Incurabili* in Venice at the Time of J. A. Hasse," *JAMS*, v. XXIII, 1970, pp. 282-301, 505-521.

_____, *The Solo Cantatas, Motets, and Antiphons of Johann Adolf Hasse*, Ph. D. Dissertation, University of Illinois, 1967.

_____, *Works for Solo Voice of Johann Adolph Hasse*, (1699-1783) (Detroit Studies in Music Bibliography, *v. 12), Detroit: Information Coordinators, Inc., 1968.*

Hawkins, Sir John, *A General History of Music*, London: T. Payne, 1776, 5 vols.

Heartz, Daniel, "Raaff's Last Aria; a Mozartean Idyll in the Spirit of Hasse," *Musical Quarterly*, v. 60, 1974, pp. 517 ff.

Heriot, Angus, *The Castrati in Opera*, London: Secker and Warburg, 1956.

Hiller, Johann Adam, *Wochentliche Nachrichten und Anmerkungen die Musik betreffend*, Leipzig: 1766-1769 (modern facsimile: Hildesheim: Olm, 1970).

Hortschansky, Klaus, ed., Hasse's *Ruggiero*, preface and notes, *Concentus Musicus*, V. 1, Volk: Köln, 1973.

Hücke, Helmuth, "Die neapolitanische Tradition in der Oper," *Report of the Eighth Congress of the International Musicological Society, New York, 1961*, Kassel: Bärenreiter, 1961, pp. 253-277.

Hughes-Hughes, Augustus, *Catalogue of Manuscript Music in the British Museum*, London: Printed for the British Museum, 1906-09, 3 vols.

Kamienski, Lucian, *Die Oratorien von Johann Adolf Hasse*, Leipzig: Breitkopf und Härtel, 1912.

Kandler, Franz Sales, *Cenni storico-critici della vita e delle opere di G. A. Hasse*, Venice: Picotti, 1820.

Keyssler, Johann Georg, *Fortsetzung neuester Reisen durch Deutschland*, Hannover: 1740.

Köchel, Ludwig Ritter Von, *Chronologisch-thematisches Verzeichnis sämtlicher Tonwerk Wolfgang Amadé Mozart*, Wiesbaden: Breitkopf und Härtel, 7th ed., 1965.

Krause, Christian Gottfried, *Von der Musikalischen Poesie*, Berlin: J. F. Voss, 1753.

Landmann, Ortrun, *Quellenstudien zum Intermezzo Comico per Musica und zu seiner Geschichte in Dresden*, Ph. D. Dissertation, University of Rostock, 1972.

Lazarevich, Gordana, "18th-Century Pasticcio: the Historian's Gordian Knot," *Analecta Musicologia*, v. 17, 1976, pp. 121-145.

Loewenberg, Alfred, *Annals of Opera*, 1597-1940, Geneva: Societas Bibliographica, 2nd ed., 1955, 2 vols.

Löffler, Fritz, *Das Alte Dresden, Geschichte seiner Bauten*, Dresden: Sachsenverlag Dresden, 1955.

[Mainwaring, John,] *Memoirs of the Life of the Late George Frederic Handel*, London: R. and J. Dodsley, 1760.

Mamczarz, Irene, *Les Intermèdes Comiques Italiens au XVIIIe Siècle, en France et en Italie*, Paris: Editions du centre national de la Recherche Scientifique, 1972.

Mancini, Giambattista, *Riflessioni pratiche sul canto figurato*, Milan: Giuseppe Galeazzi, 3rd ed., 1777, (1st ed., 1775).

Manfredini, Vincenzo, *Regole armoniche osieno precetti ragionati per apprendere principj della musica*, Venice: Guglielmi Zerletti, 1775.

Marpurg, Friedrich Wilhelm, *Historisch-kritische Beyträge zur Aufnahme der Musik*, Berlin: Schützens Wittwe, 1754-62, 5 vols.

[_____,] *Kritische Briefe über die Tonkunst*, Berlin: F. W. Birnstiel, 1760-64, 3 vols.

Marshall, Mrs. Julian, "Hasse," *Grove's Dictionary*, v. 4, pp. 129 ff. (List of works following article is by Alfred Loewenberg.)

Mattheson, Johann, *Vollkommene Kapellmeister*, Hamburg: Herold, 1739.

Mennicke, Carl, *Hasse und die Brüder Graun*, Leipzig: Breitkopf und Härtel, 1906.

_____, "Joh. Adolf Hasse. Eine biographische Skizze," *Sammelbände der Internationalen Musikgesellschaft*, v. V, 1903, pp. 230-44, 469-75,

Metastasio, Pietro Trapassi, detto, *Tutte le opere di Pietro Metastasio*, Bruno Brunelli, ed., Milan: Arnoldo Mondadori, 1943-54, 5 vols.

_____, *Dramas and Other Poems*, John Hoole, tr., London: H. Baldwin and Son, 1800, 3 vols.

Millner, Fredrick L., "Hasse and London's Opera of the Nobility," *The Music Review*, v. 35, 1974, pp. 240-246.

_____, Review of Hasse's *Ruggiero*, ed. by Kurt Hortschansky, *The Music Review*, v. 38, 1977, pp. 229-233.

Mizler, Lorenz Christoph, *Neu-eröffnete Musikalische Bibliothek*, Leipzig: im Verlag des Verfassers und bey Brauns Erben, 1736-54, 4 vols.

Mozart, W. A., *Mozart: Briefe und Aufzeichnungen*, Wilhelm Bauer and Otto Deutsch, eds., Kassel: Bärenreiter, 1962.

Monelle, Raymond, "Gluck and the 'Festa Teatrale,'" *Music and Letters*, v. 54, 1973, pp. 308-325.

Müller, Erich H., *Die Mingottische Opernunternehmungen, 1732-1756*, Dresden: 1915.

Müller, Walther, *Johann Adolf Hasse als Kirchenkomponist*, Leipzig: Breitkopf und Härtel, 1910.

Rousseau, Jean-Jacques, *Dictionnaire de Musique*, Paris: Duchesne, 1768.

Sartori, Claudio, manuscript catalogue of opera libretti, Biblioteca nazionale di Brera, Milan, Italy.

Schatz, Albert, manuscript notebooks: catalogues by composer, "Hasse," (2 vols.), Library of Congress, Washington, D.C.

Scheibe, Johann Adolph, *Critischer Musikus*, Leipzig: Breitkopf, 2nd ed., 1745.

Schnoor, Hans, *Dresden. Vierhundertjahre deutsche Musikkultur*, Dresden: Dresdner Verlagsgesellschaft, 1948.

Seiffert, Max, "Zur Biographie J. A. Hasses," *Sammelbände der Internationalen Musikgesellschaft*, v. VII, 1905-06, pp. 129-31.

Sonneck, O. G. T., "Die drei Fassungen des Hasseschen Artaserse," *Sammelbände der Internationalen Musikgesellschaft*, v. XIV, 1912-13, pp. 226-42.

_____, *Library of Congress. Division of Music. Catalogue of Opera Librettos Printed before 1800*, Washington: Government Printing Office, 1914, 2 vols.

Strohm, Reinhard, "Händels Pasticci," *Analecta Musicologia*, v. 14, 1974, pp. 208-267.

_____, Hasse, Scarlatti, Rolli," *Analecta Musicologia*, v. 15, 1975, pp. 220-257.

_____, *Italienisch Opernarien des frühen Settecento (1720-1730)*, *Analecta Musicologia*, v. 16 I/II, 1976.

_____, Review of Hasse's *Ruggiero*, ed. by Klaus Hortschansky, *Die Musikforschung*, v. 28, 1975, pp. 365-67.

Tintori, Giampiero, *L'Opera napoletana*, Milan: G. Ricordi, 1958.

Viertel, Karl-Heinz, "Neue Dokumente zu Leben und Werke Johann Adolf Hasses," *Analecta Musicologia,* v. 12, 1973, pp. 209-223.

Vogler, Abt. Georg Joseph, *Betrachtungen der Mannheimer Tonschule,* Mannheim: 1778-81, 3 vols.

Walther, Johann Gottfried, *Musikalisches Lexikon oder musikalische Bibliothek,* Leipzig: Wolffgang Door, 1732.

Weichlein, William J., *A Comparative Study of Five Settings of Metastasio's Libretto, La Clemenza di Tito,* (1734-1791), Ph. D. Dissertation, University of Michigan, 1956.

Wiel, Taddeo, *I teatri musicali veneziani del settecento. Catalogo delle opere in musica rappresentati nel secolo XVIII in Venezia,* Venice: Fratelli Visentini, 1897.

Wotquenne, Alfred, *Catalogue de la bibliothèque du Conservatoire royal de musique de Bruxelles,* Brussels: J. J. Cousemans, 1898-1912, 4 vols.

Yorke-Long, Alan, *Music at Court; Four Eighteenth-Century Studies,* London: Weidenfeld and Nicolson, 1954.

Záloha, Jiří, "The First Opera Repertoire of the Castle Theater in Ceský Krumlov," *Current Musicology,* No. 15, 1973, pp. 64-72.

Zanetti, Girolamo, *Memorie per servire all'istoria della inclita citta di Venezia* [1742-43], Arcivio Veneto, Anno XV, Nuovo Serie, Tomo XXIX, Parte I, 1885, pp. 93-148.

Zeller, J. G. Bernhardt, *Das Recitativo accompagnato in den Opern Johann Adolf Hasses,* Halle: Buchdruckerei Hohmann, 1911.

(B) Libretti Observed

(This does not attempt to be a complete list of Hasse libretti.)

Adriano in Siria, Dresden: Vedova Stössel, (1752). (Italian only)

_____, Dresden: Vedova Stössel, (1751). (German-Italian libretto)

Alcide al Bivio, Vienna: Ghelen, (1760).

_____, Copenhagen: H. J. Graae, 1774.

Alcides an der Doppel-strasse, Vienna: Ghelen, (1760).

L'Alessandro nell'Indie, Venice: Marino Rossetti, 1736.

_____, Venice: Marino Rossetti, 1738.

_____, Verona: Dionigi Ramanzini, (1740).

Alessandro nell'Indie, Pressburg: Eredi Royeriana, (1741), (Hasse not named)

_____, n.p. (Venice, 1743).

_____, Verona: Giambattista Saracco, (1754).

_____, Lucca: Filippo Maria Benedini, 1759.

Alessandro Rè d'Epiro, Parma: Monti, 1752 (-1753).

Alfonso, n.p., (Dresden, 1738). (Italian only)

_____, Dresden: Vedova Stössel, (1738). (German and Italian).

Antigono, Lucca: Domenico Ciuffetti, 1744 (not for a performance).

_____, Verona: Dionigi Ramanzini, (1748).

Antioco, Wolfenbüttel: Christian Bartsch, (1721).

Arminio, Milan: Giuseppe Richino Malatesta, 1730.

_____, Dresden: Vedova Stössel, (1745).

_____, Vienna: Giov. Pietro van Ghelen, 1747.

Artaserse, Venice: Carlo Buonarigo, (1730).

_____, Verona: Jacopo Vallarsi, (1733).

_____, London: Charles Bennet, 1734.

_____, Venice: Marino Rossetti, 1734. (Hasse not named)

_____, Bergamo: Fratelli Rosse, 1737.

_____, Dresden: Vedova Stössel, (1740).

_____, n.p., (Bologna, 1745).

_____, Ferrara: Giuseppe Barbieri, 1745.

_____, London: G. Woodfall, 1754.

_____, Naples: Girolamo Flauto, 1760.

_____, Ferrara: Bernardino Pomatelli, (1765).

Artemisia, Dresden: Vedova Stössel & Giov. Carlo Krause, (1755).

Asteria, n.p., (Dresden, 1737).

Attalo, rè di Bitinia, Naples: Francesco Ricciardo, 1728.

_____, Ferrara: Giuseppe Barbieri, (1739).

Attilio Regolo, Friedrichstadt: Vedova Harpeter, (Dresden, 1750).

Il Bevitore, n.p., (Dresden, 1747).

Il Bottegaro Gentiluomo, Venice: Marino Rossetti, 1739.

_____, Venice: Domenico Lovisa, 1739.

Caio Fabbricio, London: T. Wood, 1733. (Hasse not named)

Cajo Fabricio, Rome: Antonio de' Rossi, (1732).

_____, Naples: n.p., 1733.

_____, Venice: Marino Rossetti, 1735.

_____, Salzburg: Eredi di Giovanni Giuseppe Mayr, 1737.

_____, Lucca: Francesco Marescandoli, 1739, (Leghorn, 1740).

Cajo Fabrizio, t.p. missing, (Berlin, 1766)

Cajus Fabritius, Dresden: Gottlob Christian Hilschern, 1734.

Il Capitan Galoppo, Venice: Marino Rossetti, 1741.

Catone in Utica, Turin: Giov. Battista Valetta, 1731 (-1732).

Cesare in Egitto, Bruna: Massimiliano Swoboda, (Holleschau, 1736).

Il Ciro riconosciuto, Stuttgart: Giovanne Giorgio Cotta, (1752).

La Clemenza di Tito, Verona: Dionigi Ramanzini, (1738).

_____, Berlin: Christiano Sigismondo Bergemann, 1743.

_____, Hamburg: Spiering, (1748).

Cleofide, Dresden: Giovanni Corrado Stössel, (1731).

_____, Berlin: Haude e Spener, (1777).

Cleonice, Venice: Marino Rossetti, (1740).

La Contadina, Venice: Carlo Buonarrigo, 1721 (sic), (Trieste, 1731).

_____, n.p., (Bologna, 1738).

Dalisa, Venice: Carlo Buonarigo, (1730).

_____, Florence: Piero Matini, (1742).

Il Demetrio, Venice: Marino Rossetti, 1732.

_____, Verona: Jacopo Vallarsi, (1733).

_____, Ferrara: Giuseppe Barbieri, 1737.

L. Demetrio, Venice: Giuseppe Bettinelli, (1737).

Demetrio, n.p. (Parma, 1737).

Il Demetrio, Reggio: Vedrotti, (1739).

Demetrio, Dresden: Stössel, (1740).

_____, Venice: Gasparo Girardi, 1744, (Gorizia, 1745).

Il Demetrio, Ferrara: Giuseppe Barbieri, (1746).

Demetrio, n.p., (Venice, 1747).

_____, Turin: Pietro Giuseppe Zappata e figluolo, (1748).

Il Demetrio, Rè della Siria, Parma: Monti, (1737).

Demofoonte, n.p., (Dresden, 1748).

_____, Venice: All'Insegna della Scienza, 1749.

_____, Venice: Modesto Fenzo, 1753, (Vicenza).

Il Demofoonte, Valletta: Stamper. di S.A.S., 1765.

Didone, London: G. Woodfall, 1748.

Didone abbandonata, Berlin: Haude e Spener, (1753).

_____, Berlin: Haude und Spener, 1769.

La Donna accorta, Florence: Gio. Paolo Giovannelli, 1751.

Il Don Tabarano, Finte turco per amore, n.p., (Dresden, 1763).

Don Tabarano, t.p. missing, (Dresden, 1737?)

Don Tabarrano, n.p., (Dresden, 1747). (Hasse not named)

Egeria, Vienna: Ghelen, (1764).

Die erkannte Semiramis, Wolfenbüttel: Bartschischen Schrifften, (Brunswick, 1748).

L'eroe cinese, Berlin: Haude und Spener, 1773.

Euristeo, Venice: Carlo Buonarigo, (1732).

_____, Venice: Carlo Buonarrigo, (Ljubljana, 1733).

_____, Venice: Modesto Fenzo, 1747, (Padua).

Eurymedonte e Timocleone, ovvero I Rivali Delusi, Venice: Luigi Pavini, 1746.

Ezio, Naples: n.p., 1730.

_____, Dresden: Vedova Stössel, (1755).

La Finta tedesca, Potsdam: C. F. Voss, 1749. (Hasse not named: pasticcio)

Galatea ed Acide, Potsdam: C. F. Voss, 1748. (Hasse not named; pasticcio)

Gerone, tiranno di Siracusa, Naples: Francesco Ricciardo, 1727.

Die Grossmüthige Tomyris, Wolfenbüttel: Christian Bartsch wittwe u. Erben, (Brunswick, 1749).

Die Gutigkeit des Titus Vespasianus, Wolfenbüttel: Christian Bartsch, (Brunswick, 1744).

L'Ipermestra, Vienna: Gio. Pietro v. Ghelen, (1744).

Ipermestra, Naples: Cristoforo Ricciardo, (1746).

_____, Friedrichstadt: Vedova Harpeter, (Hubertusburg, 1751).

Irene, Dresden: Vedova Stössel, 1738.

Leucippo, n.p., (Dresden, 1747).

_____, n.p., (Venice, 1749).

_____, Prague: Ignazio Pruscha, (1752). (Hasse not named)

_____, Pressburg: Giovanni Mich. Landerer, (1759).

Lucio Papirio, Berlin: Haude e Spener, 1766.

_____, Berlin: Haude e Spener, 1784.

Lucio Papirio Dittatore, Naples: Ricciardi, (1746).

La Nitteti, Florence: Stamperia dirimpetto all'Oratorio di S. Filippo Neri, (1758).

Numa, n.p., (Dresden, 1743).

Olimpiade, Dresden: Vedova Stössel e Giovanni Carlo Krause, (1756).

L'Olimpiade, Turin: Gaspare Bayno, (1765).

Pandolfo, Venice: Marino Rossetti, 1739.

Partenope, n. p., (Vienna, 1767).

_____, Berlin: Haude e Spener, 1775, (Sans-Souci).

Pharamundus, Wolfenbüttel: Christian Bartsch, (Brunswick, 1748).

Piramo e Tisbe, Berlin: Haude e Spener, 1771, (Potsdam).

Pirro, Vienna: Gio. Battista Schilgen, 1734, (Jaromeriz).

Il Rè Pastore, Dresden: Vedova Stössel e Giovanni Carlo Krause, (Hubertusburg, 1755).

_____, Berlin: Haude e Spener, 1770.

Romolo & Ersilia, Vienna: Ghelen, (Innsbruck, 1765).

Romolo, ed Ersilia, Rome: Carlo Barbiellini, 1765, (Innsbruck).

Ruggiero, Vienna: Ghelen, (Milan, 1771).

Semiramide riconosciuta, Venice: n. p., (1745).

La Semiramide riconosciuta, n.p., (Dresden, 1747).

_____, London: G. Woodfall, 1748.

Semiramide riconosciuta, (Warsaw): Micaele Groell, (1760).

Senocrita, n. p., (Dresden, 1737).

La Serva Scaltra, Berlin: Haude e Spener, 1752.

Il Sesostrate, Naples: Angelo Vocala, (1726).

Siroe, n. p., (Parma, 1742).

Il Siroe, Bologna: Lorenzo Murtetti, (Rimini, 1743).

Siroe, Lucca: Filippo Maria Benedini, 1748.

_____, n. p., (Dresden, 1763).

Il Siroe, Siena: Francesco Rossi, 1765.

_____, n. p. (Brunswick, 1767).

Siroe, rè di Persia, Padua: Giambatista Conzatti, 1737.

_____, Parma: Monti, (1742).

_____, London: G. Woodfall, 1764.

Siroës, Warsaw: Michael Gröll, (1763).

Siroes, King of Persia, London: Charles Bennett, 1736. (Hasse not named)

Solimano, Dresden: Vedova Stössel, (1753).

_____, Dresden: Vedova Stössel, (1754).

La Spartana generosa, ovvero Archidamia, n.p., (Dresden, 1747).

Lo Starnuto d'Ercole, Venice: Luigi Pavini, 1746.

Il Tabarano, n.p. (Bologna, 1744).

_____, Brunswick: Reitel, (1749).

_____, Wolfenbüttel: Jo. Gott. Ant. Mattheen, (1750).

Il Tigrane, Naples: Francesco Ricciardo, 1729.

Tigrane, Naples: Cristoforo Ricciardi, (1745).

Tito Vespasiano, ovvero la clemenza di Tito, Pesaro: Niccolo Gavelli, 1735.

Il Trionfo di Clelia, Vienna: n.p., (1762).

Il Tutore, Dresden: n.p., 1738.

_____, n.p. (Bologna, 1746).

Il Tutore or the Tutor, London: G. Woodfall, (?)

Il Tutore e la Pupilla, Vienna: n.p., 1747.

L'Ulderica, Naples: Francesco Ricciardo, 1729.

Die verlassene Dido, Dresden: Stösselin, 1742.

Viriate, Venice: Marino Rossetti, 1739.

Die Wahl des Herakles, n. p., (Dresden, 1883).

(C) Printed Music of Hasse

Alcide al Bivio, Leipzig: Breitkopf, 1763.

Arminio, Rudolf Gerber, ed., *Das Erbe deutsche Musik*, vols. 26-27, Leipzig: Breitkopf und Härtel, 1957.

Le Delezie dell opere, Being a Collection of all the Favourite Songs on Score collected from the Operas Compos'd by BACH, etc., London: Walsh, 1776.

Draomira, Naples: 1729. (Chorus to Act V)

Farinelli's Celebrated Songs &c. Collected from Sig.r Hasse, Porpora, Vinci, and Veracini's Operas, Set for a German Flute, Violin, or Harpsicord. . . London: I. Walsh, [1736-1755?].

The Favourite Songs in the Opera Antigono, London: R. Bremner, [c. 1773].

The Favourite Songs in the Opera call'd Anibale in Capua, London: Walsh, [1746].

The Favourite Songs in the Opera Call'd Artaxerxes, by Sig.r Hasse, London: Walsh, [1734].

The Favourite Songs in the Opera Call'd Dido, by Sig.r Hasse, London: I. Walsh [1748].

The Favourite Songs in the Opera Call'd Ezio, by Sig.r Perez, London: I. Walsh, [1754].

The Favourite Songs in the Opera Call'd Ezio, with some Songs in Ipermestra never before Printed, London: I. Walsh, [1754-55].

The Favourite Songs in the Opera Call'd Il Demofoonte, London: Walsh, [1755].

The Favourite Songs in the Opera Call'd Il Re Pastore, by Sig. Hasse, Sung by Sig.ra Mingotti, London: I. Walsh, [1757].

The Favourite Songs in the Opera Call'd La Ingratitudine Punita, by Sig.r Hasse, Pergolisi, &c, London: Walsh, [1748].

The Favourite Songs in the Opera Call'd Siroe, by Sig.r Hasse, London: I. Walsh, [1736].

The Favourite Songs in the Opera Leucippo and Zenocrita, London: R. Bremner, [1765].

The Favourite Songs in the Operas Call'd Merode & Olimpia as Perform'd at the Theatre in the Hay-Market, London: Walsh, [1740].

The Maid of the Mill, a Comic Opera, As it is performed at the Theatre Royal in Covent Garden, London: R. Bremner, [1765].

Ruggiero, Klaus Hortschansky, ed., *Concentus Musicus*, v. 1, Volk: Cologne, 1973.

The Summer's Tale, A Musical Comedy As it is perform'd at the Theatre Royal in Covent-Garden, The music by Abel. . ., London: I. Walsh, [1765].

A Valuable Collection of the most Favourite Songs Selected from the latest Italian Opera's, Composed by the following eminent Masters, Sig.r. Bach. . .Adapted for two German Flutes or Violins, By. Sig.r Ghiluni di Asuni, London: John Welcker, [1776].

(D) Manuscript Scores of Hasse Operas

(Titles are extremely varied and in some cases are missing; accordingly, they have been standardized. This list includes only the scores that were actually observed, except where otherwise stated.)

Achille in Sciro, I-Mc, Part. Tr. ms. 166 (autograph)

Adriano in Siria, I-Mc, Part. Tr. ms. 176 (autograph)

_____, I-MOe, Mus. F. 548

Alcide al bivio, I-Mc, Part. Tr. ms. 154 (autograph)

_____, I-MOe, Mus. F. 546

_____, US-Wc, M 1500 .H35A5

Alessandro nell'Indie, D-D1, Mus. 2477/F/9 (as *Cleofide*; Dresden copy)

_____, D-Mbs, ms. mss. 213 (as *Cleofide*; arias only)

_____, GB-Lbm, Add. 30838 (version IIa; Venetian copy)

Alfonso, D-D1, Mus. 2477/F/27 (Dresden copy)

Andromeda, A-Wn, 18033 (pasticcio)

Antigono, A-Wn, 17206 (Dresden copy)

_____, GB-Lbm, Add. 32144

_____, I-Mc, Noseda 041 1-10 (ten loose arias)

_____, US-Wc, M 1500 .H35A6

Antonio e Cleopatra, A-Wn, Fond Kiesewetter S. A. 68B 33

Armida placata, A-Wn, 18021 (pasticcio)

Arminio, D-Mbs, mus. mss. 193 (version IIb)

_____, D-W, Codex Guelferbytanus 119 mus. hs. (Berlin version)

_____, F-Pn, Cons. D. 5392-4 (version IIb)

_____, I-Mc, Part. Tr. ms. 152 (as *Egeste e Tusnelda*)

_____, PL-Wn, Mf. 539 (version I; arias only)

_____, US-NH, Cupboard, Mq 20/H27e (version IIa; arias only)

_____, US-Wc, M 1500 .H35A65 (version IIb)

Artaserse, A-Wn, S.m. 1061 (version Ic)

_____, D-D1, Mus. 2477/F/2 (version Ic; Dresden copy)

_____, D-D1, Mus. 2477/F/4 (arias only)

_____, GB-Lam, ms. 72 (version Ia)

_____, GB-Lbm, Add. 32582 (version Ia)

_____, GB-Lbm, Add. 39568 (version Ia)

_____, I-Mc, Part. Tr. ms. 171 (version II; autograph)

_____, I-Nc, Rari 7.4.5. (version II)

_____, I-Nc, Rari 7.4.6 (version II; arias only)

_____, I-Vnm, Cod. It. IV-481 (=10005) (version Ia; Venetian copy)

Artemisia, I-Mc, Part. Tr. ms. 164 (autograph)

L'Asilo d'amore, I-Mc, Part. Tr. ms. 181 (autograph)

_____, US-BE, uncat. Ms. 834 (sinfonia and one aria only)

Astarto, I-MC, 125/A/2 op. 1-3

Asteria, D-Dl, mus. 2477/F/21 (Dresden copy)

_____, D-Mbs, mus. mss. 194 (arias only)

Atalanta, I-Mc, Part. tr. ms. 162 (autograph)

Attalo, I-Vnm, Cod. It. IV 483 (=10007) (Venetian copy)

Attilio Regolo, I-Mc, Part. Tr. ms. 172 (autograph)

Cajo Fabrizio, A-Wgm, Q 1748 (version a)

_____, B-Bc, K. 2136 (version a)

_____, D-Bpk, Amalien-Bibliothek 305 (version b; arias only)

_____, D-Bpk, mus. ms. 9542 (version b)

_____, D-Bpk, mus. ms. 9542/1 (version b; Dresden copy, with corrections by Hasse)

_____, D-Bpk, mus. ms. 9542/2 (Berlin version of 1766; mostly version b)

_____, D-Dl, mus. 2477/F/11 (version b; Dresden copy)

_____, F-Pn, Cons. D. 5399-5401 (version b)

_____, I-Mc, Part Tr. ms. 157 (as *Pirro*: version a; autograph)

_____, I-Vc, Ospedaletto XIX 323 (version b; Act I only: autograph)

_____, US-Wc, M 1500 .H35C2 Case (version b; arias only)

Ciro riconosciuto, D-Mb, mus. mss. 192/1-3 (Dresden copy, with corrections by Hasse)

_____, GB-Lbm, Add. 32026 (voice and bass only)

_____, I-Mc, Part. Tr. ms. 161 (autograph)

_____, D-Bpk, Amalien-Bibliothek 307 (version Ib)

_____, D-Bpk, mus. ms 9544 (version Ib; arias only)

_____, D-Bpk, mus. ms. 9544/1 (as *Tito*; version Ib)

_____, D-Dl, Mus. 2477/F/22 (version Ib)

_____, D-Mbs, mus. mss. 6312 (version Ib; voice and bass only)

_____, D-W Codex Guelferbytanus 117 mus. hs. (as *Tito Vespasiano*; version Ib; Dresden copy, with corrections by Hasse)

_____, F-Pn, Cons. D. 5244 (version II)

_____, I-Mc, Noseda G3 (version II; arias only)

_____, I-Mc, Noseda G7 (version II)

_____, I-Mc, Noseda H21 (version II; Act I only; arias only)

_____, I-Mc, Part. tr. ms. 174 (version II; autograph)

_____, I-Nc, Rari 7.4.7. (version II)

_____, I-Nc, Rari 7.4.10 (version Ia; perhaps a pasticcio in Act III)

_____, I-Nc, Rari 7.4.11B (version II)

_____, US-AA, M 1500 .H35C6 1737 (version Ia; Acts I and II only)

_____, US-BE, uncat. ms. 714, (version Ib; arias only)

La Contadina, D-Bds, ms. autogr. J. A. Hasse 4 (as *Don Tabarano e Scintilla*; autograph)

_____, D-SW1, Am. Dom. 2. 2478 (as *Don Tabarano*)

_____, D-W, Codex Guelferbytanus 121 mus. hs. (as *Don Tabarano*)

_____, I-Rc, 2507 (as *Don Tabarano e Scintilla*)

_____, US-Wc, M 1500 .H35C7 Case

_____, US-Wc, M 1500 .H35D5 (as *Don Tabarano*; copy of Dresden manuscript)

Demetrio, A-Wn, 17257 (pasticcio; Reggio, 1739)

_____, D-Dl, mus. 2477/F/12 (version b; Dresden copy)

_____, F-Pn, Cons. D. 5471-73 (version b; Dresden copy)

_____, I-Vnm, Cod. It. IV 482 (=10006) (version a; Venetian copy)

Demofoonte, DK-Kk, C I, 259e (version Ia; end of Act II only)

_____, F-Pn, Cons. D. 5426-5428 (combination of versions Ia and Ib)

_____, F-Pn, X 43-45 (version Ia)

_____, F-Pn, X 116 A-C (version II)

_____, F-Pn, X 1032 1-3 (version Ia)

_____, GB-Lbm, Add. 32025 (version Ia; arias only)

_____, I-Mc, Noseda H9 I & II (version II; Acts I and III only)

_____, I-Mc, Part. Tr. ms. 156 (version Ia; autograph)

_____, I-Nc, Rari 7.4.12. (version Ia)

_____, I-Vc, Ospedaletto XIX 325 (version II; Acts I and II only; autograph)

_____, US-Wc, M 1500 .H35D3 (version Ia)

_____, US-Wc, M 1500 .H35D4 (version II)

Didone abbandonata, D-Bpk, mus. ms. 9549

_____, D-Bpk, mus. ms. 9549/1

_____, D-W, Coden Guelferbytanus 118 mus. hs. (arias only)

_____, F-Pn, Cons. D. 5947 (Dresden copy)

_____, F-Pn, Rés 1351 (Although marked "autograph" in card catalogue, this is not in Hasse's hand.)

_____, I-Mc, Noseda F67 (slightly altered version)

_____, I-Nc, Rari 7.4.13-15

_____, I-Vc, Ospedaletto XIX 324

_____, US-NYp, *MS

_____, US-Wc, M 1500 .H35D43

Enea in Caonia, I-Nc, 21.3.15

Egeria, I-Mc, Part. Tr. ms. 151 (autograph)

_____, I-MOe, Mus. F 547

_____, US-Wc, M 1500 .H35E4

L'Eroe cinese, GB-Lbm, Add. 32031 (Berlin version of 1773)

_____, I-Mc, Part. Tr. ms. 160 (autograph)

Euridice, A-Wn, 18032 (pasticcio)

Euristeo, F-Pn, Cons, D. 5476-5478 (Dresden copy)

Ezio, A-Wn, 17292 (version II)

_____, GB-Lk, 22.17 (version I; not observed)

_____, F-Pn, Cons. D. 5431 (Version II; arias only; voice and bass only)

_____, I-Mc, Part. Tr. ms. 173 (version II; autograph)

La Fantesca, I-MC, 124/G/28 op. 1

_____, US-Wc, M 1500 .H35D5 (as *Capitan Galoppo*; copied from a D-Dl manuscript).

Gerone, A-Wn, 17280

_____, I-Mc, Part. Tr. ms. 179 (autograph)

_____, I-MC, 124/G/30 op. 1

Ipermestra A-Wgm, Q 1463 (version a; Acts II and III only)

_____, A-Wn, 17285 (version a; Act II only)

_____, F-Pn, Cons. D. 5433 (version b; Dresden copy)

_____, F-Pn, X 52-54 (version b: Dresden Copy)

_____, I-Mc, Noseda G4 (version a)

_____, I-Mc, Part. Tr. ms. 167 (version b; autograph)

Irene, D-Dl, mus. 2477/F/24

_____, US-Wc, M 1500 .H35I7 Case (arias only)

Issipile, I-Mc, Noseda A31 (Act I only)

_____, I-MC, 124/G/31 op. 1-3

Larinda e Vanesio, D-Dl mus. 2477/F/99 (as *L'Artigiano gentiluomo*; Dresden copy)

_____, I-MC, 125/A/2 op. 1-3 (with *Astarto*)

_____, I-Rc, 2507

Leucippo, A-Wgm, Q1474 (version a; opening only)

_____, D-Bpk, mus. ms. 9558 (version a)

_____, D-Bpk, mus. ms. 9558/2 (version c)

_____, D-W Codex Guelferbytanus 122 mus. hs. (version a; Dresden copy)

_____, DK-Kk, C I, 259e (version a)

_____, F-Pn, Cons. D. 5435-37 (version a, with version c differences in appendix; Dresden copy)

_____. GB-Lbm, Add. 32027 (version c)

_____, I-Mc, Part. Tr. ms. 155 (version d; autograph)

_____, I-Nc, 27.2.22 (version a)

_____, US-Wc, M 1500 .H35L3 (version c)

Lucio Papirio, D-Dl, mus. 2477/F/32 (Dresden copy)

Miride e Damari, US-Wc, M 1500 .H35C7 Case (version matches neither libretto nor remnants in score of *Sesostrate*)

Il Natal di Giove, I-Mc, Part. Tr. ms. 181 bis (autograph)

Nitteti, D-Mb, mus. mss. 195

Numa, I-Mc, Part. Tr. ms. 169 (Acts I and II only; autograph)

_____, US-AA, M 1500 .H35N8 17..b

L'Olimpiade, A-Wgm, Q 1473 (version a)

_____, D-Dl, mus. 2477/F/84 (version a)

_____, F-Pn, Cons. D. 5439 (version a; voice and bass only; arias only)

_____, F-Pn, Cons. D. 5482-4 (version a; Dresden copy)

_____, F-Pn, Vm^4.35 (version b; arias only)

_____, I-Mc, Part. Tr. ms. 153 (version a, remnants of version b; autograph)

_____, I-Tn, Foà 52 (version a; Dresden copy)

Pantaleone e Carlotta, I-MC (microfilm copy in possession of Sven Hansell)

Partenope, I-Mc, Part. Tr. ms. 159 (incomplete; autograph)

Pimpinella e Marcantonio, US-AA, M 1500 .H35N8 17..b, (with *Numa*)

Piramo e Tisbe, I-Mc, Noseda G6 I e II

_____, I-Mc, Noseda G97

_____, I-Mc, Noseda H7 I e II

_____, I-Mc, Part. Tr. ms. 170 (autograph)

Porsugnacco, GB-Lam, ms 125

Il Rè pastore, I-Mc, Part. Tr. ms. 165, (autograph)

_____, US-NYp, Drexel 4898 (soprano and bass only; arias only)

Rimario e Grillantea, D-Dl, mus. 2477/F/102 (Dresden copy)

Romolo ed Ersilia, A-Wn, 17288

_____ US-Wc, M 1505 .A2H38 (one aria only)

Ruggiero, GB-Lbm, Add. 16025 (arias only)

_____, I-Mc, Part. Tr. ms. 168 (autograph)

Semele, A-Wgm, Q 1476

Semiramide, D-W, Codex Guelferbytanus 120 mus. hs. (version b; arias only)

_____, F-Pn, Cons. D. 5449 (version b; arias only)

_____, F-Pn, Cons. D. 5454-5 (version a; Venetian copy)

_____, GB-Lbm, Add. 16026 (version b)

_____, I-Bc, FF 241 (version a)

_____, I-Vc, Ospedaletto XX 326 (version b; autograph)

Senocrita, A-Wgm, Q 1479

_____, D-Mbs, mus. mss. 191 (arias only)

La Serva scaltra, I-Rc, ms 2506

_____, I-MC, 124/G/29 op. 1

_____, US-Wc, 1500 .H35S2

Sesostrate, A-Wgm, Q 1477

Siroe, A-Wn, 17256 (version a)

_____, A-Wn, 19058 (version a)

_____, I-Mc, Part. Tr. ms. 178 (version b; autograph)

_____, US-Wc, M 1500 .H35S8 (version b)

Solimano, D-Mbs, mus. mss. 191m, (voice and bass only; arias only)

_____, D-Mbs, mus. mss. 826 (voice and bass only; arias only)

_____, D-Mbs, mus, mss. 4294 (voice and bass only; arias only)

_____, GB-Lbm, Add. 32146 (arias only)

_____, I-Mc, Part. Tr. ms. 175 (autograph)

_____, US-Wc, M 1500 .H345S6

_____, US-Wc, M 1500 .H35S6

La Sorella amante, D-Dl, mus. 2477/F/98 (as *Lavinia;* autograph*)*

La Spartana generosa, D-Dl, mus. 2477/F/48 (Dresden copy)

Tigrane, A-Wgm, Q 1475

_____, GB-Lam, ms. 73

_____, I-Mc, Part. Tr. ms. 177 (Acts II and III only; autograph)

Il Trionfo di Clelia, A-Wgm, Q 1464

_____, I-Mc, Part Tr. ms. 158 (autograph)

_____, I-MOe, Mus. F. 545

Il Tutore, D-Mbs, mus. mss. 196

Viriate, I-Mc, Part. Tr. ms. 180 (Venetian copy)

Zenobia, I-Mc, Part. Tr. ms. 163 (autograph)

(E) Significant Hasse arias in manuscript

Alessandro nell'Indie IIb, "Non temer, rasciuaga il ciglio," I-Vnm, Cod. It. IV 478 (=10002) (6).

_____, "Pensa che offeso io sono," I-Vnm, Cod. It. IV 478 (= 10002) (5).

Antioco, Six Arias in D-SWl, 4721, No. 59, 68-72 (not observed).

Catone in Utica, "Che legge spietata," DK-Kk, C I, 259e; F-Pn, Cons. D. 5465 (10); GB-Lbm, Add. 31529 (25).

_____, "Chi mai saper desio," F-Pn, Cons. D. 5470 (5); F-Pn, Cons. D. 5465 (6); I-Mc, Noseda Q7-9, Q8-29.

_____, "Chi un dolce amor," D-Dl mus. 2477/F/107, D-Mbs, mus. mss. 27/141 28 199.

_____, "Confusa, smarrita," GB-Lbm, Add. 14180 (24), I-MC 124 G 21.

_____, "In che t'offende," GB-Lbm, Add. 31637 (passim.) (3). Also found in all scores of *Demetrio a.*

_____, "Mi lusinga il dolce affetto," D-Dl, mus. 2477/F/107, D-Mbs, mus. ms. 24/141 25 149; GB-Lbm, Add. 31603 (2); I-Mc, Noseda Q8-31.

_____, "Nell'ardire che il seno," D-Dl, mus. 2477/F/107, D-Mbs, mus. mss. 25/141 26 151.

Catone in Utica, "Non ha più pace," A-Wn, s.m. 4081; GB-Lbm, Add. 31592 (16); GB-Lbm, Add. 31595 (1); I-PLc, Pisani 27, pp. 11-157 (#3); I-Rsc, A. Ms. 3709.2 Also found in all scores of *Cajo Fabrizio a.*

_____, "Non ti minaccio sdegno," US-BE, uncat. ms. 129/7.

_____, "O nel sen di qualche stella," D-Dl, mus. 2477/F/107, D-Mbs, 141.

_____, "Sarebbe un gran diletto," D-UMs 1981.

_____, "So che pietà non hai," B-Bc, 4166; F-Pn, Cons. D. 5466 (24).

La Clemenza di Tito Ia, "Getta il nocchier," B-Bc, 4121. The manuscript reads "Pesaro 1735, Sig.ra. Bordoni-Hasse." The only other source for Act III (I-Nc, Rari 7.4.10) includes a suspect terzetto at this point.

_____, "Vo disperato a morte," I-Mc, Noseda Q 7-9. The manuscript reads "Sig.r. Carestini, in Pesaro." It matches the only other source for Act III (I-Nc, Rari 7.4.10), suggesting that the latter may be a pasticcio only for the last scenes of the opera.

Dalisa, "Che pena o mio tesoro," A-Wn, s.m. 4101.

_____, "Lasciami in pace addio," D-Dl, mus. 2477/F/107; D-Mbs, mus. mss. 22/141 23/143 6; D-MUs, 1982; I-MC 124 G 22.

_____, "Non chiamarmi ingrato core," A-Wn, 17546; A-Wn, s.m. 1075; D-MUs, 1981; F-Pn, Cons. D. 5466 (8); F-Pn, ms 948; GB-Lbm, Add. 31603 (3); I-PLc, Pisani 27, pp. 11-157 (#1); I-Vc, Correr 157-43-1. This aria was also used in *Ezio I.*

_____, "Perdonare oh ciel non deggio," D-MUs, 1982.

_____, "Priva dal caro bene," D-MUs, 1981; GB-Ob Mus. e. 10: I-Mc, Noseda I-93 (12); I-Mc, Noseda O 41-19; I-MC 124 G 22; I-Rc, ms 2252.

_____, "Se fosse il mio diletto," D-Dl, 2477/F/107; D-Mbs, mus. mss. 19/141 20 136; I-MC 124 G 22.

_____, "Un raggio di stella," in pasticcio of *Catone,* London 1732 (Strohm).

Demetrio c, "Da quel cor virtude," D-Dl Mus. 1/F/28, 12.

_____, "Io già so chiedendo," D-D1, Mus. 1/F/28, 12.

Didone abbandonata, "Ombra cara, ombra tradita," I-Bc, FF 244 (1). A mixture of autograph and Dresden copyist with autograph corrections.

Nitteti, "Si ti credo, amato bene," I-Mc, Mus. Tr. ms. 570. Copy, with autograph corrections.

_____, "Si ti credo, amato bene," I-Mc, Mus. Tr. ms. 575. Autograph. Different from above.

Il Rè pastore, "Vanne a regnar ben mio," I-Mc, Mus. Tr. ms. 571. Copy, with autograph corrections.

Senocrita, "Ah se di te mi privi," I-Mc, Mus. Tr. ms. 569/II. Autograph.

Ulderica, "Da me tu brami ancor," I-Nc, 33-2-17.

_____, "Fissa nei sguardi miei," A-Wn 17661; A-Wn, s.m. 4073; D-D1, mus. 2477/F/110; GB-Lbm, Add. 31601 v. 1 (3); I-Vc, Correr 157-43-1.

_____, "Già sento nel seno," D-Mus, 1982; GB-Lbm, Add. 31603 (5); I-Mc, Noseda O 42-6; I-Nc, 33.2.17.

_____, "Io non ho diadema al crine," I-MC 124 G 22.

_____, "Io ti lascio, idolo mio," GB-Lam, RM 34 d4(4); GB-Lk, 23 d 4; I-Mc, Noseda Q 8-17.

_____, "Le momorande imprese," found in *Enea in Caonia* (I-Nc, 21.3.15).

_____, "Mi disarma amore il braccio," I-MC, 124 G 21 and 22.

_____, "Pria di darmi un si bel vanto," I-MC 124 G 22; in pasticcio *Ormisda* (1730) (Strohm).

_____, "Tu vedi un pastorello," GB-Lbm, Add. 14180 (2); US-BE, uncat. ms. 129/17.

_____, "Vaghe labbra voi ridete," in pasticcio *Catone* (London, 1732) (Strohm); I-MC, 124 G 20.

_____, "Vien la speranza al core," D-Hs, M B/1923.

(F) Manuscript scores of music not by Hasse

Feo, Francesco, *Siface, rè di Numidia*, I-Nc, 32.3.27

Porpora, Niccolò, *Flavio Anicio Olibrio*, GB-Lbm, Add. 14121

Scarlatti, Alessandro, *Gerone, tiranno di Siracusa*, GB-Och, ms. 990

Vinci, Leonardo, *Artaserse*, US-Be, uncat. ms. 138

_____, *Astianatte*, I-Nc, 33.6.2

_____, *Catone in Utica*, I-Nc, 3.1.9

GENERAL INDEX

Page numbers of plates and musical examples are italicized.

Accompanied recitative. *See* Recitativo; obbligato
Achille in Sciro (Chiarini), 18
Adolfati, Andrea, 295 n.78
Aesthetics, eighteenth-century views on, 253-57
Affect, or relationship of music to text, 177-84
Albuzzi, Ottavio, 130
Albuzzi, Teresa, 25, 26, 27, 31, 115, 116, 151-52, 175, 297 n.101, 297 n.102, 304 n.19; salary, 296 n.92
Algarotti, Francesco, 20, 28, 259, 294 n.72, 297 n.105
Allgemeine Musikalische Zeitung, 264
Amalia. *See* Maria Amalia, Saxon Electoral Princess
Amorevoli, Angelo, 17, 20, 21, 22, 23, 24, 25, 26, 27, 31, 115, 130, 141, 152, 174, 176, 290 n.31, 293 n.57, 297 n.101
Annibali, Domenico, 7, 15, 18, 19, 20, 21, 22, 26, 31, 115, 117, 129-30, 141, 150-52, 304 n.25; compared with Carestini, 129-30; pension, 31; range, 130
Appiani, Giuseppe, *detto* Appianino, 107, 303 n.15a
Arias; five-part da capo, 39-42; half da capo, 42-43, 52; method of composition of, 85; structure and form of, 26, 39-44, 153-56, 191, 193-250, 265-84, 301 n.12; types (character), 277-78, 312 n.46
Ariodante (Pollaroli), 5
Artaserse (Vinci), 4, 258, 292 n.50
Arteaga, Stefano, 259
Ascanio in Alba (Mozart), 33
Astianatte (Vinci), 211-18, 212-17
Augustus II, King of Poland. *See* Frederick Augustus I Augustus III, King of Poland.
Augustus III, King of Poland. *See* Frederick Augustus II
Aureli, Aurelio, 3
Autographs, of Hasse, 55-95; addition and removal of arias visible in, 86, 89-91, *92-94,* 133; cadences added or changed in, 77-78, *79-81,* 82, *83;* corrections in, 58, *85,* 95; copyists in, 55, 72, 74, *75,* 76-78, *79-81,* 83, 91, *92-94,* 113-16, 142-50, 153; descriptions of, 58, 76,

77, *78-81,* 82-*83,* 116-17, 119, 120, 121, 122-23, 124-26, *127,* 141-49; errors in, 76, *85,* 95; handwriting in, 152-55; haste shown in writing, 72-76, 152; instrumental placement within, 85, 126-27; organization into fascicles of, 65-73, 76-77, 89; sources of (table), 56-58; space-saving devices in, 67; survival and later history of, 187, 298 n.107, 298 n.109; use of space and paper in, 82, 177
Azioni teatrali, 49-53. *See also under specific titles in* Index of Hasse's Works

Bach, Carl Philipp Emmanuel, 7
Bach, Johann Christian, 263
Bach, Johann Sebastian, 7, 251, 252
Bach, Wilhelm Friedemann, 7
Ballets, 27
Barbieri, Antonio, 139
Belli, Giovanni, 26, 27, 115, 175, 297 n.101, 297 n.102
Bellotto, Bernardo, *detto* Canaletto, 9
Belmuro, Andrea, 4
Benda, Georg, 28, 34
Berlin, 19, 21; Hasse in, 26
Bernacchi, Antonio Maria, 284, 304 n.25
Betrachtungen der Mannheimer Tonschule (Vogler), 263
Biancardi, Sebastiano, *pseud.* Domenico Lalli, 6, 15, 18, 293 n.59
Bindi, Giovanni, 17, 18, 19, 20, 21, 22, 26, 131-32, 133, 139
Boccardi, Michelangelo, 7, 140
Boldini, Giovanni, 289 n.25
Bologna, Hasse in, 1, 15, 29
Bordoni-Hasse, Faustina, 4-5, 6, 7, 15, 16, 17, 25, 27, 31, 35, 116; conflict with Mingotti, 295 n.83; critical views of, 251, 257, 262; in London, 289 n.26; operas revised for, 108, 128, 140; range and vocal skill, 124, 128, 136-37, 304 n.26; retirement, 25, 31; roles, 5, 6, 7, 15, 16, 17, 18, 19, 20, 21, 22, 23, 24, 25, 108, 135, 194, 290 n.31, 293 n.64; salary, 7, 16, 25, 31, 291 n.42, 297 n.117
Breitkopf, J.G.I., 263
Broschi, Carlo, *detto* Farinelli, 2, 4, 15, 51
Brosses, Charles de, 257-58, 301 n.14

INDEX OF HASSE'S WORKS

For operas, intermezzi, serenate, and feste teatrali, see Table III (pp. 56-58) and Appendices.

INDEX OF ARIAS

Arias are alphabetized in strict word order; articles are considered integral parts of the poetic line. All arias are by Hasse unless otherwise indicated.